Cheap Street

Manchester University Press

Cheap Street

London's street markets and the cultures of informality, c. 1850–1939

Victoria Kelley

Manchester University Press

Copyright © Victoria Kelley 2019

The right of Victoria Kelley to be identified as the author of this work has been asserted by her in accordance with the Copyright, Designs and Patents Act 1988.

Published by Manchester University Press
Oxford Road, Manchester M13 9PL

www.manchesteruniversitypress.co.uk

British Library Cataloguing-in-Publication Data
A catalogue record for this book is available from the British Library

ISBN   978 0 7190 9922 9 hardback
ISBN   978 1 5261 6385 1 paperback

First published 2019
Paperback published 2022

The publisher has no responsibility for the persistence or accuracy of URLs for any external or third-party internet websites referred to in this book, and does not guarantee that any content on such websites is, or will remain, accurate or appropriate.

Typeset in 10/12 Apolline Std by
Servis Filmsetting Ltd, Stockport, Cheshire

cheap adj. 1. costing relatively little; inexpensive; good value. 2. charging low prices. 3. of poor quality, shoddy. 4. worth relatively little. 5. not worthy of respect, vulgar. (Old English *ceap*, barter, bargain, price, property)

Cheapside EC2. The chief marketplace of medieval London (Old English *ceap* or *chepe*, market)

Contents

	List of figures	viii
	List of plates	xi
	Acknowledgements	xii
	Introduction	1
1	What is a street market?	17
2	Things	48
3	Streets	74
4	People	109
5	Street markets, informality and the performance of London	152
	Conclusion	187
	Select bibliography	191
	Index	201

Figures

Map
1. London Street Markets 1851 and 1893, based on the lists of markets in Henry Mayhew, *London Labour and the London Poor* (1851) and London County Council's *London Street Markets* report (1893), Appendix C. Map by Robert Sinfield   2

Figures
1. 'Saturday Night in the East End', *Good Words*, November 1868   3
2. 'Saturday Night in the East End', in Richard Harding Davis, *Our English Cousins*, 1894   4
3. Laszlo Moholy-Nagy, 'Berwick Street Market: general view', in Mary Benedetta, *The Street Markets of London*, 1936 (courtesy of Guildhall Library, City of London)   5
4. 'The meat market, Smithfield, at two in the morning', *Illustrated London News*, 13 January 1870 (© Illustrated London News Ltd/Mary Evans)   23
5. 'Sunday Morning in the New Cut, Lambeth', *Illustrated London News*, 27 January 1872 (© Illustrated London News Ltd/Mary Evans)   29
6. Columbia Market in 1869, *Illustrated London News*, 1 May 1869 (© Illustrated London News Ltd/Mary Evans)   29
7. Columbia Market in a semi-derelict state in 1914 (courtesy of London Metropolitan Archives)   30
8. Plan for a market hall at Strutton Ground, Westminster (exterior), London County Council, *London Markets*, 1893 (courtesy of the Library of the Institute of Historical Research, University of London)   37
9. Plan for a market hall at Strutton Ground, Westminster (interior), London County Council, *London Markets*, 1893 (courtesy of the Library of the Institute of Historical Research, University of London)   38
10. Lewisham High Street, 1937 (© John Topham/Topfoto)   54

Figures

11 Laszlo Moholy-Nagy, 'Commercial Road: stall for housewives', in Mary Benedetta, *The Street Markets of London*, 1936 (courtesy of Guildhall Library, City of London)   58
12 Laszlo Moholy-Nagy, 'Berwick Market: "There you can get thin pure silk stockings for 1s. 3d."', in Mary Benedetta, *The Street Markets of London*, 1936 (courtesy of Guildhall Library, City of London)   59
13 John Thomson, 'Dealer in fancy ware', in John Thomson and Adolphe Smith, *Street Life in London*, 1877 (courtesy of Guildhall Library, City of London)   60
14 East Street market, Walworth, 1939 (courtesy of London Metropolitan Archives)   68
15 Street market in Hammersmith, postcard, c. 1900–14   77
16 Laszlo Moholy-Nagy, 'Petticoat Lane: general view', in Mary Benedetta, *The Street Markets of London*, 1936 (courtesy of Guildhall Library, City of London)   78
17 'The London poor at their Christmas marketing – a sketch in the New Cut', *Illustrated London News*, 1872 (© Illustrated London News Ltd/Mary Evans)   88
18 Frederick Barnard, 'Why pay a doctor?', in George Sims, *How the Poor Live*, 1883 (courtesy of Guildhall Library, City of London)   89
19 Frederick Barnard, 'Ere y'are; three shots a penny! Now's yer chance!!!', in George Sims, *How the Poor Live*, 1883 (courtesy of Guildhall Library, City of London)   92
20 'Saturday Night in Whitechapel Road', in George Sims, *Living London*, 1901 (courtesy of Guildhall Library, City of London)   93
21 'London street scene: costers' stalls in Walworth', *Daily News*, 10 August 1903 (© The British Library Board. All rights reserved. With thanks to the British Newspaper Archive, www.britishnewspaperarchive.co.uk)   94
22 'Barrows for hire', in George Sims, *Living London*, 1901 (courtesy of Guildhall Library, City of London)   96
23 'My youngest customer', in Olive Malvery, *The Soul Market*, 1907 97
24 Laszlo Moholy-Nagy, 'Petticoat Lane: "A man who sells a mysterious preparation for making brass fenders look like chromium"', in Mary Benedetta, *The Street Markets of London*, 1936 (courtesy of Guildhall Library, City of London)   101
25 'The London Costermonger', in Henry Mayhew, *London Labour and the London Poor*, Vol. I, 1861 (courtesy of Esther M. Zimmer Lederberg memorial website)   114
26 'The Jew Old Clothes-Man', in Henry Mayhew, *London Labour and the London Poor*, Vol. II, 1861 (courtesy of Esther M. Zimmer Lederberg memorial website)   118
27 'Sooner or later; or, what it must come to', *Punch*, 23 November 1867 119
28 'A civil deputation to the Home Office', *Punch*, 7 December 1867   120

29 'Returning from the Derby', in Richard Harding Davis, *Our English Cousins*, 1894 — 121
30 Phil May, 'The Londoner's Sunday – 1. Petticoat Lane', *St Paul's magazine*, 9 June 1894 (by permission of Tower Hamlets Local History Library and Archives) — 131
31 Phil May, 'From Petticoat Lane to the Lane of the Park', *Punch*, 1898 — 132
32 'Petticoat Lane on Sunday morning', postcard c. 1900 (courtesy of Bishopsgate Institute) — 135
33 Albert Chevalier in costume as a costermonger (© Victoria and Albert Museum, London) — 137
34 Laszlo Moholy-Nagy, 'Petticoat Lane: an engraver', in Mary Benedetta, *The Street Markets of London*, 1936 (courtesy of Guildhall Library, City of London) — 144
35 East Street market, Walworth, 1939 (courtesy of London Metropolitan Archives) — 162
36 'Mr Albert Chevalier singing one of his coster songs in a West-End drawing-room', *The Graphic*, 29 October 1892 (© Illustrated London News Ltd/Mary Evans) — 174
37 Kate Carney in costume as a costermonger, 1890s (© Victoria and Albert Museum, London) — 176
38 Bill Brandt, 'East End Girl Dancing the "Lambeth Walk"', 1939 (© Bill Brandt Archive) — 180

Where copyright details are not otherwise stated, images have been photographed from out-of-copyright originals in the collection of the author. Photography by Robert Sinfield.

Plates

following page 82

1. Covent Garden, postcard, *c.* 1890s
2. Chrisp Street market, postcard, *c.* 1910 (photo by Popperfoto/Getty Images)
3. 'An East End symphony of salesmanship', *National Geographic*, January 1937 (B. Anthony Stewart, National Geographic Creative)
4. John Atkinson Grimshaw, *Blackman Street, London*, 1885 (Wikimedia Commons)
5. Paul Sandby, *A Muffin Man*, *c.* 1759 (Yale Center for British Art, Paul Mellon Collection)
6. 'The Coster's Mansion', sheet music, *c.* 1899 (© Victoria and Albert Museum, London)
7. 'The Rise and Fall of the Pearly King', *Picture Post*, 2 August 1947 (photo by George Konig/Keystone Features/Picture Post/Hulton Archive/Getty Images)
8. 'The Chevalier Quadrilles', sheet music, *c.* 1893 (© The British Library Board)
9. 'If it Wasn't for the 'Ouses in Between', sheet music, 1894 (© Victoria and Albert Museum, London)
10. 'When the Summer Comes Again', sheet music, *c.* 1899 (© Victoria and Albert Museum, London)
11. 'When the Stars Are Peeping', sheet music, *c.* 1899 (© Victoria and Albert Museum, London)
12. 'The Lambeth Walk', sheet music, 1938 (© Victoria and Albert Museum, London)

Where copyright details are not otherwise stated, images have been photographed from out-of-copyright originals in the collection of the author. Photography by Robert Sinfield.

Acknowledgements

I owe sincere thanks to many people for their help and encouragement in the research, writing and making of this book. I am very grateful to the staff of all the archives and libraries who have helped me to consult the works in their care: there is full list in the bibliography, but special thanks go to the Guildhall Library, Bishopsgate Institute Library, London Metropolitan Archives, Tower Hamlets Local History Library and Archives and the British Library. Emma Brennan and her colleagues at MUP have struck the perfect balance between efficiency and patience, as well as being generous enough to commission the book in the first place. Both Central Saint Martins and the University for the Creative Arts have supported the project generously. Both institutions have given me sabbatical leave, and UCA has also contributed to image costs. In both universities, very many colleagues have offered their interest and encouragement: they include Jane Tynan, Royce Mahawatte, Caroline Evans, Janet McDonnell, Thomass Atkinson, Lesley Millar, Francis Summers, Katarina Dimitrijevic and Roni Brown. Latterly, the team in the Research Office at UCA have made it possible for me to finish: many thanks to Nino Nizharadze, Liz Baxter, George Barber, Mary O'Hagan, Sian Bennett and Tracy Crowther.

As is often the way with academic research, time with students provides a laboratory for ideas, and they shape the research with their questions and responses. I am very grateful in this regard to the BA fashion, jewellery and textiles students at Central Saint Martins, to MA students in several disciplines at UCA, and to PhD students in both institutions. Important words of encouragement along the way have come from academic colleagues including Richard Dennis, who invited me to turn a conference paper into a research seminar, and Barbara Burman, who told me that that research seminar could and should lead to a book. Peter Jones shared his research, and Ruth Mason invited me to deliver a seminar at University College London, where her colleagues offered advice that helped to set the direction of the research. Richard Harris, in a shared conference panel, confirmed that direction and engaged in generous dialogue on developing it. Jane Hamlett helped me to link my research with wider contexts in the history of retailing, as did Jon Stobart. At a pivotal moment, Sarah Hosking and the Hosking Houses Trust supported me with the miraculous gift of a writing residency (a space and a place to think and to create) as well as a welcome contribution to the cost of images.

Finally, we come to friends and family. Here, for their friendly encouragement, I would like to thank Alison Harry, Jo McCrone, Frances Nestor, Kate Quarry, Claire Pollock, Caroline Hughes, Jo Smith, Maria Parker, Neil Weerdermeester and Allison Streetly. Simon Kelley and Gerald Kelley have been unfailingly loyal and interested, and Leon and Hugo have been patient, tolerant and encouraging. Robert has photographed images, prepared the maps and, as always, helped in so many other ways that I can't begin to list them. I would like to dedicate this book to Robert, Leon and Hugo and to my mother Joan Kelley (née Grimes, 1937–2013) and mother-in-law Jean Sinfield (née Mearns, 1940–2017). Robert did not bring me to London, but he and the boys kept me here (not at all against my will), and it is because of them that I am now both a Northerner and a Londoner.

Introduction

In 1851 the social explorer Henry Mayhew counted thirty-seven street markets in London. These periodic gatherings of costermongers and street sellers sold fruit, vegetables, fish and a great range of other commodities from barrows and stalls in the open air, especially on Saturday nights:

> The sights, as you elbow your way through the crowd, are ... multifarious. Here is a stall glittering with new tin saucepans; there another, bright with its blue and yellow crockery, and sparkling with white glass. Now you come to a row of old shoes arranged along the pavement ... This stall is green and white with bunches of turnips – that red with apples, the next yellow with onions, and another purple with pickling cabbages ... Go to whatever corner of the metropolis you please ... and there is the same shouting and the same struggling to get the penny profit out of the poor man's Sunday dinner.[1]

Just over forty years later, in 1893, a London County Council report listed 112 street markets, a threefold increase during a period when London's population had roughly doubled (see map 1). The thirteen largest markets each had over a hundred stalls, and sold a wide range of products that included food, household goods and clothing. 'Nearly everything required for personal consumption or home use can be obtained here', was the report's verdict on Chrisp Street, typical of the larger markets, and it noted that the street markets 'undoubtedly fulfill a most useful purpose ... Costermongers are keenly alive in ascertaining when produce is at exceptionally low prices, and are always ready to purchase and distribute an almost unlimited quantity when this is the case.'[2]

Around forty years later still, in 1932, the London School of Economics' *New Survey of London Life and Labour* recorded another steep rise in the total number of stalls, up by around 50 per cent since the turn of the century, and therefore once more outstripping population growth.[3] By this date the street markets were serving a growing consumer culture not just with food, household

Cheap street

1 London Street Markets 1851 and 1893, based on the lists of markets in Henry Mayhew, *London Labour and the London Poor* (1851) and London County Council's *London Street Markets* report (1893), Appendix C. Map by Robert Sinfield

Introduction

goods and old clothes, but with the cheap luxuries of consumer modernity. Second-hand clothes had largely been replaced by mass-market fashions and silk stockings, and magazines, gramophones, gramophone records and even 'contraceptive devices' were now all sold on the stalls.4 The *New Survey*, like the LCC report before it, paid tribute (if slightly grudgingly) to the role of the street markets:

> In a Utopia their existence would certainly not be tolerated. In a Utopia, however, there would be no poverty, and if the street markets were abolished to-day, the poor would certainly suffer ... In poor neighbourhoods the tradition of the street markets flourishes and forms a cheerful and colourful link with a past that goes back to Bartholomew Fair and beyond.5

Across the 1850–1939 period the street markets played a vital role in supplying and provisioning London: there wasn't much that could be bought in a shop that couldn't also be had (and probably cheaper) from a market stall. As is indicated in figures 1, 2 and 3 (images that are similar in chronological span to the three written descriptions already quoted), the markets were vibrant and noisy focal points in many localities, dominating the East End's retail culture, enlivening sprawling suburbs, and inserted into the back streets of Soho and other West End areas. They formed an important part of the fabric of urban life, and as the city expanded and changed, so did they. In the mid-nineteenth century Mayhew had attempted to dissect the London character from his interviews

1 'Saturday Night in the East End', *Good Words*, November 1868

2 'Saturday Night in the East End', in Richard Harding Davis, *Our English Cousins*, 1894

with street sellers and costermongers, and by the early twentieth century the idea that working-class Londoners were the way they were because 'the streets demand quick wits and rapid, decided action' was firmly established.[6] In 1937, just a few years after the *New Survey* described the street markets' 'cheerful and colourful' nature, the musical *Me and My Girl* opened in the West End. As its central character, costermonger Bill Snibson, led a cast of Cockney characters and crusty aristocrats in dancing and singing the 'Lambeth Walk' (named after a London street market), it was clear that the street markets had not just provisioned the city, but had come to occupy a central role in its myths too.[7]

* * *

Selling from stalls on the street is recorded in London as far back as the medieval period, when Cheapside and Eastcheap were thriving shopping streets, lined with both shops and stalls. The 'cheap' element in the names of these streets derives from Old English *ceap*, to barter or bargain, and hence denotes a market.[8] Until comparatively recently the basic models used by retail historians have included an evolutionary analysis of the development of shopping that sees it change from primitive to sophisticated, from small-scale to large-scale, from markets to shops.[9] James B. Jefferys' classic 1954 account describes how from the nineteenth into the twentieth centuries, 'decaying and moribund institutions such as fairs and markets disappeared or completely changed their character and purpose'.[10] According to the economic historians Michael Ball and David Sunderland, in London 'one of the most visible signs of economic change in

4

3 Laszlo Moholy-Nagy, 'Berwick Street Market: general view', in Mary Benedetta, *The Street Markets of London*, 1936

the nineteenth century was the expansion of shopping', and Richard Tames in his *Feeding London* claims that this growth in shops meant that street selling was 'increasingly marginal' with only 'vestigial significance' by the mid-nineteenth century.[11] In this context, the London street markets of the later nineteenth and early twentieth centuries, those described by Mayhew, London County Council and the LSE's *New Survey*, with their links 'back to Bartholomew Fair and beyond', have been seen by some commentators as little more than the survival of an essentially outmoded retail form into an age when modern retailers (department stores, chain stores and co-operatives) apparently dominated. As Jon Stobart and Ilja Van Damme state, markets in the modern period have been viewed as nothing more than 'remnants of the past'.[12] Yet clearly London's street markets were growing in number, size and scope from the 1850s to the

1930s. They did not merely persist, but expanded, and the selling of novel consumer products such as silk stockings and gramophone records suggests that they found a role within consumer modernity.

In recent years economic and retail historians have begun to break from the simplicities of the evolutionary model of retail development to consider the complex ways in which different retail forms coexist and traditional structures – including markets – can respond to new times.[13] Ian Mitchell, for instance, comments that markets 'have a tendency to reinvent themselves to cope with changing circumstances', and Stobart and Van Damme support this proposal.[14] Recent studies by Judith Walkowitz (of Berwick Street market in Soho in the 1920s and 1930s) and Peter Jones (of Whitecross Street market) have analysed the development of these individual London markets squarely in the context of modernity, adding to a small older literature on the role of Britain's provincial markets within changing nineteenth- and twentieth-century retail cultures.[15] James Winter deals with some aspects of the history of the street markets in the wider context of an excellent history of London's streets, and Christopher Breward's work on Camden Market, although it considers a much later period, indicates how markets fit into the broader geographies of the consumer city.[16]

This book attempts to add a detailed account of street markets across London to this picture, exploring their history from the mid-nineteenth to the mid-twentieth centuries, from the moment when Mayhew observed a growing number of Saturday night markets, to the eve of the Blitz. At this point, the destruction caused by wartime bombing, subsequent slum clearance and the move to a regime of more assertive urban planning caused some disjuncture in the story of the street markets, and this is why this book does not extend into the post-war period. The first and most straightforward question this book asks is whether the street markets looked forward as well as backward, in a street culture of selling that had as much to do with the particular conditions of the modern urban metropolis as it did with pre-modern models of market exchange in the open air. What was the relationship between London's street markets and modernity?

* * *

The period between the mid-nineteenth century and the Second World War was one of enormous change in London. Between the 1851 Census and 1939 the population grew from 2.7 to 8.6 million, so that London on the eve of conflict had a bigger population than at any time in its history, until that high-water mark was surpassed some time in early 2015 to set a new maximum in the city's history of gigantism.[17] London's geographical area expanded rapidly as the city spread outwards to cover its rural hinterland with industry (predominantly in the east) and suburbs, linked to the centre by new transport networks.[18] And as the city grew, its old heart was simultaneously transformed, with ancient streets ripped out and areas of poverty and slum 'rookeries' cleared away to create new routes and grand buildings – with the aim both of improving circulation and rooting out degradation.[19]

As London grew, it grew more wealthy. The city had long been a centre of luxury consumption for the privileged few, and in the second half of the nineteenth century that role expanded.[20] The West End in particular provided numerous opportunities for leisure and entertainment, and a network of consuming institutions, chief among which were the department stores.[21] Throughout the nineteenth century the middle class was growing and prospering, so that consumer activity spread more widely across the social spectrum than ever before. Towards the end of the century the working classes too began at last to feel the benefits of industrialisation in gradually improving living standards.[22] Yet London was characterised by extreme contrasts of wealth and poverty, particularly acute in the earlier part of the 1850–1939 period, and by no means overcome by its end. The majority of London's population was working-class, and within that majority a substantial minority was trapped in casualised work on depressed wages.[23] In the post-1918 period, after the social, political and economic upheavals of the First World War, London's economy entered a distinct new phase with the emergence of technology-driven light industries, and a partial end to the problem of casual labour, but not of poverty.[24]

Across the whole period, the governance of London was transformed in several stages, as new institutions were created in an attempt to bring coherence to the patchwork of authorities that oversaw the administration of the unwieldy metropolis. The establishment of the city-wide Metropolitan Board of Works in 1855 allowed for infrastructure planning, and the creation of London County Council in 1888 introduced democratic city governance with a wider remit. Yet the persistence of the City Corporation (inheritor of the medieval authority that still pertained within the 'square mile' territory of the City of London, the financial district) continued as a source of tension and contestation.[25]

All these issues form a backdrop to the story of the street markets. The city's class structure, the shape of its exchange economy, its rich culture of consumption and leisure, the developing geography of its streets, and the tensions around its government were instrumental in shaping the context in which the street markets operated. In modern London, arguably the greatest (certainly the largest) of the world's 'world cities', the street markets proliferated and flourished. Their business model was a simple one, based on exchange in its purest form, and for much of the period under discussion here they were barely regulated, occupying space on the ground in defiance of urban planning or municipal control, yet always threatened by it. The street markets were often criticised by voices in local and national government and politics, yet simultaneously their utility was recognised, and for the working-class public they were an essential, and even loved, part of everyday life, the source not just of cheap food and commodities, but of sensory stimulation and social interaction, of pleasure and leisure, and of complex notions about what London was, what it looked like, and what it meant to be a Londoner. Unlike many other British towns and cities, where open-air markets were rehoused in covered buildings during the course of the nineteenth century, in London the markets stayed on the streets.[26] This diverging history contributed to the sense that the street markets helped to mark the distinct character of the capital city.

* * *

This book is founded upon its author's background as a historian of design and material culture, seeking to understand and document the materiality of ordinary lives, and particularly British working-class lives. The investigation of London's street markets sits naturally within such a concern, as the markets were the primary site of the consuming activities that supported home and family in the city. The initial impetus of this study is therefore to understand the street markets materially, using the design historian's focus upon objects – whether those objects be the diverse goods that were on sale, the barrows and stalls on which they were displayed, the lights that lit the markets, the sideshow entertainments, or even the markets themselves as 'things' – composite objects placed within the street environment, and interacting with it.

If the concern with objects and materiality remains central, then this book also spins its narratives wider. This is partly to root understanding of the street markets in the complex determining factors of the rapidly growing city, and partly to encompass the cultural ramifications of the street markets, which commenced as materially constituted spaces of exchange yet quickly became generators of culture. In order to formulate interpretive strategies, I use a number of *analytical frames* that are drawn broadly from the fields of social, cultural and economic history and related areas in anthropology and sociology. The dominant frame is captured in a single term, 'informality'. In the late nineteenth and early twentieth centuries London's 'street' markets were also known by an alternative name; they were the 'unauthorised markets', a categorisation that distinguished them from the authorised, formal markets, places such as the fruit, vegetable and flower market at Covent Garden, which was housed in a grand market building and contrasted strongly with the unplanned street markets' occupation of kerbside locations. In the early stages of my research, informality was one concept among many, but it gradually moved to the fore as a ruling interpretive principle; it is impossible to understand the street markets without first considering that they were informal, irregular, organically constituted, only erratically documented, with little or no status within the law, and largely overlooked by the developing apparatus of business regulation. This book's second big question, therefore, asks what can be discovered by applying the concept of informality to London's street markets in this period.

The concept of informality originated in the early 1970s with Keith Hart's ground-breaking ethnography carried out in Accra, Ghana, which has been developed by economists, anthropologists and sociologists as a way of making sense of small-scale productive, trading and service activities that operate on the margins of more organised economies. Hart conducted his study in a slum district where large numbers of people were 'not touched by wage employment' and where official statistics (such as the census) identified large-scale unemployment.[27] Yet Hart found not enforced idleness, but an array of enterprises that ranged from growing and selling vegetables to construction work, tailoring, vehicle repair, laundry, illegal gambling – and street selling.[28] Informal activity such as this has been defined simply as 'the myriad ways of making a living outside the formal economy', a definition that operates by identifying informality with reference to the formal institutions that it dodges or ignores (or that ignore it), and considering both economic and legal contexts.[29] A further characteristic is the issue of visibility: the sort of economic activity that Hart analysed was very apparent on the street, yet completely overlooked, to the point of being rendered invisible, in the economic analyses that formed the basis, in the Ghanaian context, of government and World Bank policy.[30] And informality concerns not just the type of activity involved, or its documentation (or otherwise) by official bodies, but also the people involved in it, who are often economically and socially marginal, and therefore unable to access the economy in more formal ways. Such people frequently include migrants (many of Hart's respondents were internal migrants from rural areas) and women.[31]

While many scholars of the informal economy stress how difficult it is to formulate simple definitions,[32] the three factors above are commonly cited, and all apply to the London street markets, suggesting that it might make sense to look at these markets through the lens of informality. London's street markets were categorised as unauthorised, defining them in opposition to the London markets that did have formal legal status, as well as in relation to rate- and tax-paying fixed-premises shopkeepers. Their invisibility to certain sorts of state-led information gathering is exemplified in the inquiry of the Royal Commission on Market Rights and Tolls (1888–91), which excluded the street markets from its investigation on the grounds that they were not authorised, failing to record their activities.[33] The development of the London street markets across the period of this study was driven in large part by the small-scale entrepreneurial efforts of people otherwise marginalised in London's economy. Such people included migrants to the city, and women who turned to informal work because it offered the flexibility to balance normative domestic obligations with earning.[34]

The idea of informality originated in developing economies, although economists and sociologists have more recently recognised its appearance in developed nations in the contemporary post-industrial world.[35] Can it also be useful in historical analysis? There have been polite nods of recognition between early proponents of informality and historians. Hart's 1973 paper briefly mentions 'the high degree of informality in the economic lives of the nineteenth-century London poor', and historians Gareth Stedman Jones and John Benson have both recorded their debts to ethnographic accounts of developing-world economies in making sense of nineteenth-century casual and informal labour.[36] However, on the whole historians have been slow to examine the implications of informality, as is noted by Danielle van den Heuvel, whose own analysis of street selling in the early modern period in continental Europe is an exception to this lack.[37] Thomas Buchner and Philip R. Hoffmann-Rehnitz's work on 'shadow economies and irregular work' is another significant contribution: these historians, and others, have developed the idea of informality in a largely early-modern and continental European context; I apply the idea to London in the modern period, drawing also on John Benson's *Penny Capitalists* (1983), which was an early attempt to uncover some aspects of the informal economy in nineteenth-century Britain.[38]

Informality is a concept founded upon the tension between more or less firmly established legal and economic frameworks, and certain sorts of activities that ignore, bypass or oppose such frameworks. I am neither a historian of the law, nor of the economy: Andrew Godley (who is an economic historian) asks what happens when we put culture into economics.[39] I reverse the formulation, asking what happens when we take a phenomenon that is defined by economic (and legal) characteristics, and investigate not only these characteristics but also their cultural (and material-cultural) effects. This book commences with an examination of the economic and legal characteristics of informality in the London street markets, and traces this through the things that were traded, the material qualities of the streets themselves, and the people who sold and bought. From here I move to the street markets' role in the 'performance' of London, taking the concept of informality through a cultural turn. My third big question is to ask how understanding London's street markets as essentially informal allows us to see the city differently.

Within the ruling frame of informality, I deploy a number of (often related and overlapping) concepts. These include the aforementioned material culture approaches, which I access in part through a focus on the street markets as complex (and sometimes overwhelming) *sensory* environments; analysis of materiality and sensory properties overlaps, and 'the senses ... are the medium' though which material culture can be accessed.[40] The street markets occupied both space and time in London's streets, and unlike fixed shops, which are static in space and constantly present in time, street markets are fluid in relation to both. They appear at the start of the day and disappear at its end, and while tenacious in their occupation of certain streets, as informal entities they may shift in constitution, and even be cleared away entirely. Henri Lefebvre's *rhythmanalysis* attempts to understand cities through this relationship of space and time: 'everywhere where there is interaction between a place, a time, and an expenditure of energy, there is *rhythm*', says Lefebvre: 'time and space, the cyclical and the linear, exert a reciprocal action'.[41] The sometimes uneven rhythms of the street markets perhaps represent an alternative, or overlooked, aspect of modernity, just as the informal economy shadows the development of modern capitalist exchange.

The idea of informality implies a converse notion of formality, or control, and to understand this further I have turned to notions of *governmentality*. As Patrick Joyce has shown, the nineteenth century was the period when the liberal 'rule of freedom' was instituted in many cities.[42] Liberalism was about creating conditions in which freedom could flourish, and for the street market the freedoms at stake might be contradictory: street selling conflicted with circulation, for instance, yet limiting street stalls restricted the operations of free trade. Alongside consideration of mechanisms of control I place the *carnivalesque*. Mikhail Bakhtin centres his analysis of this phenomenon in the physical space of the marketplace, and it is difficult to ignore his characterisation of the market as the centre of popular festivity and rituals of misrule that symbolically challenge authority.[43] The cultural historians Peter Stallybrass and Allon White have used Bakhtin to analyse many aspects of British and European culture, taking forward the idea of transgression, the confusion of cultural categories of high and low.[44] The idea of the carnivalesque allows a sophisticated appreciation of the combative play between high and low in culture, and is a useful tool in understanding how the street markets were enthusiastically represented in depictions of London's 'low' culture. Control and freedom; rule of law and the territory of the street; high and low – all these are important in analysing the street markets, and all can perhaps be better understood by juxtaposing ideas of governmentality with the inversions of carnival.

The analytical frames that shape this research are not discrete. As might be expected of contexts that are all useful for the analysis of a single empirical subject, the London street market, they overlap and intersect, drawing on some common theorists and common themes. Yet they are diverse, and I am keenly aware that this is a varied set of analytical tools. I make only half an apology for this, however, and for cross-pollinating ideas across disciplines (and geographies and historical periods), on the pragmatic grounds that all these frames have been useful to generate plausible interpretations. I have been careful in my application of these ideas, qualifying them where necessary and making them servant to my evidence and not its master. The London street market was, in any case, a very diverse, heterodox and contradictory thing, and it thus seems appropriate to approach it with diverse tools. As Peter Stallybrass and Allon White comment in their discussion of the market, 'only hybrid notions are appropriate to such a hybrid place'.[45]

* * *

How is it best to structure a history in which events-based narrative, while present, is not dominant? While there were clear and important changes and developments in London's street markets that took place between 1850 and 1939, there were also many continuities, and a straightforwardly chronological structure that retells events in time-based divisions will hardly do for a subject that is about the fine grain of everyday experience, and activities that often persisted across time. It might have been possible to use the analytical frames just discussed as a structuring mechanism, but this too would be unsatisfactory, in that dealing with these frames one at a time would separate out modes of analysis that will serve better if they can be brought into juxtaposition and interaction. I have chosen instead to shape my chapters in response to the street markets themselves. Chapter 1 asks 'What is a street market?' and is this book's chief attempt at a narrative history. It is my opening gambit in defining the street markets as informal entities, setting out not just their growth and development, but also their changing relationship to the law and their ongoing unauthorised status. The following chapter, 'Things', develops further the idea of informality by placing the street markets and the goods they sold into the context of London's broader economy. Chapter 3, 'Streets', deals with the places where the markets occurred and the claim they made upon both space and time there. Chapter 4, 'People', analyses the traders who did the selling, looking at how the street markets generated types and stereotypes that moved gradually to the centre of definitions of the working-class Londoner. The final chapter deals with 'Performance', both as an aspect of the street market itself, but also as the primary mode by which it came to influence wider culture in staged representations of London and Londoners.

* * *

The journey to this research commenced in two different places. One was in Saturday morning trips to my local street market in an inner suburb of southeast London, a place I came to love as the source of fruit and vegetables that were cheap, abundant and varied (in quality as well as type), where I slowly began to be recognised by a few of the friendlier stallholders, and where I rubbed shoulders with a cross-section of the magnificently diverse community in which I live. The other was in the archives, where, in the course of an earlier research project, I met repeated references to London's street markets in autobiographies, social explorations and journalism. The markets were vivid in these accounts, and the descriptions of crowded streets lined with stalls, heaped with things, filled with noise, in which sensual enjoyment and easy-going sociability were contrasted with desperation, poverty, chaos and filth seemed to offer a rich seam of analysis for understanding the material culture of the city, especially for its poorer inhabitants. I am keenly aware that these routes into the subject might suggest the danger of either romanticism or nostalgia. All I can say in reply is that this book is an exploration and not a celebration, and to make a final assertion (a bold one for a historian) that the street markets might not just have useful lessons to teach us about history, but also a role to play in the contemporary world of global capitalism with its big-business blandness, of corporate domination of the high street, and of the resurgence of informality in the 'gig economy'.

Notes

1 H. Mayhew, *London Labour and the London Poor*, Vol. I (London: Griffin, Bohn and Co., 1861 [1851]), pp. 9–10. Mayhew cites Dr Johnson in claiming that 'costermonger' derived from 'costard-monger', a seller of a particular type of apple. Mayhew defined costermongers as sellers of 'fish, fruit and vegetables', distinguishing (although not too rigorously) between them and the many other sellers of non-food goods (pp. 7–8). Charles Booth followed a similar definition in *Life and Labour of the People in London*, Series II, Vol. III (London: Macmillan, 1902–03), p. 260; other commentators used 'costermonger' to mean all street traders, whatever the goods they sold.

2 London County Council Public Control Department, *London Markets, Special Report of the Public Control Committee Relative to Existing Markets and Market Rights and as to the Expediency of Establishing New Markets in or Near the Administrative County of London* (London: London County Council, 1893) (hereafter LCC, *London Markets* 1893).

3 London School of Economics, *New Survey of London Life and Labour*, Vol. III (London: P.S. King, 1932), p. 291. Mayhew's *London Labour*, the LCC *London Markets* report of 1893 (and an updated version of 1901) and the LSE's *New Survey* form a spine of detailed quantitative and descriptive accounts of London's street markets, to which should be added Charles Booth's monumental *Life and Labour of the People in London* (1902–03). All these arose from official or quasi-official attempts to understand London's working-class inhabitants and the problem of poverty. Other major classes of sources used are national and local government investigations and commissions of inquiry (The Royal Commission on Market Rights and Tolls (1888–91); J. W. Sullivan's *Markets for the People* (1913) and Mary Benedetta's *The Street Markets of London* (1936)); records of national and local government processes (Hansard for parliamentary debates, the minute books and documents of London County Council and borough councils); journalistic accounts; autobiographical accounts; accounts by social explorers and observers; legal textbooks and cases; sheet music and song lyrics; and extensive visual material. For the more complex sources there is consideration at key points in the coming chapters of interpretive issues around their use; for Mayhew and Booth these issues are considered in Chapter 4, where they are most pertinent.

4 LSE, *New Survey*, p. 292; *Hansard*, 13 May 1926, vol. 195, cc. 1059–90; M. Benedetta, *The Street Markets of London* (London: John Miles, 1936) pp. 48–9.

5 LSE, *New Survey*, p. 300.

6 Anon., *The City of London: The Times Book* (London: Times Publishing, 1927), p. 133.

7 C. Madge and T. Harrisson, 'Doing the Lambeth Walk', in *Britain by Mass Observation* (London: Faber and Faber, 2009 [1939]), pp. 140–1.

8 I. Archer, C. Barron and V. Harding (eds), *Hugh Alley's Caveat: The Markets of London in 1598* (London: London Topographical Society, 1988), pp. 1–5; *Collins English Dictionary* (Glasgow: Harper Collins, 1991).

9 G. Shaw and M. T. Wild, 'Retail patterns in the Victorian city', in J. Benson and G. Shaw (eds), *The Retailing Industry, Volume II: The Coming of the Mass Market 1800–1945* (London: I.B. Tauris, 1999), pp. 99–100; see also M. Phillips, 'The evolution of markets and shops in Britain', in J. Benson and G. Shaw (eds), *The Evolution of Retail Systems* (Leicester: Leicester University Press, 1992), p. 62, citing this tendency in H.-C. and L. Mui, *Shops and Shopkeeping in Eighteenth-century England* (London:

Routledge, 1989). A further recent example of the evolutionary model is S. Isenstadt, 'The spaces of shopping: a historical overview', in D. C. Andrews (ed.), *Shopping: Material Culture Perspectives* (Newark, DE: University of Delaware Press, 2015), pp. 1–32.
10 J. B. Jefferys, *Retail Trading in Britain 1850–1950* (Cambridge: Cambridge University Press, 1954), p. 39.
11 M. Ball and D. Sunderland, *An Economic History of London 1800–1914* (London: Routledge, 2001), p. 121; R. Tames, *Feeding London: A Taste of History* (London: Historical Publications, 2003), pp. 153–4.
12 J. Stobart and I. Van Damme, 'Introduction: markets in modernization: transformations in urban market space and practice, c.1800–c.1970', *Urban History*, 43.3 (2016), 358–71, p. 364.
13 M. Casson and J. S. Lee, 'The origin and development of markets: a business history perspective', *Business History Review*, 85 (2011), 9–37, p. 17
14 I. Mitchell, *Tradition and Innovation in English Retailing 1700–1850* (Farnham: Ashgate, 2014), pp. 2–4; Stobart and Van Damme, 'Markets in modernization'.
15 J. Walkowitz, *Nights Out: Life in Cosmopolitan London* (New Haven, CT: Yale University Press, 2012), ch. 5; P. Jones, 'Redressing reform narratives: Victorian London's street markets and the informal supply lines of urban modernity', *London Journal*, 41.1 (2016), 60–81; see also J. Stobart and I. Van Damme (eds), *Urban History*, special issue on *Markets in Modernization*, 43.3 (2016), and Jerry White's magnificent three-volume history of London, particularly the volumes on the nineteenth and twentieth centuries: J. White, *London in the Nineteenth Century: 'A Human Awful Wonder of God'* (London: Vintage, 2008 [2007]); J. White, *London in the Twentieth Century: A City and its People* (London: Vintage, 2008 [2001]). For consideration of markets outside London, see R. Scola, *Feeding the Victorian City: The Food Supply of Manchester, 1770–1870* (Manchester: Manchester University Press, 1992); J. Blackman, 'The food supply of an industrial town: a study of Sheffield's public markets 1780–1900', *Business History*, 5 (1963), 83–97; D. Hodson, 'The municipal store: adaptation and development in the retail markets of nineteenth-century urban Lancashire', *Business History*, 40 (1998), 94–114. See also recent research within food history focusing attention on street vending, in various localities and historical periods, for example M. Calaresu and D. van den Heuvel (eds), *Food Hawkers: Selling in the Streets from Antiquity to the Present* (London: Routledge, 2016).
16 J. Winter, *London's Teeming Streets 1830–1914* (London: Routledge, 1993); C. Breward, *Fashioning London: Clothing and the Modern Metropolis* (London: Berg, 2004).
17 GLA London Datastore (http://data.london.gov.uk/census/), Historical Census tables; 'London Population Confirmed at Record High', Greater London Authority press release, 2 February 2015.
18 See Ball and Sunderland, *Economic History of London*, pp. 171–5.
19 White, *London in the Nineteenth Century*, pp. 31–2, 56; White, *London in the Twentieth Century*, pp. 8–9; Winter, *London's Teeming Streets*, p. 207.
20 Ball and Sunderland, *Economic History of London*, pp. 121–2.
21 E. D. Rappaport, *Shopping for Pleasure: Women in the Making of London's West End* (Princeton, NJ: Princeton University Press, 2000).
22 Ball and Sunderland, *Economic History of London*, ch. 5.
23 Ball and Sunderland, *Economic History of London*, ch. 5; G. Stedman Jones, *Outcast*

London: A Study in the Relationship Between Classes in Victorian Society (London: Penguin, 1984 [1971]), Part 1.

24 Stedman Jones, *Outcast London*, preface to the revised edition (London: Verso, 2013).
25 Ball and Sunderland, *Economic History of London*, ch. 16; White, *London in the Nineteenth Century*, pp. 471–6; White, *London in the Twentieth Century*, pp. 355–7.
26 J. Schmiechen and K. Carls, *The British Market Hall: A Social and Architectural History* (New Haven, CT: Yale University Press, 1999), pp. xi–xii.
27 K. Hart, 'Informal income opportunities and urban employment in Ghana', *Journal of Modern African Studies*, 11.1 (1973), 61–89, p. 62.
28 Hart, 'Informal income opportunities', p. 69.
29 M. Leonard, 'Coping strategies in developed and developing societies: the workings of the informal economy', *Journal of International Development*, 12.8 (2000), 1069–85; S. Sassen, 'The informal economy: between new developments and old regulations', *Yale Law Journal*, 103.8 (1994), 2289–304.
30 Hart, 'Informal income opportunities', p. 62; see also Casson and Lee, 'Origin and development of markets', p. 15, for much older examples of 'invisibility' in informal markets.
31 Hart, 'Informal income opportunities'; D. van den Heuvel, 'Selling in the shadows: peddlers and hawkers in early modern Europe', in M. M. van der Linden and L. Lucassen (eds), *Studies in Global Social History, Volume 9: Working on Labour: Essays in Honour of Jan Lucassen* (Leiden: Brill, 2012), pp. 125–51; T. Buchner and P. R. Hoffmann-Rehnitz, 'Introduction: irregular economic practices as a topic of modern (urban) history – problems and possibilities', in T. Buchner and P. R. Hoffmann-Rehnitz (eds), *Shadow Economies and Irregular Work in Urban Europe, Sixteenth to Early Twentieth Centuries* (Vienna and Münster: Lit Verlag, 2011).
32 See, for instance, Buchner and Hoffmann-Rehnitz, 'Introduction: irregular economic practices': the warning is, however, repeated by very many other authors.
33 Royal Commission on Market Rights and Tolls, *Final Report of the Commissioners* (London: Her Majesty's Stationery Office, 1891), p. 2.
34 A. J. Kershen, 'Jewish and Muslim married women don't work: immigrant wives and home-work in the late nineteenth and late twentieth centuries', *Home Cultures*, 8.2 (2011), 119–32.
35 Sassen, 'Informal economy'.
36 Hart, 'Informal income opportunities', pp. 67–8; J. Benson, *The Penny Capitalists: A Study of Nineteenth-century Working-class Entrepreneurs* (Dublin: Gill and Macmillan, 1983), p. 4; Stedman Jones, *Outcast London*, preface to the 2013 edition.
37 van den Heuvel, 'Selling in the shadows', p. 125.
38 Buchner and Hoffmann-Rehnitz (eds), *Shadow Economies*; Benson, *Penny Capitalists*.
39 A. Godley, *Jewish Immigrant Entrepreneurship in London and New York, 1880–1914* (Basingstoke: Palgrave, 2001), ch. 1.
40 D. Howes, 'Hyperesthesia, or, the sensual logic of late capitalism', in D. Howes (ed.), *Empire of the Senses: The Sensual Culture Reader* (Oxford: Berg, 2005), p. 295; M. Paterson, 'Haptic geographies: ethnography, haptic knowledges and sensuous dispositions', *Progress in Human Geography*, 33.6 (2009), 766–88, p. 775; A. Gerritsen and G. Riello (eds), *Writing Material Culture History* (London: Bloomsbury, 2014), p. 7.
41 H. Lefebvre, *Rhythmanalysis: Space, Time and Everyday Life*, trans. S. Elden (London: Bloomsbury, 2013), pp. 25, 18.

42 P. Joyce, *The Rule of Freedom: Liberalism and the Modern City* (London: Verso, 2003).
43 M. Bakhtin, *Rabelais and his World*, trans. H. Iswolsky (Bloomington, IN: Indiana University Press, 1984 [1965]).
44 P. Stallybrass and A. White, *The Politics and Poetics of Transgression* (London: Routledge, 1986).
45 Stallybrass and White, *Politics and Poetics*, p. 27.

∽ I ∾

What is a street market?

What is a street market? And how did London come to have a growing number of them from the mid-nineteenth century onwards? The answer to the first question at least might seem obvious, but in fact this issue requires some consideration in the context of a broader, complex history of market provision and retail development in London and beyond. The report of the Royal Commission on Market Rights and Tolls (1888–91) defined a market as 'an authorised public concourse of buyers and sellers of commodities, meeting at a place, more or less strictly limited or defined, at an appointed time'.[1] This is a neat definition – people buying, people selling, commodities, a set place and a set time; together these constitute a *market*. The Royal Commission (which examined the whole of Great Britain and Ireland) identified in London thirteen markets, including Smithfield, Billingsgate, Spitalfields, Borough Market, Leadenhall and Covent Garden. But as we have already seen in the Introduction, Henry Mayhew had counted 37 markets in 1851, and London County Council was to find 112 when it studied the issue in 1893. Why then did the Royal Commission in 1888 list just thirteen markets?

The Commission's definition of a market contains one more term, apart from buyers, sellers, commodities, place and time, and that is the word 'authorised'. In the Commission's view, a market was only a market if it had some sort of legal sanction or basis, a market charter or a grant of market rights. It is this part of the definition that led the Royal Commission to restrict its efforts, in London, to the investigation of certain markets only – those such as Smithfield or Billingsgate which had emerged from the medieval period onwards, founded upon royal or parliamentary grant or charter, and which all had long histories in the provisioning of London.[2] The reason why the Royal Commission reached such a different figure for the number of markets from Henry Mayhew and London County Council was that it was counting different markets, and did not include the street markets in its tally.

In contrast to the formal (or 'authorised') markets, street markets are usually referred to as 'unauthorised' by nineteenth-century commentators, although I prefer the more straightforward term 'street market', which was also used commonly (as indeed was 'informal').[3] 'Street market' is descriptively accurate: with just one exception (Whitechapel Hay Market), by the mid-nineteenth century the authorised markets were all housed in off-street premises, while almost without exception, the unauthorised markets took place on the street. In its thirteen volumes the Royal Commission devoted just a few pages and a few scattered references to London's street or unauthorised markets, and when it did consider them, it was only to question their traders in their role as customers of the authorised markets, costermongers who bought their stock in Billingsgate, Covent Garden or Spitalfields and sold it in the street markets. Many other contemporary accounts of London's markets commence with the proviso that their authors will only describe the authorised markets, and are not interested in the street markets.[4] Sidney Webb, in a Fabian tract of 1891, dismissed them as 'a few insignificant so-called "street markets"'.[5] Trade directories did not list market stalls: using just *Kelly's Directory* as a source, and looking at Middlesex Street in Whitechapel as an example, the historian could form the wholly erroneous view that the businesses operating in this street were limited to the shops listed. In fact Middlesex Street, under the customary name 'Petticoat Lane', was famous for its huge street market, emerging by the early twentieth century as one of the sights of London.[6]

The fact that so many observers felt able to overlook or dismiss the street markets, which were nevertheless widespread, quantitatively significant and spectacular, says something about the status of the informal economy during the period of this study. One of the problems of applying the idea of informality to historical subject matter is to show that a concept originating in the recent and contemporary developing world, and then applied to developed post-industrial economies, is also applicable in earlier periods. One simple route to demonstrate this relevance might be to draw a parallel between London's nineteenth-century street markets and the communities in which they developed, and non-Western socio-economic practices. There are hints of precedents here: Keith Hart, in looking at Accra, was influenced by the 'proto-ethnography' of Henry Mayhew's description of nineteenth-century London's poor street sellers, while Gareth Stedman Jones, in *Outcast London* (a study of the 'casual labour problem' from the 1860s to 1914), notes how his thinking was influenced by 'the economics and politics of development … I had acquired a vivid sense of the shantytowns of the Third World from reading *Tristes Tropiques* by Claude Lévi-Strauss.'[7]

Thomas Buchner and Philip Hoffmann-Rehnitz's volume on the 'shadow economy and irregular work' goes some way to addressing the gap in historical studies of the informal economy, and provides a rather more sophisticated means of applying the idea of informality historically than simple East End/shanty town parallels.[8] Buchner and Hoffmann-Rehnitz place the history of informality – defined in the broadest terms – firmly into Western economic history, noting that it has been an overlooked feature of many economies and can be viewed alongside its more regulated and recognised counterpart in the formal economy as 'two dimensions of one comprehensive economic (capitalistic) order with emphasis on the interrelations between them'.[9] Buchner and Hoffmann-Rehnitz provide a brief periodisation that fits informality into historical changes in economic organisation: it was strongly present in Europe in the seventeenth and eighteenth centuries, the period in which guild organisation was at its tightest (proving the point made by many commentators that informality cannot exist without formality, and vice versa). From the early nineteenth century the growth of free trade economic policy might have been expected to erode informality (for the same reason), but in fact it persisted, and was reinforced late in the nineteenth century and into the twentieth by the emergence of a growing concept of formality in waged labour as the norm.[10] Although the British economy and legal frameworks developed on a slightly different trajectory to those European countries that provide the evidence drawn upon by Buchner and Hoffmann-Rehnitz, the fact that the Royal Commission and other sources failed to recognise the London street markets already begins to suggest that, for a variety of reasons, they were viewed not just as unauthorised, but also illegitimate. For the purposes of historical analysis it makes sense to think about them as *informal*.

It is a peculiarity of researching this particular historical subject that while some observers treat us to vivid descriptions of the street markets that stress their size, spectacular nature, auditory impact and the assault they made on all the other senses, other sources barely seem to see them at all, because they did not fit into accepted categories of economic activity. Understanding the street markets' informality is crucial not just to knowing their character and how they functioned, but also to handling some sorts of evidence which may be predisposed not to recognise them, or to describe them in certain ways: as Buchner and Hoffmann-Rehnitz have noted, accounts of irregular or informal economic activities often show 'a specific bias' towards a critical stance.[11] This chapter will examine the street markets through their informality, in their relationship to the law and its attempts, unsuccessful and successful, first to capture or to 'see' their activities, and secondly to regulate them. Almost any historical phenomenon is influenced by the legislative frameworks that surround it, but in the case of the London street markets that context is particularly important because they were formed in a position of uncertainty and insecurity, balanced on the precarious boundary between *laissez faire* policies and urban regulation, and it was in this context that they responded to both economic and social change. This chapter sets out a chronology of how the street markets developed and grew, establishing a story that will then be embellished thematically in the chapters to come, exploring aspects of the street markets' character over the period between the mid-nineteenth century and the Second World War.

1850s–1860s: a gap in the market

If there were established and formally constituted authorised markets in London, how and why did growing numbers of unauthorised street markets appear? Was there a gap in the formal economy that the informal street markets were able to fill? One way to answer this question is to contrast what happened in London with the development of markets elsewhere in the country. According to James Schmiechen and Kenneth Carls in their history of the British market hall:

> The market hall was an original but not surprising invention that by the second half of the nineteenth century had become arguably the most important public building in the British townscape and one that continued to evolve well into the twentieth century. It stands as an outstanding example of nineteenth-century municipal social policy and urban planning, and in it lay the embryo of the modern environmentally controlled retail spaces: the department store, the supermarket, and the shopping mall.[12]

Schmiechen and Carls depict a clear evolution of retail practices from open markets to market halls, supermarkets and malls, an evolution that is similar in principle to those models of retail change discussed in the Introduction, which also see the street stall as a primitive point of origin from which modern retailing has descended (or ascended). They further note that, unlike the towns and cities of Britain outside the capital, London 'had no public retail markets to match its great public wholesale markets': London is excluded from their study as a result.[13] Kathryn A. Morrison, in her architectural history of English shops and shopping, reinforces the point: 'while northern cities were being graced by magnificent market halls with modern amenities, Londoners resorted once again to their street markets'.[14] Historical analysis of British markets largely depicts London as anomalous, and even backward, in not building covered market halls for its retail trade. The development of market halls was not completely uniform outside London, and some street (and informal) markets were present in other large urban centres: the *Glasgow Herald*, for instance, gave a lively account in 1861 of Irish street vendors in the city, and the presence of costermongers' unions in Manchester, Leeds and other cities evidences street selling beyond the capital.[15] Such activity outside London awaits historical analysis to determine its extent and significance, but it was certainly less prominent than was the London informal economy of street retailing. Schmiechen and Carls note that 'by 1886, two-thirds of Britain's principal municipal boroughs had, in theory at least, prohibited marketing on the street': this was not the case in London.[16]

From the medieval period until the nineteenth century the legal standing of all markets, in London and elsewhere, was based upon market charters and monopolies granted by the Crown or Parliament. The right to hold a market had been closely connected from the medieval period with the development of urban centres and trade.[17] Market rights conferred a geographical monopoly: the right to hold a market included the right to prevent any other market setting up in competition nearby. Markets could be profitable enterprises, as charters often allowed their owners to levy tolls on transactions.[18] There were laws prohibiting practices such as forestalling (selling outside the market to avoid paying tolls), regrating (buying and then selling the same goods within the same market), and to enforce the correct use of weights and measures.[19]

Schmiechen and Carls describe how during the course of the nineteenth century in many English towns and cities, markets shifted from private to public hands. Private ownership of markets (often by the local landowner, and descended from the manorial rights of earlier centuries) was increasingly replaced by civic ownership as market improvement commissioners and local authorities bought out market rights and instituted reform, usually by replacing open-air markets with market halls.[20] A number of Acts of Parliament legislating on local government and public health enabled these changes: significantly, much of this legislation did not apply in London.[21] London's government had been in the hands of its Mayor and Corporation since medieval times, when certain privileges of self-rule were granted to recognise the city's pre-eminent status as England's chief trading centre. The jurisdiction of the Corporation persisted down to modern times even as London grew – it was neither revoked, but neither was it geographically enlarged, and the result was that as London spread many miles beyond its original boundaries, its ancient heart, what came to be called the City of London, continued to be ruled by the Corporation, while what we might call London-the-city which extended all around was governed by a patchwork of parish authorities, the vestries. In the mid-nineteenth century groups of vestries amalgamated to form district boards, and a number of pan-London bodies were created to deal with specific issues: these included the Metropolitan Board of Works (1855) which oversaw projects such as the new sewer system built in the 1850s–1860s, and the London School Board (1870). Throughout these changes, the Corporation of London retained its ancient jurisdiction over the 'square mile' of the City.[22]

In 1327 Edward III had granted the Mayor and Corporation of London control of all the city's markets, with a monopoly extending to a radius of around seven miles.[23] By the mid-nineteenth century, the majority (eight out of thirteen) of London's authorised markets belonged to the City of London.[24] The remaining five were in private hands, owned by individuals who had been granted later market privileges (despite the City's supposed monopoly). Covent Garden market, for instance, was owned by the Dukes of Bedford on the basis of a royal charter of 1670.[25] Thus, what was an ancient privilege, passing in most places outside of the capital into the public hands of local government, had in London long been vested in the local authority, the City of London and its Corporation, alongside a number of private individuals. On most matters, the writ of the Corporation only held within the 'square mile' of its territory, and beyond this London was governed by its local parish vestries and district boards, and after 1888 by London County Council. However, on the matter of the markets the City Corporation's authority extended well beyond its limited territory, because of that extensive seven-mile monopoly.[26] This meant that the Corporation of London could in theory restrict the setting up of new markets across the capital, as could the private market owners. Several attempts to set up new markets were halted in the courts, and in a particularly notorious case in the 1880s the owner of Spitalfields market was able to block the opening of a new market by the Great Eastern Railway Company. A later commentator noted of this case that 'Spitalfields market is interesting, not so much as a market as an illustration of the prevalence of ancient law over present convenience in certain of London's public affairs.'[27]

During the course of the nineteenth century the operations of many of London's authorised markets increased in scale (while others, such as Newport market, Hungerford market and Oxford market failed or were displaced by urban development).[28] Associated with this was a period of improvement in the middle years of the nineteenth century, as these markets were put under pressure from reformers seeking better hygiene in food supply and greater order on the city streets. George Dodd in *The Food of London* (1856) describes how this pressure had gathered pace from early in the nineteenth century, citing a pamphlet from 1814 that condemned 'with much severity' the 'mean and filthy' state of London's markets.[29] As a result new buildings were constructed and facilities were improved. The notoriously bloody and chaotic livestock trade of Smithfield market, with its associated slaughterhouses, was rehoused at the Metropolitan Cattle Market in Islington in 1855, and the Smithfield site was redeveloped as the London Central Markets (Meat, Poultry and Provisions) in stages between 1864 and the 1880s (see figure 4).[30] Newgate market (which sold meat) was closed and its activities relocated to Smithfield,[31] and Billingsgate fish market (described by Dodd in its early nineteenth-century form as 'a group of sheds and stalls, accumulated – no one knew how') was rehoused on its ancient site in the 1850s and again in the 1870s, although it continued to attract criticism for the congestion of the approach roads and the monopolistic practices of its traders.[32] The fruit, vegetable and flower market at Covent Garden, described by Dodd as 'unsightly and incommodious', was given new premises in the 1830s, and further improved in the 1870s (see plate 1).[33]

This period of improvement coincided with Schmiechen and Carls's description of nineteenth-century market reform across the country which tended to curtail (though not to completely eliminate) open-air markets and street selling outside the capital.[34] In London this reform took the shape of material improvements in the authorised markets. All the Corporation of London's new market buildings were designed by Horace Jones, the Corporation architect, and in 1877 he looked back over the work done, with a confident assertion of its value that seems designed to rebut criticism on the matter of the ancient market monopoly:

> No-one knows, or seems to care to know how much the four millions of people composing this metropolis are indebted to the chartered Lords of the markets

What is a street market?

4 'The meat market, Smithfield, at two in the morning', *Illustrated London News*, 13 January 1870

of London, 'and seven miles around it'; these Lords being the Lord Mayor and Corporation of the City of London.[35]

Yet the Corporation's development of its markets did nothing to provide new retail provision, which was increasingly stretched. As the city grew and spread, larger and larger numbers of people found themselves living at some distance from the authorised markets, which were no longer convenient for everyday shopping for the bulk of the population.[36] The authorised markets began to concentrate more and more on wholesale trade, selling to retailers who in turn sold to the public, and it is to this that we can trace the growth of the street markets.

For the working classes, the retailers were costermongers, who bought fish, fruit and vegetables wholesale in the authorised markets and tramped through the city selling from their barrows. At the beginning of our period, in 1851, Henry Mayhew's concern was largely with itinerant street traders (both the costermongers and sellers of other and varied goods), but he noted that 'the street sellers are to be seen in the greatest numbers at the London street markets on a Saturday night'.[37] His thirty-seven street markets represent the regular gathering together in habitual locations of traders, many of whom also spent at least some of their time on the move through the city's streets. Over time, itinerant street trading declined, and street markets continued to grow. Looking back from the turn of the century, Charles Booth (in *Life and Labour of the People in London*) gave an account of this process, as the authorised markets switched to wholesaling and the itinerant traders settled into more or less regular street markets:

> As a natural result of the growth of London, the original retail markets [i.e. the authorised markets] have assumed an almost strictly wholesale character. From these markets the retail shops obtain their supplies, and to them the costermonger repairs to replenish his stock ... The first and proper business of the coster is to push his barrow and sell his goods from street to street; but it has come about that itinerant vendors, seeking their customers, gather together in certain places during a portion of the day or evening, and in these places their customers finally learn to look for them. Thus the circle is complete, and an informal, unauthorized market is the result.[38]

Despite work to improve the authorised markets, as these turned to wholesale trade the City Corporation made no attempt to institute new retail markets, and its market monopoly meant that no other local authorities or private bodies could do so either. It was into the resulting vacuum that the street markets expanded, energetically, chaotically and quite without formal organisation or legal sanction. The informal economy filled a gap left by the City of London and private market owners' defence of their ancient market rights, and the failure of these bodies to develop retail markets. As Buchner and Hoffmann-Rehnitz note, 'irregular practices of distribution often serve economically as a means of opening up a market not, or only insufficiently, covered by official trade'.[39]

What was the street markets' position in the law in the 1850s and 1860s? There were a number of laws that could be used to control both itinerant street trading and street markets. These included the Metropolitan Paving Act of 1817 (also known as Michael Angelo Taylor's Act), the Metropolitan Police Act of 1839 and the Metropolis Management Act of 1855.[40] David Green analyses the use of such legislation (and that on Sunday trading), concluding that swelling numbers of street hawkers in the 1840s and 1850s were to some extent hounded off the streets, or at least displaced from central London to more peripheral areas.[41] However, Green acknowledges that the Metropolitan Police were often reluctant to act too assertively against street selling, and that many cases brought by parish vestries were unsuccessful.[42] Had street selling been under really effective attack, we would expect the numbers of both itinerant sellers and those operating in markets to fall, or at least to stagnate relative to population. Itinerant hawkers appear to have dwindled somewhat over time, but settled markets grew strongly both during and after the period covered by Green's analysis, as Mayhew's whirling maelstrom of 'those who obtain their living in the streets' resolved itself into a more structured pattern of street markets.[43] Itinerant selling did not disappear altogether: many of the costermongers who sold in the markets also did some perambulatory trade, and many city streets had lone barrows on regular pitches, as well as wandering kerbside traders who sold from their hands or from baskets. But the general direction of change was towards settled, if informal, street markets.

A number of sources across the period of this study enumerate the street markets: for the middle decades of the nineteenth century the relevant accounts are Henry Mayhew's 1851 description, and London County Council's report of 1893, which looked back as far as the 1830s. Where these two sources overlap they are consistent in the (growing) numbers of markets they list: the LCC's figures indicate that there were around thirty markets in the 1840s, Mayhew lists a total of thirty-seven in 1851, the LCC records forty-two or more in the 1850s, and sixty or more by the 1860s.[44] Clearly by this date street markets were an established and expanding feature in London's retail landscape: how did they develop from this point onwards?

1867–71: informality confirmed

London's street markets were an informal response to the growth of the city and growing demand from a rapidly swelling population, conditions that led the authorised markets to turn to wholesale trade. The ancient market monopolies acted to prevent the setting up of new retail markets, and bricks-and-mortar retailers could not meet the demand from the urban poor for cheap food and goods. By the 1860s London's swelling number of street markets played an increasingly important role in provisioning the city, but they did so on an informal basis that meant that their activities were vulnerable to legal challenge and police pressure. The late 1860s was a pivotal moment in the history of the street markets, bringing both attempts at legislative change that threatened to outlaw the markets altogether, as well as a scheme to build a new market hall that might, had it succeeded, have set a precedent leading to the formalisation of retail market facilities.

In 1867 the Conservative government of the Earl of Derby introduced a Metropolitan Streets Act. This was not primarily focused upon the street markets or itinerant street sellers, but was intended to tackle traffic problems caused by congestion and obstructions, and to ensure safe freedom of movement for pedestrians. It contained a clause prohibiting the placing of goods on the roadway or pavement 'for a longer time than may be absolutely necessary for loading or unloading'.[45] As the street markets had no explicit market rights to protect them, the effect of this was to make the setting up of a stall or parking of a barrow illegal, which would have outlawed both street markets and itinerant traders, unless they kept moving constantly. As the historian James Winter notes: 'few who supported the bill noticed that they had just given the police direction to end all street commerce and [they] had to be reminded by vigorous protests and demonstrations'.[46] *The Times* reported:

> It would appear that henceforth the costermonger's occupation is gone … We are not surprised to hear that a meeting has already been held, and a society is

being formed, to preserve this useful class of retail dealers from extinction. It is hardly possible to suppose that such was the real intention of the Legislature, and it is certain that, so construed, the Act would inflict a cruel injustice, not only on them, but on the large class which is mainly supplied by them.[47]

When the law, quickly condemned as the 'Starvation Act', came into force on 1 November 1867 there was a widespread outcry.[48] Many newspapers spoke out on the street traders' behalf, estimating that approximately 50,000 'peaceable, orderly and industrious' people would be deprived of their livelihood, and that they and their dependents would be thrown on to the Poor Law for support.[49] Their customers, the mass of the working-class population, would be deprived of the 'cheap and convenient' provisions and household goods sold by the street traders.[50] The right to free trade, a key tenet of nineteenth-century liberal economic thinking since the battle over the Corn Laws in the 1840s, was also seen to be under serious challenge.[51] The more radical press even depicted the affair as class war: 'if the costermonger's barrow is to be removed from the street as an obstruction, why permit the carriages of the nobility and the gentry to blockade frequented thoroughfares where balls, breakfasts, and morning concerts are going forward?'[52] As Buchner and Hofmann-Rehnitz note, urban authorities are frequently caught between the need to protect 'pillars of urban society', while also 'enabling the poor to earn a living and satisfy their basic needs in terms of clothing and food, essential goods they could frequently only afford through the use of irregular trade channels'.[53] In 1867 public opinion as orchestrated in the press came down on the side of the informal street sellers and their customers.

This controversy came at an awkward moment: parliamentary business in the first half of 1867 had been dominated by machinations over the Second Reform Act. There had been agitation over electoral reform dating back to 1866, with public demonstrations in support of extending the franchise. One of the Second Reform Act's most recent historians, Robert Saunders, plays down the level of unrest, which was certainly much less threatening than that which had accompanied other key moments of real or potential political reform, notably the Great Reform Act of 1832 and the Chartist agitation that ebbed and flowed throughout the 1830s and 1840s. Nonetheless, it seems plausible that the government was anxious to avoid confrontations over the unintended consequences of the Metropolitan Streets Act so soon after the Reform Act controversy.[54] The result of press criticism and public meetings was therefore a Metropolitan Streets (Amendment) Act, passed through Parliament as rapidly as the original law had been, which excepted costermongers and street hawkers from the controversial clause 'so long as they carry on their business in accordance with the regulations from time to time made by the Commissioner of Police, with the approval of the Secretary of State'.[55]

The amended Metropolitan Streets Act became the basis of the street markets' relationship to the law for the next sixty years, placing jurisdiction into the discretionary hands of the Metropolitan Police, and thereby reinforcing the markets' uncertain legal status. The government's climb-down did not, however, end criticism of the Act. As a number of press reports noted, the result of the whole affair had been to challenge the street sellers' perceived common law or customary right to trade and to place them 'under the control of the police' without the protection of clear statute law.[56] Nevertheless, as the legal historian Mariana Valverde has pointed out, police power is generally regarded as more legitimate if wielded at a local than a state level, and despite fears, the relationship of the Metropolitan Police to the street markets was not always an antagonistic one.

The workings of police jurisdiction can be seen in the proceedings of the Royal Commission on Market Rights and Tolls when it took evidence from a number of costermongers in their capacity as buyers in the authorised markets. The witnesses included John Denton, who bought fruit and vegetables wholesale in Spitalfields market to sell retail in Chapel Street market in Islington. In the following extract, Denton is being questioned by Lord Balfour of Burleigh, chair of the day's proceedings:

> Burleigh: Are you exposed to any inconvenience from the police or from other people trying to move you away from where you have been accustomed to sell?
> Denton: They cannot very well move us, because it is a *bonâ fide* market street, ours is. We have to have nine-foot boards, and three feet wide, and four feet in between.
> Burleigh: Is there any parish or other authority that gives you leave to take up your particular place?
> Denton: No.
> Burleigh: But the street has been a market street for a great many years?
> Denton: For a great many years.
> Burleigh: When you first took up your stall there, had you to get anybody's leave to go there?
> Denton: No; we put our boards on trestles and started selling; only the police came up and told us to have our boards measured nine feet long, and three feet wide, and four feet in between; that is all.
> Burleigh: Once having taken your position, you are not liable to be interfered with?
> Denton: No; as long as we keep the place clean, and there are no rows, nobody interferes with us.
> Burleigh: If you were away for two or three days, and did not occupy your stall, would anybody else take possession of the place?
> Denton: Of course, if anybody put in there, I could do nothing.
> Burleigh: All that you have to be sure of is that your stall is occupied every day?
> Denton: Yes.
> Burleigh: If so, nobody interferes with you?
> Denton: No.
> Burleigh: You get a sort of right or privilege to remain there?
> Denton: Yes; as long as we keep our things in proper order, nobody interferes.
> Burleigh: You pay no footing, or anything of that sort?

Denton: No.
Burleigh: And you do not pay the police anything?
Denton: Certainly not.[57]

This exchange reveals clearly how the Metropolitan Streets (Amendment) Act played out, with the Police Commissioner's regulations specifying the dimensions and spacing of stalls and barrows (the reference to stalls that are nine feet long and three feet wide with a gap of four feet between each one). Lord Burleigh, a man steeped in late nineteenth-century government and politics, was wrestling in his role as commissioner with the complexity of how to legislate effectively to regulate and control the authorised markets. Regulation is clearly the question uppermost in his mind in this exchange – and he is preoccupied with both rights and restrictions. He struggles to comprehend the notion that Chapel Street market exists entirely without regulation, except for that Metropolitan Police ruling. He seems to be baffled by the idea that Denton pays no rent, has no one's permission to pitch his stall, and has only a tenuous right to ongoing occupation of his habitual pitch. Denton, conversely, is nonplussed by Burleigh's interest in regulation, and downright offended by his final suggestion that costermongers bribe the police to leave them in peace. The conversation illustrates perfectly the delicate balance of the street markets' position, with no legal status, but immune from prosecution at the discretion of the police. Figure 5 shows the street market in New Cut on a Sunday morning in 1872. In the right foreground of the image are two police constables: many (if not most) popular depictions of the street markets from the mid-nineteenth century onwards include such figures, watching over the market from a peripheral surveying position (see also figures 1, 2, 17, 20, 30 and 31).

Even before the 1867 Act was passed or amended, a project was underway that would influence how the street markets' history played out over the following decades. This was Columbia Market in Bethnal Green, a private, charitable venture to build a retail market hall to give the poor of the East End clean and modern facilities for their selling and shopping. It was planned and funded by Angela Burdett Coutts, a philanthropist who dedicated her huge inherited wealth to a succession of projects to improve the lives of the London poor. Burdett Coutts was able to circumvent the market monopoly by obtaining market rights by Act of Parliament, and in May 1869, eighteen months after the controversy over the Metropolitan Streets Act, she unveiled to the public a market complex that had been planned since 1864.[58] Columbia Market (see figure 6), designed by architect Henry Darbishire, was massive in scale, imposing in grandeur, and was launched by a opening ceremony attended by the Archbishop of Canterbury, the Bishop of London and various members of the royal family.[59] The press heaped praise upon the splendour of the market: the *Builder*, for instance, commented on 'the endeavour here nobly made to establish a market and to bring order and elegance, as well as economy and comfort, into the midst of poverty, squalidness, and misery'.[60] *The Times*

What is a street market?

5 'Sunday Morning in the New Cut, Lambeth', *Illustrated London News*, 27 January 1872

6 Columbia Market in 1869, *Illustrated London News*, 1 May 1869

compared Columbia Market to Westminster Abbey, noting that 'it is really impossible to over-praise the beauty of the whole structure', with its soaring clock tower and pointed arches in polished granite emulating the gothic beauty of a fourteenth-century cathedral.[61] The market cost the huge sum of £250,000, covered a two-acre site, and incorporated shop units, a market hall, colonnaded arcades and a large covered courtyard for costermongers and their barrows. It also had wholesale facilities, as Burdett Coutts was critical not just of London's street markets, but also the domination of the existing wholesale markets.[62]

Yet within six months of its opening Columbia Market had closed, having failed to attract sufficient traders or customers, wholesale or retail. Baroness Burdett Coutts ploughed in more money to convert her splendid building into a wholesale fish market to rival Billingsgate, but this too failed, and Columbia Market was passed to the Corporation of London in 1871. The Corporation likewise could not make it flourish, and it went back once more to Burdett Coutts in 1874. Various further schemes came to nothing, and the building was closed as a market for the last time in 1885 (see figure 7).[63]

Many reasons were suggested for Columbia Market's failure. Shortly after

7   Columbia Market in a semi-derelict state in 1914

it closed for the first time the journalist Blanchard Jerrold collaborated with the French artist Gustave Doré on a book entitled *London: A Pilgrimage*. In it Jerrold claimed that the fault for the market's demise lay with those who it was supposed to benefit:

> so sunk were those for whom the good was intended in ignorance and the wantonness of vice, that they would not use the gift ... the hosts of half-fed creatures massed far and wide around the building would not take the comfort and economy the new market offered, but went to the street shambles and road-side barrows as of old.[64]

Other commentators admitted that the building's scale and opulence were out of step with its purpose. As *The Times* noted, 'the chief impression left on the spectator's mind is a doubt whether a building so fine in its design, so elaborate in its exquisite ornamentation, is quite fit for the rough-and-ready purposes of an every-day market'.[65] There was certainly a mismatch of huge proportions between the size and style of the building and the activities and people it was intended to house. It is difficult to think of a greater architectural contrast than that between Columbia Market's soaring neo-Gothic monumentality and the usual sites and structures of the street markets, with their informal and ever-shifting arrangement of barrows and stalls on the open street, a model that, however much it was condemned by commentators, was clearly popular with both buyers and sellers.

Some historians have speculated that the religious overtones of the new market's architecture may have made it particularly forbidding to costermongers and their customers, especially as the lavish interior was decorated with repeated carved exhortations, including 'Be Sober, Be Pitiful, Be Vigilant, Be Courteous', not all characteristics widely associated with costermongers and street sellers.[66] However, when the *Builder* sent its correspondent to report on the market, he came across several observers struggling and failing to make out the inscriptions, so heavily elaborated was their Gothic script.[67] It seems unlikely that this architectural detail would have troubled many users of the market, although the overall atmosphere of the church-like building may have done so. More off-putting, perhaps, was the long list of bye-laws, which included strict provisions on the management of refuse and rubbish, regular washing and cleaning of stalls, rigorously enforced opening and closing times, and an absolute prohibition on Sunday trading. Penalties for infringement ranged from five shillings to five pounds.[68] Street sellers were known for their independence and resistance to rules and regulations: on the streets they came and went as they pleased, and they paid no rent, as John Denton explained to Lord Burleigh. London County Council's 1893 report on markets gave the costermongers' dislike of both regulations and the rent charged as the key reasons for Columbia Market's failure.[69] If it was architecturally overblown, then it was also out of step in other respects with the informality of the street economy that it attempted to replace, and in the end even Blanchard Jerrold, who had commenced by blaming the poor for failing to appreciate Baroness Burdett Coutts's magnificent market, was forced to wonder whether 'perhaps Lady Coutts is wrong after all, and marketing of the lowest kind is best done in the rain, on the kerb-stone'.[70]

If the Metropolitan Streets Act had been enforced in its original form, sweeping trade from the streets, might Columbia Market have been a success? Would the history of London's markets have been a different one, with further schemes to take the markets off the streets, and a concerted effort to do away with the monopoly of the authorised markets? If Columbia Market had been a success, would new attempts have been made to legislate on street trading? The prolonged drama of Columbia Market and its difficulties was headline news for years, partly because of the huge scale of the financial losses involved. As a prominent case study in failure, it helped to set the tone for thinking about markets thereafter, and in particular suggested to observers that the London street market was an organic entity, something that grew naturally and could not be artificially created, transplanted or controlled. *The Times* noted that the scheme had ignored 'the well-beaten path of custom' and that 'people who have been accustomed for years – perhaps for generations – to buy and sell certain commodities in certain places will not easily be persuaded to change their habits'.[71]

Other, albeit smaller and less high-profile, examples of failed market schemes suggest that Columbia Market's lack of success was as much to do with the specific conditions and characteristics of London's retail market trade as with any excess of grandeur and lack of architectural sensitivity in the Burdett Coutts scheme. In Poplar, for instance, in the early 1870s attempts were made to move an informal market from the High Street. A new market building, named Randall's Market, was built on a site nearby by a private landlord, yet the displaced costermongers ignored this and instead took to trading on neighbouring Chrisp Street, which by the 1890s had become one of the biggest and busiest of the East End street markets.[72] In Clare market, just off the Strand, a tangle of pre-Great Fire streets housed a chaotic street market clustered around a small and decrepit authorised market building dating from the seventeenth century.[73] Here, according to London County Council, 'proper accommodation was provided', yet 'the market drifted from the actual market area, and is carried on in the surrounding streets'.[74] There are other examples of attempts to move street traders into off-street sites, or to create formal retail markets, all failures, and the lesson seemed to be that, Columbia Market's particular drawbacks notwithstanding, street markets could only flourish on the streets.[75] London's various local authorities learned from these examples that, in the capital at least, there was something rather delicate about the economy and ecology of a retail market which meant that what grew haphazardly on the streets could not be artificially created in purpose-built premises. In its 1893 report on the city's markets the LCC concluded that:

> The fundamental principle in connection with markets that almost all authorities appear to agree upon, is, that their growth must be natural, and that they cannot be successfully made. Wherever an attempt has been made to create a market by the erection of market buildings ... failure has resulted.[76]

1870s–1930s: regulating the status quo

The lack of planned retail market facilities in London is usually viewed not just as an anomaly, but as a failure, both by historians and by contemporary commentators who saw the absence of market halls as a matter of regret and even shame.[77] As the street markets fulfilled the role played by market halls elsewhere, views of them were and are often coloured by unfavourable comparisons with the purpose-built and regulated facilities that still survive in many towns and cities throughout Britain. In 1872 Blanchard Jerrold reported the reactions of the artist Gustave Doré to the places they visited on their London 'pilgrimage'. Observing the crowds of working-class shoppers in the shabby surroundings of the New Cut street market, Doré declared that London should 'build twenty district markets for them, all over your city, like our arrondissement markets. *C'est logique*.'[78]

Yet despite their lack of premises and their shabby and ad hoc nature, London's informal retail markets persisted and expanded on the streets through the late nineteenth century and into the twentieth. Evidence from London County Council's 1893 report on markets suggests that twelve or more new street markets appeared in the 1870s, and sixteen or more in the 1880s. The report listed a total of 112 markets, with the majority of these sufficient in scale and frequency to make a significant contribution to retailing in their local area or, in many cases, well beyond it.[79] The total number of stalls in 1893 was 5,292, with thirty-eight of the markets having over fifty stalls, and thirteen having more than a hundred. When the LCC updated its investigation with a new report in 1901, the number of markets had dropped by two, but the number of stalls had risen by around a third to 7,055.[80] Map 1 shows clearly the growth and spread of the street markets.

The street markets continued to function under the delicate but more or less workable balance instituted by the Metropolitan Streets (Amendment) Act and its delegation of discretionary powers to the Metropolitan Police. Yet this delicate balance was frequently challenged. Guildhall Library in London contains a volume in which are bound together transcripts of a cluster of legal cases from the late 1880s and 1890s on the right or otherwise of local authorities in London to remove costermongers and their barrows from the streets (usually on the grounds that they caused an obstruction) and, conversely, the right of costermongers to trade freely, demonstrating how ambiguity continued even after the Act of 1867.[81] Most of these cases were brought under earlier legislation and most were ultimately unsuccessful. The standard legal textbook, Pease and Chitty's *Law of Markets and Fairs* (first published in 1899), contains references to many such cases, and concludes that as long as street traders complied with the Metropolitan Police directives (the 'nine by three and four between' rule) they should be safe from prosecution under any other law.[82] Although enough cases were brought to make the street traders' position always open to question, sufficient of the cases failed as to make local government jurisdiction also very uncertain.

Pease and Chitty discuss the right to trade in the streets in terms that frame it as a fundamental and ancient liberty, not to be entirely superseded by the imperative of circulation:

> It was ... a common practice in early times to hold a market or fair either wholly or in part in public streets leaving a sufficient portion of the streets open for public passage ... Where the origin of both the highway and the market or fair is immemorial, the practice, if shown to be ancient, is justifiable, although it somewhat abridges the right of the public in the use of the highway as such.[83]

Although the context to this remark is a discussion of ancient, chartered markets held in the streets, and not the informal street markets of the nineteenth century, it indicates the extent to which, despite increasing pressure to regulate London's streets, there was recognition that street trade – the ancient practice of buying and selling in public – had some protection in customary practice, as was noted at the time of the 1867 furore. The historian James Winter defines the street as both a *passage* and a *place*: in the liberal state certain freedoms were held dear, and among these was a basic assumption that the streets should be free and open to all, and not just for circulation.[84] There was marked reluctance to limit street trade as a result. Even as London's traffic increased and diversified, there was recognition that managing it might involve managing complex conflicts between different users, as Winter explains:

> Why ... should [it] be that priority be given, for example, to speeding up the pace of wheeled vehicles if the result of doing so were to inhibit pedestrians in their use of all parts of the street. Was it unambiguously obvious that the freedom of the respectable gentleman to walk without needing to make his way around a costermonger's barrow was more valuable to the welfare of the city than the freedom of the street-seller to carry on his occupation?[85]

The notion persisted that the street market had some standing in custom, if not in law, as John Denton's confident assertion in his evidence to the Royal Commission on Markets and Fairs that Chapel Street was a '*bona fide*' market street indicates.

Despite the workable solution provided by the Metropolitan Police's application of the 'nine by three and four between' rule, from the 1890s there was some pressure to legislate further and more fundamentally on the street markets. In 1888 London County Council was formed as the first city-wide local authority for London, and from the start it established itself as a progressive body, eager to develop rational government and administrative modernity.[86] The LCC's relationship with the City of London Corporation, with its ancient privileges and peculiar position in control of a small enclave of territory within the much larger area now governed by the LCC, was fractious from the start, and over the issue of markets this tension was greatly heightened by the anomalous power that the ancient market monopoly held by the Corporation, with its seven-mile radius, gave it over market development across much of London. The LCC moved to draw up its 1893 report on markets relatively soon after it was formed, lamenting the fact that 'London ... almost alone of the great cities of the world, has no control over its markets', and using the report to make a confident claim that it should be the markets authority (wholesale and retail) for the entire capital.[87] Looking back from 1913, the American J. W. Sullivan found the ongoing influence of ancient monopoly and the City Corporation perturbing:

> The London market system has come down with time, and not only have the reformers of this generation, despite their efforts, failed to remedy its incongruities, but they have been compelled to stand aside while these were made worse: the London County Council's attempts to readjust the wholesale market ownership and administration of the metropolis have for twenty years been frustrated at every important point. The stubborn City fathers refuse to be reformed.[88]

There was a tangle of powers competing over market policy, with considerable tension between the City of London and the LCC. The lowest tier of local government, the parish vestries and district boards, which were replaced in legislation of 1899 by metropolitan borough councils, formed a third strand in this complex web of legislative influence, with national government occasionally stepping in as a fourth, as seen in the 1867 Metropolitan Streets Act and the Royal Commission on Market Rights and Tolls, and several investigations of the early twentieth century.[89] Yet all of these bodies demonstrated some hesitation over how best to approach the issue of the street markets. The reasons for this include the caution induced by the 1867 Metropolitan Streets Act fiasco and the disquieting example set by Columbia Market's monumental failure to formalise retail marketing. A further cause arose from competing ideas about the most effective legislative instruments for local government, and particularly for regulating activities that take place upon the street.

The notion of governmentality – what government can do and the techniques through which it operates – originated with Michel Foucault.[90] Foucault's writing, and that of many others on this subject, is largely concerned with government at the level of the state, and particularly the emergence of the modern liberal state in which ideas of the limits of government, what it should and should not do, are clearly relevant to the informal economy as well as to regulation of the streets.[91] The political scientist James Scott's influential and provocative book *Seeing Like a State* suggests that in the modern period certain governments have taken 'exceptionally complex, illegible, and local social practices' and, through techniques of gathering and representing knowledge, simplified them to achieve 'legibility' upon which action can be built.[92] The Royal Commission's treatment (or rather non-treatment) of the street markets in London fits this description: it sidelined the street markets by excluding them from its definition of a market, concentrating on achieving a clear and comprehensive overview of authorised market provision upon which recommendations were made for reform. In doing so, it ignored the burgeoning street retail trade that was nonetheless responsible for provisioning a large part of London's population. Scott notes how practices that are informal in legal or economic terms are often overlooked in such 'seeing like a state' approaches – as for instance in Keith Hart's 1973 ethnography of Accra, where the census (a classic state mode of information gathering) failed to uncover a poor but vigorous informal economy of small-scale enterprise.[93]

Scott might thus seem to provide a way to understand the marginalisation and official invisibility of London's informal street markets. Yet not every government body followed the Royal Commission in failing to see the street markets and the informal economy in which they played a vital role, with the LCC's 1893 report a case in point, demonstrating a more complex approach than that taken by the Royal Commission. Here the socio-legal ideas of Mariana Valverde might be useful: Valverde takes Scott's idea of 'seeing like a state', and suggests that we might also consider 'seeing like a city', a mode of vision in which, at the local level, older techniques of administration often persist or reappear alongside newer ones within modern contexts, and the 'state simplifications' that Scott identifies are tempered with more pragmatic and relational approaches.[94] Valverde's ideas help to explain the long history of legislative hesitancy over London's street markets, which were sometimes ignored, often criticised, *and* left to develop organically with little interference throughout the period covered by this book.

Unlike the Royal Commission which preceded it, the LCC's 1893 investigation did not let the legal marginality of the street markets blind it to their existence. It went to some lengths to gather information and to enumerate the phenomenon, recording the markets, their constituent stalls and the types of goods sold. The street markets were depicted as chaotic, unplanned, lacking facilities, and creating mess, dirt and obstruction: 'we ... consider it a disgrace that so necessary and extensive a trade ... should be forced into the public streets for want of proper market accommodation'. The report summed up the street markets as 'a serious nuisance', yet the detail of its description seems rather more enthusiastic, praising the markets' scale and scope, and criticising them on rather fewer grounds (chiefly to do with the obstruction of both vehicle and pedestrian traffic) than they are praised.[95]

Despite this recognition of the informal economy, in some respects the LCC report is reminiscent of Scott's 'seeing like a state' mode of governing: it contained detailed standardised tables of information that selectively captured the activities of the markets, their location and in particular their effect upon the circulation of traffic. And it proposed that the street markets should be housed in covered market halls, with plans and drawings for three trial schemes, at Strutton Ground, Clare Market and Leather Lane (see figures 8 and 9).[96] These

What is a street market?

8   Plan for a market hall at Strutton Ground, Westminster (exterior), London County Council, *London Markets*, 1893

would take the markets off the streets, regulate their hours, provide facilities for waste collection and public health inspection, and even bandstands and rooftop children's playgrounds. Yet what is most noteworthy about these proposals, with their beautifully idealised architects' drawings, is that they were never built: by the time the council updated its study of London's markets in 1901 they had already been dropped.[97] From the start the utopian visualisations were couched in caution: 'We have come to the conclusion', states the 1893 report, 'that the only possible way of successfully dealing with street markets is to provide them with accommodation *actually on the spot on which they have grown*, and where experience has shown they are most needed.'[98]

Some aspects of the LCC's report signal a flirtation with rather grand planning, while others fall clearly into Valverde's definitions of relational, local, 'seeing like a city' practices, a mix of strategies that uses 'both old and new gazes, premodern and modern knowledge formats'.[99] In particular, Valverde suggests that city governance (in both North America and Britain) continued to make use of the legal concept of 'nuisance', and the long-established and flexible regulatory tool of the licence.[100] Both of these became prominent in the relationship of the London street markets to the law, as was the prevalence of

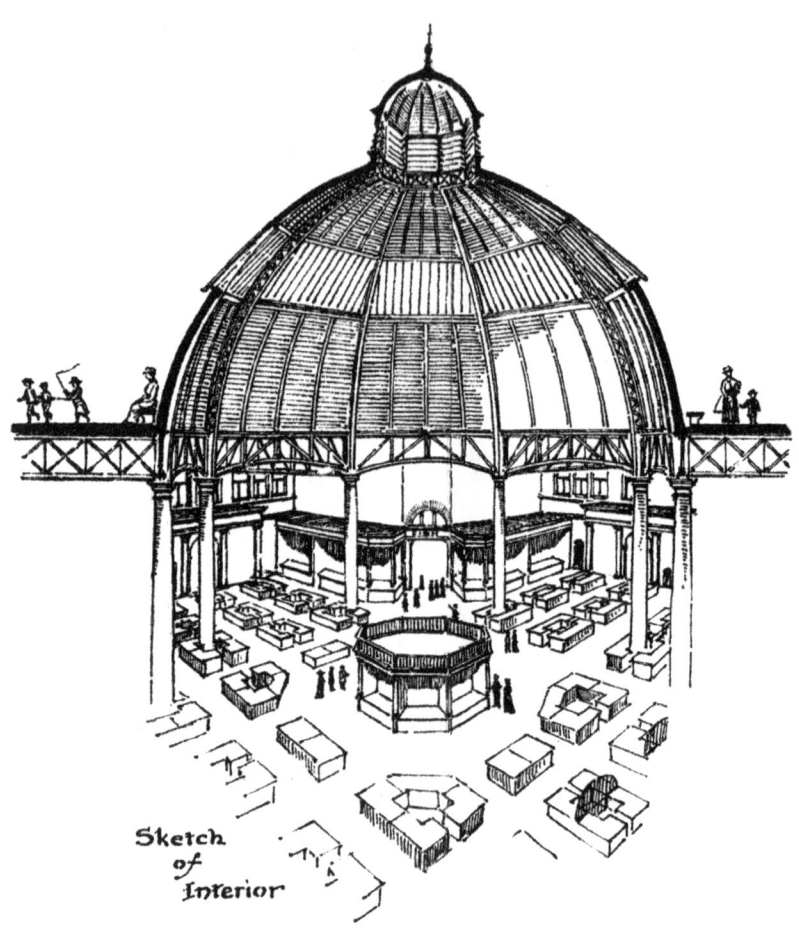

9   Plan for a market hall at Strutton Ground, Westminster (interior), London County Council, *London Markets*, 1893

police surveillance that Foucault depicted as primarily a characteristic of the condition of government before the emergence of the liberal state, but that, as far as the London street markets were concerned, sat alongside attempts to use more modern techniques of quantification and categorisation.

We have already seen how the LCC described the street markets as a 'nuisance'. Valverde notes that 'nuisance is an inherently relational and thus embodied category'. Something cannot be a nuisance in any abstract or absolute sense, but only if it can be shown that it is a nuisance *to* somebody, that it interferes with property rights or freedom of movement, for instance. Valverde further comments that nuisance law, despite its many contemporary applications, is 'backward looking, locally specific … and intersubjective' and as such it is 'in sharp contrast to the knowledge formats typically found in modern governmental projects of the seeing like a state variety'.[101] The LCC report of 1893, despite its grand ambitions, thus also embodies quite clearly Valverde's idea of 'seeing like a city', a somewhat contradictory mixture of older and newer conceptions of the purposes of government and its most appropriate tools, a pragmatic blend derived from the relational pressures of urban life.

The social investigator Charles Booth read the LCC's report and commented on it in his huge study, *Life and Labour of the People in London*, noting the LCC's somewhat contradictory blend of general criticism with particular praise for the street markets. 'If the details given in the report are studied', he noted, it was difficult to see how the LCC had reached the conclusion that the street markets were a nuisance. He recognised the relational characteristic of the category of nuisance, asking 'to whom are these markets a nuisance?':

> Not to those who frequent them, for they do so voluntarily; not to those who have shops in these streets, for their trade is increased; not to the general inhabitants of the neighbourhood, who are the people whose wants are served. The litter and refuse may indeed be accounted a nuisance, but this is inseparable from the utility of the market. The only persons whose comfort may suffer are passers-by, whose progress may be hindered by the crowd; but they in most cases might as well proceed by a different route. In truth, the nuisance is theoretic rather than practical, an offence against a rather visionary idea of civic order.[102]

As noted, the LCC quickly dropped most of its recommendations from 1893, and this pattern was repeated with several later inquiries too. In the early 1920s both the LCC and, at national level, the Home Office considered legislation on the control of street trading. The file of the relevant LCC committee on this matter is full of consultations, correspondence, reports and evidence, but in the end, a terse one-page document records the fact that, due to differing opinions, the council has decided that 'legislation not be promoted'.[103] Legislative hesitancy flowed from caution about the possibility of failure, a respect for the ancient right to trade on the streets, and profound unease about interfering with a system that, as an informal entity, fed the bulk of London's population.

It took until 1927 for legislation on London's street markets to be finally enacted: the LCC appointed the metropolitan borough councils as market authorities for their areas, with powers to license traders. This was the most minimal of interventions, a recognition in their existing form of the unauthorised markets. It was an attempt to control some of their activities, but not to remove, relocate or rehouse them. Valverde notes that the licence as a legal tool is ancient, flexible, and concentrates in its conditions on 'spaces, temporalities and activities'.[104] In setting certain conditions for the holding of a licence, it passes to licensees the responsibility to limit and control their own activities, at the risk of losing both their licence and their livelihood. The licensing of the street markets was enacted under the LCC General Powers Act of 1927, which gave authority to the borough councils to pass bye-laws on street markets. These bye-laws, based on a common template, certainly concentrate, as Valverde suggests, on space, time and activity. *Space* is covered in detailed prescriptions on the size and placing of stalls and barrows, elaborating but not fundamentally altering the previous 'nine by three by four' regulations with additional rules on the height of stalls and their placement in relation to carriageway and pavement. *Time* is covered with licences stipulating permissible days and hours of trading, as well as detailed rules about the temporary nature of stalls: they must be able to be cleared away quickly. And *activities* are set with licences granted for particular classes of goods to be sold, subject to existing public health legislation. Finally, the disposal of refuse is stipulated (one of the complaints against the street markets had always been about the mess that they left behind), with councils levying a small annual fee for the licence and a weekly charge for refuse collection.[105] In 1932 the LSE's *New Survey of London Life and Labour* (which found continued significant growth in the number of stalls in the street markets) concluded that licensing did little to alter the fundamental character of the markets, and that councils granted the majority of licence applications made by existing stallholders.[106] The only part of the capital not covered by the new licensing scheme was the City of London under its Corporation. Here street selling had been licensed since 1911, and in the mid-1920s a decision was made not to license any new street sellers, with the eventual aim of removing all street stalls and hawkers from the Square Mile: the *New Survey* notes that street selling had dwindled away there by 1932.[107]

The legal marginality of the street markets was not just about the hesitations and vacillations of London's competing local authorities. It reveals a profound though delicately balanced contest between different conceptions of the street – as a place of circulation, control and modernity, or the site of exchange, free trade and customary liberties. Valverde asserts that although '"seeing like a state" techniques of visualization and spatialization' are 'useful and important', work like James Scott's may 'have come to blind ... scholars of law and urban governance to the unpredictable dynamic by which older knowledge formats and older legal forms ... suddenly revive'.[108] Certainly in the case of London and its street markets, Valverde's notion of 'seeing like a city' helps to make sense of the fact that successive and competing local authorities, over a prolonged period, condemned and denigrated the informal street markets, proposed planned solutions to replace them with market halls, debated various legislative measures to control them, yet in the end opted for the least radical solution possible, to issue licences which did little more than wrap a cloak of formality around the informal retail provision that had grown organically with the growth of the city.

* * *

What then is the answer to the question, what is a street market? An example may serve to answer the question. Chrisp Street market, in Poplar, is recorded in the LCC report of 1893 as having first appeared in the 1860s. By 1893 it had 215 stalls, including 44 selling vegetables, 13 fruit, 22 fish and 27 meat.[109] The core business of Chrisp Street was that done by the costermongers selling fresh produce, but many other commodities were traded there too, so that as well as being a major source of food, the market was where many people furnished and equipped their homes, and clothed themselves and their families. By 1893 Chrisp Street was attracting custom from beyond the immediate area, with shoppers 'from all parts of the district, and from distances as far as Canning Town', and like most London street markets, it was busiest on Saturday nights when crowds blocked the street and no traffic could pass.[110] Plate 2 is a photograph of Chrisp Street from around 1910, seventeen years after it was described in the LCC's report, and about a decade before Dolly Scannell knew the market. Scannell grew up in Poplar, and her autobiography describes Chrisp Street market in great detail: 'a long wide road stretching from Poplar to Bromley-by-Bow, a lively, happy thoroughfare full of exciting stalls and people'. It was lit at night by 'huge naphtha flares which hissed and spluttered and turned lovely colours, yellow, orange, red and blue. The fruit was all shiny and polished and the vegetables always fresh.'[111] Later again, photographic evidence depicting Chrisp Street in the 1930s shows the market crowded in the daytime, and stalls selling magazines and radios attest to the emergence of these and other consumer commodities among the fruit and vegetables.[112]

Chrisp Street emerged from the informal economy of mid-nineteenth-century London, and it was relatively untouched by legislative control throughout almost the whole period covered in this book. Like London's other street markets, it was nothing more nor less than the habitual gathering on the open street of sellers who sold from barrows and stalls, attracting a wide working-class custom and many middle-class shoppers too. The markets' locations were determined by habit, in conjunction with the tolerance or otherwise of the Metropolitan Police, whose limited powers to remove market stalls formed the only effective legislative restraint on the street markets until licences were introduced in 1927. Sellers paid no rent for their space and pitches were allocated by informal means within the trading community. There were no special facilities – water, lighting or refuse collection – and the markets operated in streets that were open to traffic in the usual way, although the stalls often blocked that traffic in the streets they occupied. The hours and days of operation were also determined by custom and by the market sellers themselves, who decided when to set up their stalls and how late to keep them open. Some markets opened every day, others just for a few days a week. In Jewish areas Sunday trading was common (in defiance of the law), but most markets were busiest on Saturdays, and particularly on Saturday nights.

While the rest of the country got new retail market halls in a line of some continuity with ancient market sites, London had seen its ancient markets become wholesalers, and retail demand displaced to the streets. It is necessary to know about the authorised markets in order to understand how the unauthorised markets came to be, as the latter emerged to fulfil a need left unmet by the former.

Many accounts have insisted on treating the authorised markets as if they *were* London's markets, *in toto*, downplaying or even ignoring the buying and selling that took place on the streets, or assuming that it was dwindling over time, becoming outmoded. In fact the street markets flourished in and adapted to modernity, and the legal accommodations of the Metropolitan Streets (Amendment) Act and London County Council's licensing law allowed them to do so.

The street markets occupied a persistently liminal position, neither within nor beyond the law, but precariously on its margins and constantly contested: the relationship in law of informal practices to formal institutions serves as a starting point for examining many further characteristics of the London street markets. It is possible to identify a number of dominant institutions against which the street markets were defined by contemporary commentators as a subaltern opposite – but one that was often closely enmeshed with the more formal institutions it shadowed. Thus the street markets were the unauthorised analogue not just of the authorised markets but of the bricks-and-mortar shop-based retail activities that have attracted so much attention in histories of London as a consumer city. Unlike the department stores, they were located not on the broad avenues of the West End, but tangled into its back streets. And they expanded to fill the congested highways of the East End, always 'other' in the imaginative geography of London. In their material constitution, the street markets were at odds with conventional narratives of urban development, as will be seen when we examine the things that were sold in the markets and the 'architecture' of their barrows and stalls. The people who ran them were a symptom of a London labour market that was notorious for its disorganised and casualised nature. The complex play between formality and informality suggested by this initial analysis of London's street markets in comparison to its authorised markets will have other applications in the chapters that follow.

Notes

1. Royal Commission on Market Rights and Tolls, 1888–1891, *Final Report of the Commissioners* (London: Her Majesty's Stationery Office, 1891), p. 2.
2. Today only Smithfield meat market still operates on its original site, but New Covent Garden, New Billingsgate and New Spitalfields have all kept a sense of history by preserving their names as they have moved to less central sites (Nine Elms, the Isle of Dogs and Leyton).
3. For an example of 'informal', see London County Council Public Control Department, *London Markets, Special Report of the Public Control Committee Relative to Existing Markets and Market Rights and as to the Expediency of Establishing New Markets*

in or Near the Administrative County of London (London: London County Council, 1893) (hereafter LCC, *London Markets 1893*), p. 7.
4   For example, W. J. Passingham, *London's Markets: Their Origin and History* (London: Sampson Low, Marston, 1935), p. xiii; C. Maughan, *Markets of London* (London: Pitman, 1931).
5   S. Webb, *The Scandal of London's Markets*, Fabian Tract no. 36 (London: Fabian Society, 1891), unpaginated.
6   *Kelly's Post Office London Directory* (1928), p. 474.
7   J. D. Conroy, 'Intimations of Keith Hart's "informal economy" in the work of Henry Mayhew, P. T. Bauer and Richard Salisbury', available at SSRN: http://dx.doi.org/10.2139/ssrn.2031291, p. 10 (accessed 12 March 2012); G. Stedman Jones, *Outcast London: A Study in the Relationship Between Classes in Victorian Society* (London: Verso, 2013 [1971]), 'Preface'.
8   T. Buchner and P. R. Hoffmann-Rehnitz, 'Introduction: irregular economic practices as a topic of modern (urban) history – problems and possibilities', in T. Buchner and P. R. Hoffmann-Rehnitz (eds), *Shadow Economies and Irregular Work in Urban Europe, Sixteenth to Early Twentieth Centuries* (Vienna and Münster: Lit Verlag, 2011), p. 9.
9   Buchner and Hoffmann-Rehnitz, 'Introduction: irregular economic practices', p. 15.
10 Buchner and Hoffmann-Rehnitz, 'Introduction: irregular economic practices', pp. 25–35; Richard Harris, 'Modes of informal urban development: a global phenomenon', *Journal of Planning Literature*, 33.3 (2018), 267–86, doi.org/10.1177/0885412217737340; Conroy, 'Intimations', p. 3.
11 Buchner and Hoffmann-Rehnitz, 'Introduction: irregular economic practices', p. 19.
12 J. Schmiechen and K. Carls, *The British Market Hall: A Social and Architectural History* (New Haven, CT: Yale University Press, 1999), pp. 33–4.
13 Schmiechen and Carls, *The British Market Hall*, pp. xi–xii, 33–4.
14 K. A. Morrison, *English Shops and Shopping* (New Haven, CT: Yale University Press, 2003), p. 120.
15 *Glasgow Herald*, quoted in R. Swift, *Irish Migrants in Britain 1815–1914: A Documentary History* (Cork: Cork University Press, 2002), pp. 107–8; A. I. Marsh and J. Smethurst, *Historical Directory of Trade Unions*, Vol. 5 (Aldershot: Ashgate, 2006) pp. 142–9.
16 For a detailed recent account drawing on evidence from a number of towns and cities outside London, see I. Mitchell, 'Retail markets in Northern and Midland England, 1870–1914: civic icon, municipal white elephant, or consumer paradise?', *Economic History Review*, 71.4 (2018), 1270–90, doi.org/10.1111/ehr.12653; for a contemporary report, see George Augustus Sala's description of Whitechapel in Liverpool, *Gaslight and Daylight* (London: Chapman and Hall, 1859), pp. 34–5; Schmiechen and Carls, *The British Market Hall*, p. 27.
17 M. Casson and J. S. Lee, 'The origin and development of markets: a business history perspective', *Business History Review*, 85 (2011), 9–37, pp. 15–24; M. Girouard, *The English Town: A History of Urban Life* (New Haven, CT: Yale University Press, 1990), ch. 1.
18 H. Parrish, *Pease and Chitty's Law of Markets and Fairs*, 2nd edn (London: Charles Knight and Co., 1958), p. 3.

19 Casson and Lee, 'Origin and development of markets', pp. 20–1.
20 Schmiechen and Carls, *The British Market Hall*, ch. 3; I. Mitchell, *Tradition and Innovation in English Retailing 1700–1850* (Farnham: Ashgate, 2014), p. 159.
21 Schmiechen and Carls (*The British Market Hall*, pp. 39–40) name the following legislation as significant in the nineteenth-century development of market halls: Municipal Reform Act 1835, Markets and Fairs Clauses Act 1847, Public Health Acts 1848 and 1875, and Local Government Acts 1858 and 1875. See also Royal Commission on Market Rights, *Final Report*, p. 12 which notes that the Local Government Act 1858 and Public Health Act 1875 gave greater powers to local authorities to act on markets, but are not applicable in London.
22 M. Ball and D. Sunderland, *An Economic History of London 1800–1914* (London: Routledge, 2001), ch. 16.
23 Royal Commission on Market Rights, *Final Report*, p. 7. The original unit of measurement was the obsolete *leucœ*, approximately 6½ miles (p. 12). The standard legal textbook on markets gives the measurement as *leucae*, and the distance as roughly 7 miles; J. G. Pease and H. Chitty, *Law of Markets and Fairs* (London: Knight and Co., 1899), p. 77.
24 Royal Commission on Market Rights, *Final Report*, p. 12.
25 Royal Commission on Market Rights, *Final Report*, p. 22.
26 Ball and Sunderland, *An Economic History of London*, p. 395.
27 Spitalfields market's charter had been granted by Charles II in the late seventeenth century, and therefore the Great Eastern Railway argued that it had no validity from its inception as it contradicted the Corporation of London's market monopoly conferred by Edward III in the fourteenth century. The courts upheld the Spitalfields charter. J. W. Sullivan, *Markets for the People: The Consumer's Part* (New York: Macmillan, 1913), p. 242.
28 C. Knight, *Knight's Cyclopædia of London* (London: George Woodfall, 1851), p. 795; R. Tames, *Feeding London: A Taste of History* (London: Historical Publications, 2003), pp. 73–4.
29 G. Dodd, *The Food of London* (London: Longman, Brown, Green, and Longmans, 1856), p. 232.
30 Dodd, *Food of London*, pp. 233, 261–4; H. Jones, 'On the new metropolitan markets', *Royal Institute of British Architects Sessional Papers 1877–78* (London Metropolitan Archives CLA/009/01/083), pp. 116–19.
31 Pease and Chitty, *Laws of Markets and Fairs* (1899), p. 42.
32 Dodd, *Food of London*, p. 346; Corporation of London Fish Supply Committee, correspondence and press cuttings, London Metropolitan Archives COL/CC/FSC/02/2.
33 Dodd, *Food of London*, p. 370.
34 The picture was not one of unblemished improvement, however, which was why the Royal Commission on Market Rights and Tolls was appointed in 1888. This identified the dead hand of ancient privileges and monopolies still at work in some places. It recommended sweeping changes but its recommendations were not legislated upon (Parrish, *Pease and Chitty's Laws of Markets and Fairs* (1958), p. iii). See T. Cleaver, 'Sic semper monopoliis: modernising the law of markets and fairs', Bar Council Law Reform Essay Competition winner 2009, http://www.barcouncil.org.uk/2374.aspx (accessed April 2017), which analyses how market law still retains some ambiguities in the twenty-first century.

35 Jones, 'On the new metropolitan markets', p. 124.
36 Knight, *Knight's Cyclopædia*, p. 795.
37 H. Mayhew, *London Labour and the London Poor*, Vol. I (London: Griffin, Bohn and Co., 1861 [1851]), p. 9.
38 C. Booth, *Life and Labour of the People in London*, Series II, Vol. III (London: Macmillan, 1903), p. 260.
39 Buchner and Hoffmann-Rehnitz, 'Introduction: irregular economic practices', p. 25.
40 Parrish, *Pease and Chitty's Law of Markets and Fairs* (1958), pp. 35–7; J. Winter, *London's Teeming Streets, 1830–1914* (London: Routledge, 1993), p. 42.
41 D. R. Green, 'Street trading in London: a case study of casual labour 1830–60', in J. H. Johnson and C. G. Pooley (eds), *The Structure of Nineteenth-Century Cities* (London: Croom Helm, 1982), pp. 129–51.
42 Green, 'Street trading in London', pp. 141–4.
43 Mayhew, *London Labour*, Vol. I, p. 3.
44 Mayhew, *London Labour*, Vol. I, pp. 9–11; LCC, *London Markets 1893*, Appendix C.
45 Metropolitan Streets Act 1867, www.legislation.gov.uk.
46 Winter, *London's Teeming Streets*, p. 109.
47 *The Times*, 13 November 1867, p. 7.
48 'The costermongers' grievances', *Illustrated Police News*, 14 November 1867, p. 3; 'The London costermonger', *Reynolds's Newspaper*, 15 December 1867, p. 1.
49 'The new Metropolitan Street Act', *Lloyd's Weekly Newspaper*, 10 November 1867, p. 7; 'The new Traffic Act and the costermongers', *Era*, 10 November 1867, p. 9.
50 'The new Traffic Act and the costermongers', p. 9.
51 'The new Metropolitan Street Act', p. 7.
52 'The persecution of the poor', *Reynolds's Newspaper*, 17 November 1867, p. 4.
53 Buchner and Hoffmann-Rehnitz, 'Introduction: irregular economic practices', p. 28.
54 R. Saunders, *Democracy and the Vote in British Politics, 1848–1867* (Aldershot: Ashgate, 2013), pp. 226–30.
55 Metropolitan Streets (Amendment) Act 1867, www.legislation.gov.uk.
56 'The London costermonger', p. 1; 'The costermongers' grievances', p. 3.
57 Royal Commission on Market Rights and Tolls, Vol. II, pp. 166–8.
58 W. M. Stern, 'The baroness's market: the history of a noble failure', *Guildhall Miscellany*, 3.8 (1966), 353–66, p. 356.
59 'The opening of Columbia Market', *Illustrated London News*, 8 May 1869, front page.
60 'Columbia Market, Bethnal Green', *Builder*, 20 February 1869, p. 137.
61 'Miss Coutts's new market at Bethnal-Green', *The Times*, 29 April 1869, p. 5.
62 Stern, 'The baroness's market', p. 356.
63 Stern, 'The baroness's market', pp. 353–66.
64 G. Doré and B. Jerrold, *London: A Pilgrimage* (London: Grant and Co., 1872), p. 178.
65 'Miss Coutts's new market at Bethnal-Green', p. 5.
66 S. S. Lewis, 'The artistic and architectural patronage of Angela Burdett Coutts', PhD dissertation, Royal Holloway University of London, 2012, Vol. 1, pp. 275–6; D. Orton, *Made of Gold: A Biography of Angela Burdett Coutts* (London: Hamish Hamilton, 1980), p. 211.
67 'Columbia Market', *Builder*, 8 May 1869, pp. 370–1.
68 'The Bye-laws of Columbia Square Market', printed poster, Tower Hamlets Local History Library and Archives, Press Cuttings Box 652.3–652.34, 1869

69 LCC, *London Markets 1893*, p. 18.
70 Doré and Jerrold, *London: A Pilgrimage*, pp. 189–90.
71 'Great acts of public generosity', *The Times*, 14 February 1874, p. 9.
72 LCC, *London Markets 1893*, p. 56; Denton & Co., Letter to the Editor of an unnamed newspaper (possibly *East End News*), Tower Hamlets Local History Library and Archives, Press Cuttings file 652.21–652.25, 18 August 1919.
73 W. Thornbury and E. Walford, *Old and New London*, Vol. III (London: Cassell, Petter and Galpin, 1878), accessed at British History Online (www.british-history.ac.uk), no pagination.
74 LCC, *London Markets 1893*, p. 26.
75 Examples include Woolwich, where an informal market and an ancient market charter overlapped, and costermongers resisted several attempts to move them (P. Guillery [ed.], *Woolwich: Survey of London*, Vol. 48 [London/New Haven, CT: English Heritage/Yale University Press, 2012], p. 226; LCC, *London Markets 1893*, p. 24); Lewisham (Lewisham Borough Council minute books, 1901–1934); Elephant and Castle (Sullivan, *Markets for the People*, p. 221); and Chiswick (M. Benedetta, *The Street Markets of London* [London: John Miles, 1936], pp. 129–33).
76 LCC, *London Markets 1893*, p. 7.
77 Schmiechen and Carls, *The British Market Hall*, pp. 33–4; Morrison, *English Shops and Shopping*, p. 120; Webb, 'The scandal of London's markets', unpaginated.
78 Doré and Jerrold, *London: A Pilgrimage*, p. 189.
79 The LCC claimed 112 as its total figure, but a few of the markets listed are described as 'removed', as no more than a gathering of flower-sellers selling from baskets, or as containing two or fewer stalls (LCC, *London Markets 1893*).
80 LCC, *London Markets 1893*, p. 3.
81 'Walworth Road costermongers: the case of Keep and Austin v. the Vestry of St. Mary, Newington', bound with other similar cases, Guildhall Library, shelf number PAM 3407.
82 Parrish, *Pease and Chitty's Law of Markets and Fairs* (1958), pp. 4, 36.
83 Parrish, *Pease and Chitty's Law of Markets and Fairs* (1958), p. 34.
84 Winter, *London's Teeming Streets*, p. 11.
85 Winter, *London's Teeming Streets*, p. 11.
86 Ball and Sunderland, *Economic History of London*, ch. 16; J. White, *London in the Nineteenth Century: 'A Human Awful Wonder of God'* (London: Vintage, 2008 [2007]), pp. 471–6.
87 LCC, *London Markets 1893*, p. 6.
88 Sullivan, *Markets for the People*, p. 234.
89 London County Council General Purposes Committee, Conference on Streets and Street Trading, London Metropolitan Archives, LCC/CL/GP/01/229, 1899–1901; Home Office Departmental Committee on Street Trading Report, London Metropolitan Archives, LCC/CL/GP/01/210, 1922.
90 M. Foucault, 'Governmentality', in G. Burchell, C. Gordon, P. Miller (eds), *The Foucault Effect: Studies in Governmentality* (Chicago: University of Chicago Press, 1991).
91 M. Dean, *Governmentality: Power and Rule in Modern Society* (London: Sage, 2010), p. 133; P. Joyce, *The Rule of Freedom: Liberalism and the Modern City* (London: Verso, 2003), p. 4.

92 J. Scott, *Seeing Like a State* (New Haven, CT: Yale University Press, 1998).
93 K. Hart, 'Informal income opportunities and urban employment in Ghana', *Journal of Modern African Studies*, 11.1 (1973), 61–89.
94 M. Valverde, 'Seeing like a city: the dialectic of modern and pre-modern ways of seeing in urban governance', *Law & Society Review*, 45.2 (2011), 277–312.
95 LCC, *London Markets 1893*, pp. 25–6.
96 LCC, *London Markets 1893*, Appendix C, Appendix D and unpaginated plans and drawings.
97 London County Council Public Control Department, *Street markets: report of the chief officer of the public control department as to the street markets in the county of London* (London: London County Council, 1901).
98 LCC, *London Markets 1893*, p. 26.
99 Valverde, 'Seeing like a city', p. 281.
100 Valverde, 'Seeing like a city', pp. 298–9.
101 Valverde, 'Seeing like a city', p. 297.
102 Booth, *Life and Labour*, Series II, Vol. III, p. 264.
103 Home Office Departmental Committee on Street Trading Report, 1922.
104 M. Valverde, 'Police science, British style: pub licensing and knowledge of urban disorder', *Economy and Society*, 32.2 (2011), 234–52. See also Valverde, 'Seeing like a city', pp. 297–9.
105 In Lambeth, the licence fee was 5s and the weekly charge from 1s to 3s, charges typical of other borough councils (draft bye-laws and survey of charges, Lambeth Borough Council, Town Clerk's Department, Lambeth Archives Street Trading files, MBL/TC/R/268, November 1927). Draft bye-laws of 30 July 1927 can also be found in London Metropolitan Archives, London County Council General Purposes Committee Departmental Committee on Street Trading, LCC/CL/GP/01/210. Also in the London Metropolitan Archives are the bye-laws as enacted by the London Borough of Bermondsey in 1928, D.G/AE/ROL/22/18–23.
106 London School of Economics, *New Survey of London Life and Labour*, Vol. 3 (London: P.S. King, 1932), p. 299. For licence applications, see for instance Paddington Borough Council Minutes, 1928, Westminster City Archives (see index under 'street trading'); Borough of St Marylebone Council Minutes Volume XXVII, 1927–1928, Westminster City Archives (see index under 'street trading'); and Westminster City Council Minutes, 1927, Westminster City Archives, pp. 557–8.
107 London Metropolitan Archives, Home Office correspondence on street trading, CLA/048/AD/07/027 (see in particular letter from Chief Clerk of the City Police Office to the Ministry of Transport, 17 February 1928); LSE, *New Survey*, Vol. 3, p. 298.
108 Valverde, 'Seeing like a city', p. 309.
109 LCC, *London Markets 1893*, Appendix C.
110 LCC, *London Markets 1893*, p. 56.
111 D. Scannell, *Mother Knew Best: An East-End Childhood* (London: Pan, 1975), p. 34.
112 Chrisp Street market *c.* 1937, photograph, Age Exchange.

Things

What was for sale in London's street markets? Henry Mayhew gives us a vivid if not always totally disciplined baseline account, dating from the mid-nineteenth century. He starts with the fruit, vegetables and fish sold by costermongers, and also lists an unclassifiable array of other products – from old clothes to bonnet-boxes, corn-salves to 'last dying-speeches', as well as more everyday commodities such as pails, brooms and clothes-pegs.[1] Mayhew's account does not distinguish too rigorously between goods sold by perambulating traders and those sold in the street markets where many of those traders may have halted for some or all of their time, particularly on Saturday nights: in his day the division was a fluid one. By the time we reach the late nineteenth century, London County Council provides a detailed itemisation of goods sold in the city's 112 regularly occurring street markets, divided into 'perishable' and 'non-perishable' goods. The first category contains a long list of foodstuffs, with 1,423 stalls selling vegetables, 369 selling fruit, 475 selling fish and 292 selling meat; other perishable goods included confectionery, cakes, muffins and eggs, and the only non-food category under this heading was flowers. The total number of stalls selling perishable goods was 3,471. Although the number of stalls selling non-perishable goods was significantly smaller, at 1,821, the varied list of products recorded under this heading by the LCC is even longer than in the food category, and includes old clothes, haberdashery, drapery, boots and shoes, furniture, carpets, books, toys and medicines.[2] Food was the bulk business of the street markets, but many and diverse other goods were also sold. This had been the case dating back to the mid-nineteenth century, and continued down to 1939. In 1856 George Dodd had observed of the street markets, rather more concisely than his contemporary Mayhew, that 'it would be impossible to name all the wares exposed for sale at these places on a Saturday evening … Everything that may be wanted can be obtained near at hand.'[3] In 1894 the journalist Richard Harding Davis noted tersely that a 'comprehensive enough' description of the goods on sale in the street markets was provided in a single word – 'everything'.⁴ In 1901 Ernest Richards observed that 'it would be difficult indeed to think of a branch of trade which is not represented' in the street markets of 'slum London', and in 1937 the Manchester *Guardian* reported evocatively of Caledonian market (a weekly market specialising in second-hand goods) that 'all the junk in the world seems gathered there, and among it is a certain amount of treasure'.⁵

The aim of this chapter is to understand the things bought and sold in the London street markets. I will follow London County Council's division of the goods on sale into perishable and non-perishable categories, or food and 'other', examining first of all the role of the street markets in feeding the growing city from the middle of the nineteenth century until the outbreak of the Second World War. What foodstuffs were sold via the street markets? Is it possible to say what share of London's food requirements they fulfilled? And what were the mechanisms by which a proportion of the food brought to the city found its way to consumers via the informal economy of street selling? The second section will examine all goods other than food, and again questions of supply and demand will be considered: where did the street sellers procure the goods they traded, and what place did these market things occupy in the consumer economy of the city? Both sections will address questions of *price* and *quality*, prompted by the many contemporary descriptions of the street markets in which these two issues are among the foremost concerns.

The chapter will place the street markets into the context of the broader development of the London economy. This book is not primarily a work of economic history; however, its conceptualisation of informality is based upon twin foundations – legal aspects (discussed in the last chapter) and economic ones. This chapter, in pursuing the commodities traded in London's street markets, will look to economic history and in particular recent debates on the distinct nature of London's economy in the modern period.⁶ Until comparatively recently, London's role in industrial production from the mid-nineteenth century has been regarded as anomalous, falling behind the large-scale mechanised industries of other locations even as it raced ahead in the development of services and as a great *entrepôt* city.⁷ Since the mid-1990s economic historians have revisited this assessment, and I will build on their work to locate the informal exchange that took place in the streets within wider networks of both commerce and manufacture of a distinctive and complex metropolitan type. I shall argue that just as it is not possible to understand the history of London's retailing without considering the role of the street markets, or to understand the street markets without accounting for how they fitted into the wider topographies of consumption, it is also necessary to locate them in the even more complex relations of production. The street markets may have looked like the continuation of very traditional modes of exchange, but the products they sold suggest that they were integrated closely into the modern economy of London – an economy which itself had many informal characteristics in the 1850–1939 period. Just as the street markets were the informal analogue of some more formally organised aspects of London retailing, so the London productive economy was in some respects less formal that that of other parts of the country, and was critiqued by commentators on those grounds. As Charles Booth noted, 'modern' industry was distinguished by 'an extreme division of labour, a continuously extending use of machinery, and a general complexity of organization', and such characteristics were usually associated with 'a large scale of operations'. In London, however (as in some other industrial centres), production was concentrated in small units and workshops, and home-working and other forms of casual labour competed with the factories and the 'classical wage labour' that were seen as the type-form of modern industry.[8]

Cheap food: double rations for the people

Charles Booth asserted that 'the prompt sale of perishable goods' was the core business of the street markets, and it was in the distribution of food that the markets made their largest contribution to the retail economy of London: the increasingly gigantic city had a gargantuan need for food.[9] London had long drawn supplies to itself, including geese from Norfolk and cattle and sheep from as far afield as Scotland and Wales.[10] Most fruit and vegetables came from market gardens in the city's hinterland, which spread outwards as London expanded and gobbled up the green gardens that surrounded it.[11] Kent, for instance, to the south-east of the capital, was a largely agricultural county whose orchards, hop gardens and market gardens had long been shaped to the demands of London.[12] George Dodd's *The Food of London* (1856) described a busy summer night in which goods trains brought, among other things, 120 tons of Kentish peas and 40 tons of filberts to the Bricklayers Arms railway depot in Bermondsey, to be sent on to the wholesale markets by road, so that 'the Kent Road was in a turmoil all night, – nothing but laden wagons following in a stream almost continuous'.[13] The description vividly evokes the scale of supplies that were needed to feed the hungry capital.

The period Dodd described was the mid-nineteenth-century moment when railways and steamships greatly enhanced the possibilities of transporting perishable food into London.[14] The traditional supply lines from Kent and other areas were facilitated, and goods from further afield were now retailed plentifully and cheaply on the streets. 'Railway milk', for instance, appeared from the 1860s.[15] Other, rarer products suddenly became common, as Dodd noted: 'look ... at the pine-apples in the London streets; how would our forefathers have wondered at such a choice fruit being sold in pennyworths!' Pineapples had previously been an exotic and expensive hothouse delicacy, but Dodd describes how fast steamships had enabled their import, 'and there are now said to be 200,000 pine-apples in a year thus brought', a proportion of which were sold in penny slices by street sellers.[16] London's street retailing until this point had included a contingent of sellers who travelled from the country into the city on foot, bringing supplies from surrounding areas and hawking them around the streets.[17] The growth of the city and the advent of the railways more or less ended this mode of selling around mid-century, but the costermongers retained an imaginative connection with the direct import of country goods into the heart of the city.

The street market retail trade that burgeoned from the mid-nineteenth century was in part a response to the growing size of London (both in population and in geographical spread) which left the old-established authorised markets at a distance from many areas of the expanding city, so that they turned increasingly to wholesale trade and new retailers filled the gap between. Accounts of the authorised markets are consistent in their descriptions of street sellers as these markets' customers. George Dodd describes how the auctioning of large-scale lots of fruit, vegetables and fish started in the early hours of the morning, and the 'large shopkeepers purchase first', paying a premium price for good-quality and varied produce for their middle- and upper-class customers. The costermongers arrived a little later, to 'take off all that is left, frequently at very cheap prices'.[18] The costermongers were in the business of buying food that was cheap enough to suit the pockets of their customers, and what they aimed at was not to stock a barrow or stall with a full range of products, but rather to shift large quantities of whatever was plentiful, selling to customers who were 'comparatively indifferent to variety so long as they can obtain a bargain'.[19] They were the mechanism by which gluts in the market were translated into cheap food in season, and if there was 'an extra supply' of anything, noted Dodd, 'the costermongers will buy whatever the greengrocers do not want'.[20] Around forty years later London County Council described how the street markets continued to take 'the surplus produce remaining unsold in the authorised markets' and distribute it 'among the poorer classes'.[21] Twenty years later again in 1913 the American J. W. Sullivan described a situation that was broadly unchanged.[22] Most costermongers displayed considerable flexibility as they followed gluts across the seasons. In 1877 the photographer John Thomson and journalist Adolphe Smith collaborated on *Street Life in London*, a conscious (although smaller-scale) updating of Mayhew's *London Labour and the London Poor*. They interviewed a man who described in detail the short strawberry season when many costermongers would sell the fruit at 4d or 6d a punnet, and 'there's no trouble in sellin': folks will buy anythink if it's cheap and can be swallered'.[23] Like many others, this costermonger would move on to other goods at other seasons. George Dodd observed street sellers who 'impartially share their favours between Covent Garden and Billingsgate, according as fruit or fish happen to be most cheap and abundant'.[24] This nimble switching from commodity to commodity persisted into the twentieth century: when London's borough councils issued licences to street markets in 1927 stallholders were required to state on their application the goods they would sell. This was one of the grounds for complaint from those who objected to the licensing scheme: 'most costermongers hardly know from one week to another, sometimes from one day to another, what they will want to trade in' stated a spokesman in

The Times – their trade was still closely tracked to whatever was cheap and plentiful.²⁵ Plate 3 shows the abundant fruit for sale in East End street markets in the late 1930s.

As the street markets distributed these cheap and plentiful goods from the authorised markets, they made a contribution to the London food supply that was significant in scale, although the informal nature of their trade means that there are few business records that can provide the sort of quantitative information that is often available for other retailers. In mid-century Mayhew listed the different sorts of fish sold wholesale at Billingsgate, noting the proportion of each retailed on the streets by costermongers: this amounted to a quarter of cod and whiting, for example, three-quarters of fresh herrings, all whelks and two-thirds of mussels.²⁶ Just a few years later George Dodd estimated that around half the fish wholesaled in Billingsgate for retail in London was sold via fishmongers (from fixed shop premises), while the other half was sold by street sellers, a very considerable trade at a period when fish was significant in the diet of rich and poor alike, especially in London.²⁷ If these figures are correct (and it should be noted that Dodd was more judicious in his deployment of statistics than Mayhew, who has been criticised for the uncontrolled nature of his superabundant figures) they provide a clear indicative example of the scale and importance of the informal street trade in provisioning the city.²⁸ Dodd also calculated that one-quarter (25 million) of the oranges consumed in London were sold in the streets, or in theatres, the latter served by itinerant sellers closely akin to the costermongers who operated from stalls and barrows in the streets and street markets. Mayhew's and Dodd's figures date from early in the period covered in this study: it does not seem likely that the quantity of food retailed via the street markets dropped significantly, given that later reports, although wary of citing the quantity or value of street market trade, were unequivocal about the 'very substantial increase' in the number of stalls.²⁹

There is no doubt that the street markets sold large quantities of food, and that they sold it more cheaply than most shops: this was their business model, to buy only what could be sold at bargain prices. Their overheads were far lower than those of retailers with fixed premises, and their profit margins were slim, finely attuned to price-sensitive customers.³⁰ Many sources comment on the comparative cheapness of goods sold in the streets: the journalist James Greenwood in 1867 reported on meat and other goods being sold more cheaply in market stalls in Whitecross Street than in the shops; in 1896 the social worker Helen Bosanquet described the 'variety and cheapness' of the stalls in the East End street markets she knew.³¹ In 1932 the LSE's *New Survey of London Life and Labour* examined an area of Bermondsey where shop prices were 'anything from 20 to 100 per cent. higher than those charged for similar articles of at least equal quality' in the nearest street market; and in 1936 the journalist Mary Benedetta in *The Street Markets of London* recorded observational comparisons of market prices with those in the shops – the markets were consistently cheaper.³² Competition from the street markets also had the effect of keeping prices lower in shops with a market close by, as noted by Sullivan in 1913 and the *New Survey* in 1932.[33]

Street retailing made a distinctive contribution to the variety of foodstuffs – and in particular fruit, vegetables and fish – sold in London, and there were few categories of food and drink that were not sold by costermongers and street sellers. Bread was among those few goods not commonly retailed from stalls in the street; however, bakeries were well represented among the fixed shops that lined the streets that housed the street markets. Meat too was rarely sold by costermongers, but butchers, like bakers, were common as shopkeepers in the market streets. At busy times they put their cheaper cuts on counters that jutted from the front of their shops, or even on trestle tables on the pavement, joining in market-style trading as an adjunct to their regular business. The cries of butchers were among the loudest in street markets on busy Saturday nights.[34]

In the selling of food, street stalls and fixed shops provided retail provision that may have been categorically different, but was often closely integrated in the experience of customers who bought from stalls and shops alike. Indeed, the history of the street markets and many more 'modern' retail forms are closely entwined. Sainsbury's, for instance, an early multiple food retailer, was founded with a single shop in London in 1869. When John James Sainsbury expanded into his second shop in 1873 he located it in Queen's Crescent, Kentish Town, a street that was soon also home to a street market which moved there from neighbouring Malden Road in 1876 when a tramway was laid.[35] Sainsbury clearly found the proximity of the street market to be good for business, as other early branches were located in Chapel Street, Islington, and Watney Street, Stepney, both streets with lively markets.[36] Sainsbury's was thus co-located with informal street selling almost from the outset, and many markets housed branches of other early multiple retailers, including Lipton's, Maypole Dairy and Home and Colonial Stores.[37] In some cases these multiples food retailers, like the butchers, joined in market-style retailing with stalls outside their shops on which cheaper goods were offered.[38] For many customers, street markets formed a continuum of retail provision with other sorts of outlets. In suburban Lewisham for instance, despite the efforts of the local borough council to remove a growing street market, by the interwar period the High Street was home to both the market and to multiple retailers, a small department store and a large co-operative store.[39] Figure 10 is a photograph of Lewisham High Street in 1937, with stalls hugging the edge of the wide street that also housed Woolworths (the large white building in the left foreground), Marks and Spencer, and Sainsbury's. Many shopkeepers recognised that the street markets brought valuable footfall of customers.

Cheap food was of particular importance to those at the bottom of the economic scale. The food historian Panikos Panayi provides an authoritative overview of the quantity and quality of the food available to the British people from the mid-nineteenth to the mid-twentieth centuries. He concludes that 'most authorities accept that improvement occurred for urban workers following the

10 Lewisham High Street, 1937

repeal of the Corn Laws [1846], a process which would continue into the twentieth century'. Yet despite the overall trend towards improvement, poor nutrition continued to be common in the working classes down to 1914, and 'significant pockets of poverty and malnutrition remained' in the interwar period too.[40] Many people in London subsisted on wages (or casual earnings) that were insufficient to allow them to live with any security. Charles Booth's study, published in its final iteration in 1902–03, concluded that 31 per cent of the population of London lived in poverty.[41] For these people in particular, food made up a high proportion of their weekly expenditure, and what they could afford to spend on it was therefore limited, and very sensitive to any fluctuation in their income. Throughout the period of this study a common coping strategy for the poor was to buy in the street markets: bargain supplies from market stalls were of crucial importance, and the very poorest of London's populace hunted for comparative bargains even among the cheap goods sold on the stalls. Towards the end of each evening's trading, and especially on Saturday nights, market sellers began to reduce their prices to clear off any unsold perishable stock, and it was at that point that these poorest customers started to buy. The autobiography of Jack Dash records that in Lower Marsh street market: 'people would be waiting for the perishable food to be auctioned off: women in black shawls surrounding the butcher in his striped apron ... The stallholders called it being "at the murder", murdering their prices.'[42] Bryan Magee, describing the 1930s, noted how it was still the case that as trading drew to a close, 'a new kind of shopper appeared in the market: the very poor, the very old, the very mean'.[43]

Helen Bosanquet's *Rich and Poor* (1896) is an essential source for anyone interested in the material culture of working-class London. Bosanquet was an early social worker and a leading member of the Charity Organisation Society, a body that believed that support for the poor should be kept in voluntary and not state hands, campaigning against 'indiscriminate' charity that was believed to foster dependency.[44] *Rich and Poor* is the most vividly descriptive and least programmatic among Bosanquet's many works, and in it she compares London's wealthy West End with Shoreditch, a poor East End district that was thickly populated with street markets and where she carried out social work for several years in the early 1890s.[45] Bosanquet attributed some of the poverty and hunger she observed to what she saw as the inability of poor women to plan a budget, so that days of plentiful food at the start of the week led to scarcity by its end. Yet she grudgingly admitted that there was 'something not altogether ignoble' in the lives of people who took the opportunity for good living when it presented itself.[46] Working-class consumption patterns played liberality against hunger, and the street markets, with their passing gluts of low-cost supplies, catered both to this spirit and to the absolute need for cheap food. Saturday night was the busiest, in response to the weekly payment of wages, and in anticipation of the weekly festival that was the Sunday dinner. Dodd observed in 1856 that on Saturday nights 'a joint of meat, a huge cabbage, a quartern loaf, and a saucepan, sometimes march off in procession, under the care of different members of a working man's family', and many other sources too depict Saturday nights in the street markets as a frenzy of selling, with huge quantities of food sold in an atmosphere of good cheer and sociability.[47]

How did the food sold in the street markets measure up on quality? This issue is one addressed by many observers. Dodd in the 1850s looked at the fish sold to costermongers at Billingsgate and concluded that some of it was 'the cheap and too often decayed residue' of the morning's stock (a description tempered, however, when he observed that dangerously unfit fish was removed by market inspectors and destroyed). He also noted that 'cheapness need not necessarily be accompanied by questionable freshness; for in abundant season there is plenty for all': this plenty included the shellfish and sprats that were a common part of the working-class diet, and at times the more upmarket salmon and cod too.[48]

Bosanquet's *Rich and Poor* with its comparisons of West End and East End is an illuminating source of evidence on the relative price and quality of foodstuffs and consumer goods available to the wealthy and needy populations of London. She asks:

> Do the poor on the whole buy dear or cheap? ... Facts seem to tell both ways ... [M]easuring by prices alone you live indefinitely cheaper in the East than in the West. Think of what the housekeeping books would run down to if for a penny you could buy six oranges or three eggs, or enough flowers to deck your room for an evening party; while a shilling would give you the choice between a fowl or a hare or three mutton-chops.[49]

However, 'you must be prepared to find out that half the oranges are bad, or that the oranges are half-bad; that the eggs are "extra-French" (new-laid, fresh, "eggs," extra-French is the order of merit); and that the fowl and the hare are insipid creatures of foreign extraction'.[50] She concludes that 'The prices paid in the West are largely paid for the certainty that the commodities will be up to a certain standard; in the East the quality will depend upon your own powers of selection.'[51] The age-old motto of the shopper came into force here: *caveat emptor*, or let the buyer beware, at a period when there was increasing concern over the quality of many goods, but particularly food, which came under scrutiny in terms of both hygiene and purity.[52] The Adulteration of Food and Drugs Act of 1872 (following less effectual legislation of 1860) led to the appointment of public analysts by local authorities.[53] The state, deploying scientific means of knowledge, was increasingly playing a part in regulating food quality, but the street markets, in their liminal position on the edge of the law, were not subject to the sort of formal quality control that other retailers had imposed upon them, or imposed on themselves. The informal economy could provide a multitude of goods at the slenderest of prices, and among the things on offer were undoubted bargains of cheap, fresh and good-quality produce. As Sullivan noted in 1913, comparing London's food markets with Berlin, Paris and New York, the informal street markets constituted a system that was 'at once the most ancient and the most modern. It is the cheapest of all systems – efficient, natural, democratic, rightfully communistic. It often gives the masses double rations.'[54] Yet it was also a system that provided few if any checks on quality, at a period when food standards were beginning to be the subject of state intervention.

Food and diet changed somewhat across the period of this study: as working-class living standards gradually improved in the aggregate, the proportion of meat, fish, vegetables and fruit increased, although the staples were still bread and potatoes.[55] New preservation techniques (including canning) had an impact on the foodstuffs available, as did the industrialised manufacture of packaged and branded goods that frequently used the brand as the sign of a guarantee against adulteration.[56] Although the street markets continued to specialise in fresh, unprocessed food, these branded goods appeared there too, especially in the interwar period, although they were sold more frequently in the shops that lined the market streets than from the stalls themselves: Bryan Magee in the 1930s describes how his mother 'used to buy her vegetables, fruit and flowers from the stalls, and sometimes fish too, but most other things in the shops'.[57] One of the most notable changes came as immigration brought new food cultures to London. The most influential migrants in terms of street-market food retailing were the new Jewish arrivals who came from the late 1880s, joining an established Jewish community and settling densely in the East End. By 1895 the social observer Ethel Brilliana described how the food for sale in Petticoat Lane included salted gherkins, Passover cake and kosher meat.[58] Anuradha Basu has investigated the propensity of immigrant communities to find an economic niche in entrepreneurship rather than formal employment: entrepreneurship, especially in the selling of food, offers the opportunity of a ready market of fellow immigrants, and draws on social networks to provide both labour and finance, so that 'the use of social capital ... gives immigrant entrepreneurs a competitive advantage in both formal and informal economies'.[59] We have already seen how Sainsbury's had origins that were geographically entwined with the street markets of London. Tesco, another business that was to develop into a leading supermarket chain, came directly from the stalls themselves, and from the Jewish immigrant community. Its founder Jack Cohen used his £30 demobilisation gratuity in 1919 to set up a market stall in Hackney, and developed a network of market stalls before opening his first shop in 1931.[60] The informal economy and street markets of London were not merely a relic of more ancient ways of buying and selling, but pointed towards retail modernity too, in an economy in which informal and formal trade were more closely integrated than is sometimes acknowledged. This is demonstrated even more strongly in the 'non-perishable' goods that form the LCC's second category of street-market selling.

Other things: something showy at a small cost

Mary Benedetta's 1936 book on the street markets of London includes a handy index of 'some things to be bought', commencing with American cloth (a type of waterproof fabric), animals and antiques, and ending with wireless sets, by way of beauty preparations, chair legs, corsets, field glasses, poultry, razors, tea cosies and tennis racquets – among many other items.[61] The photographs in her book, by Laszlo Moholy-Nagy, give a clear sense of this diversity: see for instance figures 11 and 12. Clearly the London street markets sold an immense variety of non-food goods: Henry Mayhew, as we have already seen, had itemised a list just as varied in the 1850s. And if there was some change between Mayhew's time and Benedetta's in the foodstuffs available in the street markets, more marked change occurred in the non-food category. When Mayhew wrote his account, almost all the clothes for sale on the streets of London were old clothes, yet by the time of the LCC's 1893 report, although old clothes were still significant, new clothes and accessories were beginning to be sold in the street markets too. By the 1930s a full range of cheap, ready-made clothing could be bought on market stalls, from underwear to dresses to stockings, a development which the *New Survey of London Life and Labour* described as 'by far the most remarkable change' in the nature of the goods the street markets sold, attributed

11 Laszlo Moholy-Nagy, 'Commercial Road: stall for housewives', in Mary Benedetta, *The Street Markets of London*, 1936

12 Laszlo Moholy-Nagy, 'Berwick Market: "There you can get thin pure silk stockings for 1s. 3d."', in Mary Benedetta, *The Street Markets of London*, 1936

to 'the arrival of the Jew in the street markets'.⁶² The *New Survey* noted a fall in the quantity of furniture, crockery and household goods on sale as 'sixpenny stores and domestic bazaars' began to compete in the sale of cheap household goods. However, there was a matching rise in some of the more emblematic products of consumer modernity, including gramophones, gramophone records and wireless sets; Benedetta lists all of these, as well as cameras, hair nets, coloured electric light bulbs and even car tyres in the street markets of 1936.

If the selling of cheap fresh food was the dominant trade of the London street markets, the retailing of many and varied 'non-perishable' products was not far behind. There were few if any categories of product for sale in London's shops that could not also be bought in the streets, and this included items strongly associated (then as now) with consumer culture, and even with luxury. In Thomson and Smith's *Street Life in London* (1877) one of the most striking entries among the short chapters on street trades and street characters is an account of the 'fancy-ware' or 'swag' trade, describing two men who sold 'modern "quasi" jewellery' on the streets of London and in street markets such as that in the New Cut (see figure 13). 'I can supply a set of real flash jewels for about three shillings – diamonds if you like, brooch, bracelets, black or gold

13   John Thomson, 'Dealer in fancy ware', in John Thomson and Adolphe Smith, *Street Life in London*, 1877

ear-drops, and finger-ring', says one of the swag dealers interviewed. The other sells a variety of items at a penny each, of which 'perhaps the most ingenious and attractive pennyworth was a pair of sleeve-links, each containing a dog's head moulded in coloured glass, and protected by a convex glass neatly set in a gilt and burnished rim of metal'.[63] This account is not unique: Mayhew had also described the swag trade, and two decades later Bosanquet, in her comparison of London's West and East, rich and poor, noted that the young women of the East End were prone 'to break out into marvellous but inexpensive jewellery (gold and diamonds and other precious stones are wonderfully cheap and plentiful in the East)'.[64] At a similar date Charles Booth's description of Berwick Street market in Soho noted 'cheap jewellery' stalls among many others.[65]

Less than twenty years before Thomson and Smith reported on the swag dealers selling sleeve-links for a penny, Henry Mayhew reported that the common price for the cheapest 'quasi' jewellery items was threepence, a sum he nonetheless considered very low.[66] The business historian Francesca Carnevali notes how the 1860s – between Mayhew's and Smith's accounts – was the key moment of acceleration in the production of cheap jewellery, with 'the application of steam power to stamping machines that punched out both the basic shape and the surface detailing of a piece in one rapid action', as well as the development of new plating techniques to apply gold and silver to base metals.[67] Smith's swag dealers bought their stock from the 'Jews in Houndsditch and such like places': Houndsditch was a centre of commercial activity in London's long-established Jewish community, and its 'swag-shops' wholesaled not just cheap jewellery but also a variety of ornamental and useful consumer goods, from 'pot' figurines to clocks to tea trays.[68] Much of the jewellery was made in Birmingham, (in)famous for its cheap 'Brummagen' ware, although Carnevali makes clear the extent to which London manufacturers also made cheap stamped jewellery on a large scale alongside the higher quality traditional wares. Birmingham craftsmen were also capable of making the latter, although their reputation for paste and gilding obscured this fact.[69]

The middle decades of the nineteenth century saw the ongoing and accelerated development of the 'consumer revolution', in which cheap and fashionable consumer goods (and not just jewellery) were produced in growing quantities and retailed at steadily falling prices. Supply factors converged with demand, as by the mid-nineteenth century real wages for the mass of the working-class population were beginning to rise, slowly but steadily (a trend that would continue, at varying rates, across the First World War and into the interwar period, despite periodic downturns).[70] The street sellers and street markets of London were closely implicated in this change. The jewellery they sold was a 'modern, democratic luxury', fashionable merchandise in which novelty and display outweighed monetary value and quality. The fact that the sparkling effects were produced by cheap gilding, shiny base metals and 'imitation' stones was not too troubling to working-class consumers eager to access the delights of shopping and to deploy the symbolic capital of a fashionable appearance.[71] As the economic historian Paul Johnson has noted of the British working classes at this period, it is necessary to recognise that 'consumption expenditure is not simply the means to individual sustenance and gratification, but is also part of a social dynamic', which helps to explain Bosanquet's observation that the young women she saw purchasing the 'cheap diamonds' of the East End prioritised such 'external finery' over decent underwear.[72] One of Thomson and Smith's swag sellers reported a similar preference for cheap jewellery over warm clothes in young girls eager to purchase fancy combs to decorate their hair, and Thomson's photograph shows just such a girl, clearly poorly dressed, and clearly very interested in the goods laid out before her.[73]

While much of the jewellery sold in London's streets was made in Birmingham, in a number of other categories of consumer goods, most notably fashionable clothing and furniture, many of the products sold in the London street markets appear to have been predominantly the product of London manufacture. There are a very few works of history that consider the London street markets and their role in the retailing of non-food goods, chief among them the cultural historian Judith Walkowitz's chapter on Berwick Street market in the 1930s.[74] Yet neither Walkowitz nor any other historian describes where the goods on sale came from, and unlike the solid nineteenth-century accounts that document how cheap food was distributed from the authorised markets via costermongers and street markets, there are no detailed historical descriptions of the source of the many and varied non-food goods sold on London's streets. There are, however, tantalising scattered fragments of evidence, some more extensive and others very fleeting. These scraps form the basis of the following analysis (which will focus on fashion and clothing), deployed in the context of modern analyses of London's economic history that suggest that it should be understood in terms of complex relationships in production and exchange. Such arrangements are consistent with my attempt to understand the street markets through the lens of informality: the informal economy of the street markets was in some sympathy with London's economy more generally.

According to Paul Johnson, London's manufacturing economy in the later nineteenth and early twentieth centuries has long been seen as a 'relic of an earlier, pre-industrial age, where production was based around workshops and artisanal skills' and economic growth was dependent on the prodigal development of the service economy and hungry consumer demand.[75] This was in strong contrast to the dynamic development of manufacturing in many areas of the North and Midlands. Although London was by no means the only place that did not see a straightforward move from workshop to factory (Birmingham, for instance, had significant continuing artisan activity),[76] there was nonetheless a general contrast between provincial enterprises and London's productive organisation. The former developed large-scale factories and mechanised processes, seeking efficiency through economies of scale and vertical integration, whereas in London manufacturers controlled their costs and improved productivity through 'a multitude of market-based transactions', complex arrangements of subcontracting between small and specialised workshops where hand working was very common, and many tasks were put out to casually employed home workers.[77] As early as mid-century, Mayhew described the 'honourable and dishonourable' trades in several fields of London manufacture, including garment making, in which legislation protecting skilled labour and the long-standing apprenticeship system was undermined by subcontractors who employed casual, semi-skilled workers.[78] These arrangements (and particularly their *lacks* – of large-scale enterprise, mechanisation and unionised labour) have been used to characterise London manufacturing as 'backward', in much the same way that the capital city's lack of planned market halls was seen as a sign of developmental failure in its retail markets.

There is no doubt that there were troubling features in the way that manufacturing in London developed. In her description of women's work in East London in Charles Booth's study, Clara Collet resorts to what she calls 'genealogical tables' to represent the bewildering number of transactions involved in the manufacture of shirts. These might be subcontracted multiple times – from the commissioning of the work by a wholesaler, to the cutting of the cloth, to the machining of the garment, to finishing processes such as sewing button-holes and adding buttons. Complexity made the process opaque: 'the sub-contractor does not know where his shirts go to; the finisher does not know where hers come from'.[79] Many contemporary commentators saw the factory model of manufacture that was more common outside London as the preferred one, fearing that London's system almost inevitably declined into 'sweating' as a multitude of small enterprises squeezed profit from the endeavours of home workers or semi-skilled labour in small workshops.[80] Such productive arrangements functioned efficiently only to the extent that they portioned the processes of manufacture into smaller and smaller divisions, choreographed in many layers of subcontractual arrangements that called for a responsive and flexible labour force, and delegating risk and many overhead costs to the workers themselves. As today, the fear was that 'flexible' labour meant exploited labour. Collet interviewed women home-workers who finished shirts for 5d a dozen, a pittance fit only to starve on. She spoke to one woman who, if she could get work direct from the workshop, was paid 1½d an hour, but who was paid only half that if the work came to her via a middle-woman.[81] The final stage of the subcontracting process often involved women home-workers paying a portion of their meagre earnings to a messenger to hurry their finished work back to the workshop or subcontractor, or even enlisting their children to help out on an order requiring speedy completion.[82]

Yet Johnson and others argue persuasively that London's manufacturing economy was not as backward as some commentators claimed, and that the 'flexible specialisation' of the small workshop and subcontracting system was in fact characterised less by 'immiserisation' than by 'economic dynamism'.[83] Charles Booth, while recognising the potential for exploitation in London's subcontracting arrangements, also noted their 'persistent vitality'.[84] This was particularly the case from the 1880s onwards when large numbers of new Jewish immigrants joined London's established Jewish community, further transforming productive arrangements in the manufacture of ready-made clothing (and in certain other trades, including furniture).[85] As a result, Andrew Godley asserts, by 1939 London's clothing manufacturers were 'more efficient than anywhere else' and were generating around 50 per cent of national production in key categories of women's clothing, including tailored outerwear and dresses, and this despite the fact that firms were smaller than the national average.[86]

Giorgio Riello's contribution to the 'economic dynamism' debate adds greater consideration of demand to that of supply, arguing for the importance of consumers in 'expanding, price-conscious markets', as well as for the role of retailers.[87] This consideration of retailing is welcome; however, it is sketchy, and relies on secondary literature on the growth of department stores. I would argue that we should also look to the street markets as retailers of cheap consumer commodities. For many working-class consumers, street stalls were accessible (financially and geographically) in a way that department stores were not, particularly in the earlier part of the 1850–1939 period. As Helen Bosanquet noted in 1896, 'the great mass of extraordinarily cheap blouses, jackets, mantles and skirts, which are turned out in thousands by the slaves of the needle, are bought and worn by women only a few degrees better off than their makers'.[88] Such cheap garments – 'something showy at a small cost' – were sold in high-street drapers in the East End and other poor areas of London, but also in street markets, as Bosanquet reports in her vivid description of a typical East End street market.[89]

When Bosanquet was writing, new ready-made clothes were a relative novelty in London's street markets. In the mid-nineteenth century Mayhew had described the familiar figure of the Jewish 'old clothes man' selling second-hand garments in the streets.[90] For many working-class people, shopping for clothes at this date might commonly involve acquiring the worn cast-offs of their economic betters (which might nonetheless still carry some sense of fashionability), and almost all clothes sold in street markets were second-hand. By the time London County Council reported on the street markets in 1893 only around four in ten clothes stalls sold second-hand garments. Others sold the new ready-made garments that Bosanquet observed, and drapery and haberdashery stalls also retailed cloth and trimmings used in the home sewing of new garments. By 1932 the *New Survey* found that only about one in ten clothing stalls in London's street markets sold old clothes, and many markets had been transformed by the influx of ready-made, mass-market fashions (particularly for women), produced under developing 'flexible specialisation' techniques by largely Jewish entrepreneurs.[91] Mary Benedetta observed in Brixton market, 'knickers at a starting price of 1s. a pair ... These are the artificial silk knickers with elastic that you buy at the draper's for 3s. 11d. and 4s. 11d.' In Petticoat Lane, the biggest of the East End street markets, where the influence of Jewish migrants had been most dramatic, she described how 'some of the stalls sell new afternoon dresses for 5s ... The kind of dress that would cost 35s to £2 in a shop.'[92]

How did street market traders manage to sell so much more cheaply than their shop-based counterparts? Partly it was a result of their lower costs. Until 1927 no street seller paid rent or fees for their stall, and even after licences were introduced, the charges were low. Shop retailers frequently complained about what they saw as unfair competition from street stalls that paid no rent or rates or taxes. The cost of setting up a stall was limited to the hire of a barrow and the purchase of stock to fill it, meaning that market trading had extremely low entry costs. And if low entry costs and overheads meant that street sellers could keep their prices low, it is apparent that they also pursued other cost-cutting strategies in sourcing the goods they sold. Some street sellers sold products they made themselves, although this was more common in food and consumables: Bosanquet knew muffin sellers who made their muffins at home – she was put off buying when she discovered the unhygienic conditions of manufacture.[93] Booth's *Life and Labour* also cites examples of this sort of simple conduit between maker and user, but he noted that it was declining.[94] Thomson and Smith's swag dealers bought their stock, made in London or Birmingham, from the Houndsditch wholesalers, and wholesalers were no doubt the source of many other street market goods, as well as supplying other retailers. For market sellers the emphasis, as Benedetta's price comparisons indicate, must always have been on pursuing the lowest priced goods on offer among the wholesalers' stock. An autobiography by Ralph Finn recalls how his widowed mother supported her family with a stall in Goolden Street (near Petticoat Lane) selling just such items – souvenirs for George V's coronation, glass, china and 'beads and baubles'.[95]

Finn's mother, with her 'beads and baubles', serves as an example not just of a market stall selling cheap, mass-manufactured consumer goods, but also as an indication of how the street markets provided relatively flexible economic opportunities for women. In an economic and social system in which women's paid labour was discouraged in favour of normative domesticity, and disadvantaged by lower rates of pay, the informal economy of the street markets provided some opportunity for women, who could balance the running of a market stall with domestic duties. Market selling offered relative autonomy that was lacking for those women, such as the shirt finishers described by Clara Collet, working in casualised production in the home.[96] Another example is Alexander Hartog's mother, who sold haberdashery from a street stall which she would prepare every morning with the help of her older children before they set out for school.[97]

Other market sellers appear to have bought direct from the factory (although the exact nature of this business relationship is unclear) and Benedetta's description of Petticoat Lane mentions knives sold by a Mrs Cohen, all sourced from the same factory, and plaster statues of animals from 'a factory in Highbury'.[98] Some goods found their way to the street markets because they were unsaleable in other contexts. Bosanquet described a market stall selling trimmings, lace and ribbons, including 'old-fashioned remainders of West End stocks', as well as 'remnants' and 'damaged lots', which were perhaps sold cheaply to street sellers from the East End's many ready-made clothing workshops.[99] The journalist Ernest Richards reported that stalls in Whitecross Street sold children's clothes that were cheap because they were ex-sample garments from wholesalers.[100] Last year's West End fashions seem to have continued to find their way East beyond Bosanquet's day, and in the 1930s Benedetta described in Petticoat Lane a stall at which 'well-known manufacturers of suitcases' sell off 'old stock'.[101]

And finally there are hints of the outer fringes of the informal economy that shaded by degrees into crime. Benedetta opens her account of Petticoat Lane by cheerfully assuring her reader that 'eighty per cent of the wares are said to be genuine' – implying that 20 per cent were not.[102] By the 1930s the development of the brand, in processed food, fashion and other goods, had already given rise to the corollary notion of the counterfeit, and Ralph Finn described the 'chocolate kings' of Petticoat Lane in the 1920s and 1930s selling with enormous performative effort boxes of branded confectionery.[103] At first glance, the goods offered seemed to be startling bargains; however, there was a catch: 'the names on the boxes were cunningly reminiscent of well-known brands, popular makes. Perhaps only a letter was changed. "Codbury" for instance, instead of "Cadbury", "Fray" for "Fry".'[104] Bryan Magee, whose autobiography records Hoxton Street market at a similar date, also observed confectionery being sold in auctions; here the goods seemed to be genuine enough, but Magee was sure that they were stolen. There are, however, surprisingly few mentions of street markets as a site for the sale of stolen goods: theft, if it is discussed, more usually takes the form of pickpockets stealing from customers and children pilfering from stalls.[105]

I have said that evidence describing where and how the street sellers sourced their stock is fragmentary, partly as a result of the informality of these businesses, which left few if any records behind, and which are documented largely through the reports of witnesses who may have been less interested in understanding their business practices than their quasi-ethnographic features. I offer an invitation to future historians to seek out further documents that will give us a better understanding of the street markets as businesses. However, I do have one final, and rather satisfyingly complete, piece of evidence to present that indicates the extent to which the street markets of London were integrated into – a product of and a contributing factor within – the 'flexible specialisation' of London's manufacturing economy. The journalist Andrew Miller's detailed and evocative biography of his grandfather Henry Feldman, based on Feldman's extensive papers and correspondence, offers a case study of one man's activities across market stall, workshop and factory.[106]

Feldman's parents were born in Galicia in the Austro-Hungarian Empire and emigrated to London, where Feldman was born in 1906. His father was a furrier who died young, so that Feldman's childhood was one of poverty, supported (like Ralph Finn and William Hartog) by his widowed mother and her stall in Petticoat Lane market. Feldman's working life started early when he too set up as a street seller in Petticoat Lane and other markets in London and beyond, selling underwear and hosiery that he bought from wholesalers: 'Atlas the hosiery specialists at the Aldgate, Kaye's in Houndsditch and the other piled-high apparel wholesalers on the edge of the City.'[107] After his marriage (to another child of Jewish immigrants), Feldman made a momentous decision in 1932 to begin manufacturing his own stock, and the story of his trajectory from market trader to manufacturer, assisted by his brothers and wife, is an eloquent case study of the enmeshed relationships that linked the informal economy of the street markets into the complex networks of London's manufacturing economy. Refused credit by a high-street bank, Feldman arranged a private loan from a distant relative who was already established in clothing manufacture. A school friend who worked in the warehouse of the textile giant Courtauld 'agreed to slip them the tail-end of a roll of a rayon locknit fabric ... so long as they came round first thing ... before the foreman arrived'.[108] Feldman took on a single employee, a skilled cutter who cut the garment pieces on Feldman's kitchen table, and the assembly of the garments was subcontracted to 'half a dozen outdoor tailors' on piece rates. The growing business provided employment for Feldman's younger brothers, who extended the business's network of contacts in the markets and workshops of the East End. After several years of selling from market stalls, Feldman surrendered his market licence in 1935, having opened his first workshop some time previously. By the outbreak of war in 1939 his business success was securely established, having grown from roots that lay in the street markets and the informal networks of London's manufacturing and retailing economy.

* * *

The London street markets were a vigorous emanation of economic informality. In the selling of fresh food, they were the mechanism by which any goods in plentiful supply, and therefore low in cost, were taken from the wholesale markets to the people, and they functioned alongside more formal retailers in high streets where consumers could pick and choose between the cheap products on the stalls and those on offer in shops, and where the branded products of consumer modernity had a presence alongside more traditional market wares (as in figure 14, where Persil washing powder is advertised prominently in East Street market, Walworth). Over the period from 1850 to 1939, as the street markets grew and diversified, the strategies by which the sellers of non-food goods sourced their stock and sold it cheaply were varied and hybrid. There may have been some illegality in the selling of stolen or counterfeit goods, but more common were strategies that took low-quality, damaged, out-of-date or otherwise compromised products and sold them cheap to customers who had limited budgets but an increasing appetite to participate in the pleasures and symbolic values of consumer modernity.

However, the majority of the non-food goods sold in London's street markets were sourced not from the fringes but from the centre of the London economy.

Cheap street

14   East Street market, Walworth, 1939

They were goods such as the cheap jewellery produced in both Birmingham and London, or the increasingly dominant mass-market, ready-made fashions that by the 1930s were made and retailed at numerous price points, with the market stalls fulfilling the hungry demands of the bottom end of this market. Despite the fact that the street markets were informal and only (and then minimally) regulated in the final decade of the period before 1939, they were nonetheless clearly integrated into London's broader economy, which was characterised by great consumer demand, and the fact that its productive basis was more complex, more relationship-based and less overtly 'formal' than that of many other centres of manufacturing. The street markets were a simple and direct, but not a primitive, form of retailing, and found their place within the distinctive, and distinctively modern, London economy.

Notes

1   H. Mayhew, *London Labour and the London Poor*, Vol. I (London: Griffin, Bohn and Co., 1861 [1851]), pp. 5–6.
2   London County Council Public Control Department, *London Markets, Special Report of the Public Control Committee Relative to Existing Markets and Market Rights and as to the Expediency of Establishing New Markets in or Near the Administrative County of*

London (London: London County Council, 1893) (hereafter LCC, *London Markets 1893*), p. 25.

3   G. Dodd, *The Food of London* (London: Longman, Brown, Green, and Longmans, 1856), pp. 515–16.
4   R. Harding Davis, *Our English Cousins* (New York: Harper and Brothers, 1894), p. 217.
5   E. Richards, 'A Saturday market in slum London', *Temple Magazine*, September 1901, p. 1048; 'London's street markets: their ten thousand pitches', *Manchester Guardian*, 13 December 1937, p. 6.
6   See *The London Journal* special issue 'Industry in London 1750–1945', 21.1 (1996), particularly M. Daunton, 'Industry in London: revisions and reflections', 1–8; P. Johnson, 'Economic development and industrial dynamism in Victorian London', 27–37; A. Godley 'Immigrant entrepreneurs and the emergence of London's East End as an industrial district', 38–45. See also A. Godley, *Jewish Immigrant Entrepreneurship in New York and London, 1850–1914* (Basingstoke: Palgrave, 2001), and G. Riello, 'Boundless competition: subcontracting and the London economy in the late nineteenth century', *Enterprise and Society*, 13.3 (2012), 504–37.
7   Daunton, 'Industry in London', p. 1; Johnson, 'Economic development', pp. 27, 28–9.
8   C. Booth, *Life and Labour of the People in London* (London: Macmillan, 1903), Series I, Vol. V, pp. 69–70; T. Buchner and P. R. Hoffmann-Rehnitz, 'Introduction: irregular economic practices as a topic of modern (urban) history – problems and possibilities', in T. Buchner and P. R. Hoffmann-Rehnitz (eds), *Shadow Economies and Irregular Work in Urban Europe, Sixteenth to Early Twentieth Centuries* (Vienna and Münster: Lit Verlag, 2011), p. 3.
9   Booth, *Life and Labour*, Series II, Vol. III, p. 260.
10 Dodd, *Food of London*, pp. 321–3; J. Burnett, *Plenty and Want: A Social History of Food in England from 1815 to the Present Day* (London: Routledge, 1989 [1966]), p. 7.
11 Dodd, *Food of London*, pp. 373–6.
12 W. Page (ed.), *The Victoria History of the County of Kent*, Vol. III (London: St Catherine's Press, 1932), p. 420.
13 Dodd, *Food of London*, p. 394.
14 P. J. Atkins, '"A tale of two cities": a comparison of food supply in London and Paris in the 1850s', in P. J. Atkins, P. Lummel and D. J. Oddy (eds), *Food and the City in Europe Since 1800* (Abingdon: Routledge, 2016 [2007]), p. 25; Dodd, *Food of London*, pp. 389–94.
15 P. Atkins, *Liquid Materialities: A History of Milk, Science and the Law* (London: Routledge, 2010), pp. xvi–xvii; Booth, *Life and Labour*, Series II, Vol. V, p. 64.
16 Dodd, *Food of London*, p. 389; Mayhew, *London Labour*, Vol. I, p. 84.
17 Dodd describes the strawberry trade thus organised; Dodd, *Food of London*, pp. 379–80.
18 Dodd, *Food of London*, pp. 363–5, 382–3.
19 London School of Economics, *New Survey of London Life and Labour*, Vol. III (London: P.S. King, 1932), p. 296.
20 Dodd, *Food of London*, p. 383.
21 LCC, *London Markets 1893*, p. 23.

22 J. W. Sullivan, *Markets for the People: The Consumer's Part* (New York: Macmillan, 1913), pp. 212–13.
23 J. Thomson and A. Smith, *Street Life in London* (London: Sampson Low, Marston, Searle and Rivington, 1877), pp. 97–8.
24 Dodd, *Food of London*, p. 364; see also Mayhew, *London Labour*, Vol. I, pp. 54–5.
25 'Fate of the London costermonger', *The Times*, 1 April 1927 (press cutting, in London County Council General Purposes Committee – Departmental Committee on Street Trading file, London Metropolitan Archive (LCC/CL/GP/01/210)).
26 Mayhew, *London Labour*, Vol. I, p. 63. Mayhew gives similar figures for British-grown fruit and vegetables wholesaled in a number of London markets and then retailed on the streets; again, the quantities are significant – half of apples, pears, strawberries and cherries, one-third of cabbages and marrows, one-eighth of lettuces and cucumbers and one-tenth of turnips (p. 80).
27 Dodd, *Food of London*, pp. 363–5; P. Panayi, *Spicing up Britain: The Multicultural History of British Food* (London: Reaktion, 2008), p. 99.
28 K. Williams, *From Pauperism to Poverty* (London: Routledge and Kegan Paul, 1981), p. 268.
29 LSE, *New Survey*, Vol. III, pp. 290–1.
30 J. Greenwood, 'Evidence to Food Committee', *Journal of the Society of Arts*, 27 December 1867, p. 92.
31 Mrs B. Bosanquet [Helen Bosanquet, née Dendy], *Rich and Poor* (London: Macmillan, 1896), p. 128.
32 LSE, *New Survey*, Vol. III, p. 293; M. Benedetta, *The Street Markets of London* (London: John Miles, 1936), for example, pp. 70, 112.
33 Sullivan, *Markets for the People*, p. 226; LSE, *New Survey*, Vol. III, p. 295.
34 Dodd, *Food of London*, p. 516; Greenwood, 'Evidence to Food Committee', p. 92. The LCC's 1893 report counted many street stalls run by adjacent shopkeepers, including examples of butcher's stalls (LCC, *London Markets* 1893, Appendix B, Appendix C).
35 R. Tames, *Feeding London: A Taste of History* (London: Historical Publications, 2003), pp. 95–6; LCC, *London Markets* 1893, Appendix C.
36 Tames, *Feeding London*, pp. 95–6; LCC, *London Markets* 1893, Appendix C.
37 See, for example, B. Magee, *Clouds of Glory: A Hoxton Childhood* (London: Pimlico, 2004), p. 65.
38 Applications for street trading licences, including an application from Home and Colonial Stores, Bethnal Green Road, for a stall outside their shop, Bethnal Green Street Trading Committee minutes, Tower Hamlets Local History Library and Archives, L/BGM/A/16/1/1, 9 May 1928; Maypole Dairy, Stepney Markets Committee minutes, Tower Hamlets Local History Library and Archives, L/SMB/A/15/1, 24 October 1927.
39 Lewisham Borough Council minute books, Lewisham Local History and Archives Centre, 22 May 1901; *Ideal Homes*, http://www.ideal-homes.org.uk/lewisham/assets/galleries/lewisham/stroud-drapers (accessed September 2013).
40 Panayi, *Spicing up Britain*, pp. 95–6 (drawing on the work of food historians John Burnett and Derek J. Oddy, among others).
41 M. Ball and D. Sunderland, *An Economic History of London 1800–1914* (Abingdon: Routledge, 2001), p. 111.

42 V. Jenkins, *Where I was Young* (London: Granada, 1976), pp. 124–5.
43 Magee, *Clouds of Glory*, p. 54.
44 R. McKibbin, *The Ideologies of Class: Social Relations in Britain 1880–1950* (Oxford: Clarendon Press, 1990), p. 172.
45 E. Ross, *Slum Travelers: Ladies and London Poverty 1860–1920* (Berkeley, CA: University of California Press, 2007), p. 64.
46 Bosanquet, *Rich and Poor*, p. 132.
47 Dodd, *Food of London*, p. 517.
48 Dodd, *Food of London*, p. 363. See also Thomson and Smith, *Street Life*, p. 87.
49 Bosanquet, *Rich and Poor*, pp. 94–5.
50 Bosanquet, *Rich and Poor*, p. 95.
51 Bosanquet, *Rich and Poor*, p. 95.
52 Atkins, *Liquid Materialities*, p. 143.
53 S. M. Horrocks, 'Quality control and research: the role of scientists in the British food industry, 1870–1939', in J. Burnett and D. J. Oddy (eds), *The Origins and Development of Food Policies in Europe* (Leicester: Leicester University Press, 1994), pp. 130–45.
54 Sullivan, *Markets for the People*, pp. 227–8.
55 Burnett, *Plenty and Want*, p. 164; Panayi, *Spicing up London*, pp. 95–6.
56 Burnett, *Plenty and Want*, pp. 224–5.
57 Magee, *Clouds of Glory*, p. 64.
58 Ethel Brilliana in Ross, *Slum Travelers*, pp. 252–3.
59 A. Basu, 'Immigrant entrepreneurs in the food sector: breaking the mould', in A. Kershen (ed.), *Food in the Migrant Experience* (Aldershot: Ashgate, 2002), p. 153.
60 Tames, *Feeding London*, p. 99; Panayi, *Spicing Up Britain*, p. 114.
61 Benedetta, *Street Markets*, pp. 199–201.
62 LSE, *New Survey*, p. 292.
63 Thomson and Smith, *Street Life*, pp. 48–50.
64 Mayhew, *London Labour*, Vol. I, pp. 346–9; Bosanquet, *Rich and Poor*, p. 105.
65 Booth, *Life and Labour*, Series I, Vol. I, p. 183.
66 Mayhew, *London Labour*, Vol. I, p. 346.
67 F. Carnevali, 'Luxury for the masses: jewellery and jewellers in London and Birmingham in the nineteenth century', *Entreprises et Histoire*, 46.1 (2007), 56–70, pp. 63–4.
68 Mayhew, *London Labour*, Vol. I, pp. 333–6; J. Greenwood, *Unsentimental Journeys: Or, Byways of the Modern Babylon* (London: Ward, Lock and Tyler, 1867), pp. 163–8; C. Dickens, Jr, *Dickens's Dictionary of London* (London: Macmillan, 1879), p. 140.
69 Carnevali, 'Luxury for the masses', p. 69.
70 G. R. Boyer, 'Living standards, 1860–1939', in R. Floud and P. Johnson (eds), *The Cambridge Economic History of Modern Britain*, Vol. II (Cambridge: Cambridge University Press, 2004), p. 280.
71 Carnevali, 'Luxury for the masses', p. 57; J. F. Fraser, 'Birmingham and its jewellery', *The Windsor Magazine*, 6 (1897), 463–73.
72 P. Johnson, 'Conspicuous consumption and working-class culture in late-Victorian and Edwardian Britain', *Transactions of the Royal Historical Society*, 38 (1988), 27–42, p. 29; Bosanquet, *Rich and Poor*, p. 105.
73 Thomson and Smith, *Street Life*, p. 50.

74 J. Walkowitz, *Nights Out: Life in Cosmopolitan London* (New Haven, CT: Yale University Press, 2012), ch. 5.
75 Johnson, 'Economic development', p. 27.
76 P. Hudson, *The Industrial Revolution* (London: Arnold, 2005 [1992]), p. 46.
77 Riello, 'Boundless competition', pp. 506, 510.
78 H. Mayhew, 'Letter XVI', *Morning Chronicle*, 11 December 1849.
79 C. Collet, 'Women's work', in C. Booth (ed.), *Labour and Life of the People*, Vol. I: *East London* (London: Williams and Norgate, 1889), pp. 411–12 (this was the earliest, partial, published version of Booth's inquiry).
80 Riello, 'Boundless competition', p. 509.
81 Collet, 'Women's work', p. 413.
82 Collet, 'Women's work', pp. 415, 417.
83 Johnson, 'Economic development', p. 32; Ball and Sunderland, *Economic History of London*, p. 56. See also Godley, 'Immigrant entrepreneurs'; Godley, *Jewish Immigrant Entrepreneurship*; Daunton, 'Industry in London'; A. Kershen, 'Morris Cohen and the origins of the women's wholesale clothing industry in the East End', *Textile History* 28 (1997): 39–46.
84 Booth, *Life and Labour*, Series II, Vol. V, p. 70.
85 On furniture, see L. D. Smith, 'Greeners and sweaters: Jewish immigration and the cabinet-making trade in East London, 1880–1914', *Jewish Historical Studies*, 39 (2004), 103–20.
86 Godley, 'Immigrant entrepreneurs', p. 42.
87 Riello, 'Boundless competition', p. 507.
88 Bosanquet, *Rich and Poor*, p. 86.
89 Bosanquet, *Rich and Poor*, pp. 129–30.
90 Mayhew, *London Labour*, Vol. II, pp. 119–21.
91 These figures are based on the LCC *London Markets* report (1893), and the LSE *New Survey*, Vol. III (1932), extrapolating the proportions of old clothes and new clothes stalls in 'market centres' to all street markets.
92 Benedetta, *Street Markets*, pp. 2, 33.
93 Bosanquet, *Rich and Poor*, p. 83.
94 Booth, *Life and Labour*, Series II, Vol. I, pp. 219–21; Series II, Vol. III, p. 270.
95 R. Finn, *No Tears in Aldgate* (London: Robert Hale, 1963), p. 12.
96 See V. Kelley, 'Home and work: housework and paid work in British homes', in J. Hamlett (ed.), *A Cultural History of the Home* (London: Bloomsbury, 2019).
97 A. Hartog, *Born to Sing: Memoirs of an East End Mantle Presser* (London: Brick Lane Books, 1979), pp. 18–19.
98 Benedetta, *Street Markets*, p. 2.
99 Bosanquet, *Rich and Poor*, p. 129.
100 Richards, 'A Saturday market', pp. 1048–9.
101 Benedetta, *Street Markets*, p. 4.
102 Benedetta, *Street Markets*, p. 1.
103 Panayi, *Spicing Up Britain*, p. 104.
104 Finn, *No Tears in Aldgate*, p. 37.
105 W. Southgate, *That's the Way it Was: A Working-class Autobiography, 1890–1950* (London: New Clarion Press/History Workshop, 1982), p. 86; Magee, *Clouds of Glory*, pp. 190–1.

106 A. Miller, *The Earl of Petticoat Lane* (London: Random House, 2006).
107 Miller, *Earl of Petticoat Lane*, p. 11.
108 Miller, *Earl of Petticoat Lane*, p. 106.

Streets

In his monumental survey of *Life and Labour of the People in London*, the social investigator Charles Booth described the less well-known corners of the West End, away from the 'rattle and blaze of the great streets', many of which had been cut through the older patterns of alleys and courts in the course of the nineteenth century. 'Step but fifteen paces' from the grand thoroughfares, he says, and 'you find yourself in another world, with another people – other habits, other thoughts, and other manners seem to prevail'.[1] As part of his description, Booth gave this account of a 'typical' market street in the district, tucked into the back lanes:

> The people crowd the streets, along which no vehicle dreams of passing, chatting with each other, chaffering with the sellers, buying what they want or looking on while others buy. The air is bright with flaring lights and resonant with voices. The street is occupied by a double line of 'costers'' barrows and three slowly flowing streams of passers-by.[2]

Even in the predominantly wealthy West End there were enclaves of poverty, reflecting the nature of a city in which, as revealed by Booth's famous poverty map, riches and want were always in close proximity and urban character could change dramatically in the space of just a few streets – what the historian Jerry White calls London's 'diverse social topography'.[3] Street markets were chiefly located in these poorer areas.[4] Berwick Street market, for instance (which had thirty-two stalls in 1893 according to London County Council, and which may have been the model for Booth's description) was at the centre of Soho, a small and densely crowded area of poverty circled by the great shopping and leisure thoroughfares of Regent Street, Oxford Street, Charing Cross Road and Shaftesbury Avenue. In Westminster, Strutton Ground market (forty-seven stalls in 1893 as listed by the LCC) was in the centre of a patch of old and crowded housing and newer working-class tenements, despite being neighbour to St James's and its royal palaces, Westminster Abbey and the Houses of

Parliament. This street and its vicinity were described by the LCC as inhabited by 'artizans, labourers and the poorer class'.⁵

The East End of London was more homogeneous, being largely working-class in character, although here, in inverse reflection of the West End, some prosperous inhabitants (chiefly of the shopkeeping class, and strung out along the major shopping streets) were interspersed within the poorer community. The East End was where London's street markets were most thickly scattered and streets such as Watney Street in Stepney (161 stalls) and Chrisp Street in Poplar (215 stalls) were identified by the LCC as 'market centres', large markets that attracted customers from beyond their immediate surroundings. From the 1880s onwards Jewish immigration boosted the growth of the street market located in Wentworth Street and Middlesex Street, Whitechapel (335 stalls in 1893), and by the early decades of the twentieth century this market, long known by the informal name of 'Petticoat Lane', had grown and spread into a network of market streets that marked the whole character of this area and even turned it into a tourist destination of sorts, where food, mass-market fashions and a whole range of other goods were sold by traders renowned for their loud and lively patter.

South of the Thames, in Lambeth and Southwark, there were a number of long-established market streets known for their particularly rough and ready character. The New Cut (forty-eight stalls) is described consistently throughout the 1850 to 1939 period as the lowest, poorest and most desperate of the street markets.⁶ By the later nineteenth century many areas of quite recent suburban growth, such as Lewisham and Peckham, had their street markets too: Lewisham's was described as 'small' by the LCC in 1901, but in 1934 the borough council issued licences to trade to fifty-four stallholders and, as we saw in the previous chapter, the street market was situated in a typical interwar suburban high street.⁷

This chapter steps into the street markets, walking between the rows of stalls. What sorts of streets did the markets occupy? How did they fit into the wider rhythms of London's networks of consumption and circulation? What did they look like and how were they materially constituted? It moves on from locating the street markets within overlapping definitions of legal and economic informality to look at the results of that informality in the material culture and what might be called the *sensory affects* that characterised the market streets of London. The first section will look at the street markets as congested and crowded places that nevertheless took large quantities of food and other goods and retailed them to the mass of the population with some efficiency. Here the notion of urban rhythms and their operation in space and time will be useful – Henri Lefebvre's *rhythmanalysis* offers ways to analyse the particular patterns of the informal economy.⁸ Section two focuses on one aspect of the street markets' material culture and sensory impact: light. Many descriptions, such as that from Charles Booth quoted above, describe the particular 'flaring' quality of the markets' lighting, the result of the naked flames of naphtha lamps, a mode of illumination that was both related to but also very different from the lighting infrastructure of the West End shops, where bright light created consumer spectacle. Lighting is one way to approach the street markets as distinct urban spaces characterised by informality, and in many ways 'other' to the respectable shopping streets of the West End. The final section will suggest that the informal constitution of the street markets may be interpreted as a type of impermanent or fragile *architecture* that is related to their sensory qualities, and that reveals something about the nature of the experience these cheap streets offered to those people who shopped in them. In Bakhtin's writings, the special character of the marketplace (which is the site of carnival) is closely linked to the fluidity of its relationship to time, and moments of 'becoming, change and renewal' mark the popular festivities that were 'hostile to all that was monumental and completed'.[9] Might this offer a means of understanding how the markets, with their shifting arrays of barrows and stalls, contrasted with the more solid and formal aspects of London's retail infrastructures?

Urban rhythms: blockage, flow and the market street

Different sources report on different aspects of the street markets. As discussed in Chapter 1, some accounts (including some of those produced by local or national government and their agencies) failed to 'see' the street markets at all, or at least rapidly dismissed them as unworthy of consideration because of their informal, a-legal nature. When such accounts did consider the street markets, one of their chief concerns was with circulation and the way in which street selling could impede the passage of traffic and pedestrians. In its 1893 report, London County Council included summary descriptions of many of the street markets. These run through standard categories of information, apparently supplied by local officials in response to set questions, and always include an assessment of the market's impact on circulation. Certain phrases come up again and again: traffic is 'seriously incommoded', the street is 'impassable', or the market constitutes a 'great impediment' to vehicles and walkers.[10]

There is no doubt that many street markets caused congestion in the streets they occupied (see figure 15, the busy Hammersmith market). This was particularly the case at the busiest times (Saturday nights and in some cases Sunday mornings) when the largest numbers of stalls and customers were present. The social worker Helen Bosanquet described the typical street markets she knew on a Saturday night, when 'the pavements are so thronged with busy bargainers as to be impassable without a great expenditure of force in pushing, and the middle of the road is occupied by a stream of potential buyers'.[11] The American journalist Richard Harding Davis described, in terms similar to Charles Booth's account quoted at the start of this chapter, the three lanes of pedestrians channelled in a 'long continuous stream' between the market stalls and the shops on either side, a stream that halted at points of particular congestion.[12] Laszlo Moholy-Nagy's 1936 photograph of Petticoat Lane (figure 16) shows an even

15   Street market in Hammersmith, postcard, c. 1900–14

more crowded scene, with the elevated viewpoint revealing the double line of stalls that hugged the kerbs. Also visible in Moholy-Nagy's photograph are the three lines of shoppers, in the roadway and on the pavements on right and left. Pedestrians were channelled along these lanes, and people who wanted to look for goods on both sides of the road would have to cross and re-cross, pushing through the narrow gaps between the stalls and traversing the flow of pedestrians on each pavement and in the road. The shops on either side formed the solid infrastructure of the market street, bounding the more transitory spectacle of stalls and crowds.

The street markets constituted great tangles of people and goods as the barrows and stalls narrowed the width of the road, making it difficult or impossible for vehicles to pass. These tangles of congestion were just one instance of blockage in a city that had long appeared to be outgrowing its ability to keep people and vehicles moving freely. James Winter, in his history of *London's Teeming Streets*, notes how bodily metaphors informed many critiques of the nineteenth-century city, with the circulation of blood analogous to movement in the streets. Winter cites an article in the *Illustrated London News* which described how 'the life blood' of the 'huge giant' that was London was forced to run through inadequately narrow veins and arteries, with the result that 'there is dangerous pressure in the main channels and morbid disturbance of the current, in all causing daily stoppages of the vital functions'.[13] This was written

16 Laszlo Moholy-Nagy, 'Petticoat Lane: general view', in Mary Benedetta, *The Street Markets of London*, 1936

in 1846: the following decades saw a massive further expansion of the city and its problems of circulation, and was also the period in which the street markets proliferated: it was perhaps inevitable that there was some tension between these two developments.

As discussed in Chapter 1, there were attempts to legislate to keep the streets free of obstruction. The 1867 Metropolitan Streets Act had just this intention, but it was quickly amended to exempt the costermongers and street traders from its provisions after protest and a vigorous campaign in the press. Although the amended Act gave police discretionary powers to move costermongers on, these powers were used relatively sparingly. On the whole, the 1867 Act seems to have had the effect on the ground of empowering the police to move individual perambulating traders where they caused a genuine blockage, but to tolerate them, and the street markets, where their presence was regular and habitual. Plate 4, a painting by John Atkinson Grimshaw, shows a lone barrow tolerated in a kerbside position in Blackman Street, Borough. A few markets were moved from main roads to side streets during the latter half of the nineteenth century: just south of Elephant and Castle, for instance, a street market occupied both East Street and sections of the Walworth Road until tram tracks were laid in the main road in 1871, when the market was confined just to East Street.[14] The only street market that caused genuine traffic chaos was the Whitechapel Hay Market, which was in fact one of London's *authorised* markets, the only one, by the mid-nineteenth century, that did not have an off-street location and dedicated market buildings. It occupied a stretch of Whitechapel Road outside the London Hospital that was also the terminus of several tram routes, and the location of a costermongers' street market.[15] In late 1924 London County Council proposed removing the costermongers, but the hospital's chair, Viscount Knutsford, engaged in a correspondence with the Council's General Purposes Committee in which he argued stridently that the hay wagons were far more disruptive than the costermongers' barrows, and that it was the former that should be removed.[16]

All attempts to regulate the street markets were halting and cautious until the 1927 introduction of licensing effectively recognised them in their existing form. There was by no means a consensus in favour of clearing the streets of stalls and barrows, even to facilitate circulation: Winter describes the long-held tradition that 'all might claim the right' to use the street, 'foreigner as well as native born, women as well as men, young as well as old, poor as well as rich'. Thus, would-be reformers,

> a high proportion of whom were committed liberals, had this tradition ... to contend with whenever they gave orders or sponsored campaigns to move idlers and vagrants along, stop prostitutes from carrying on their form of free enterprise on the streets, remove costermongers' barrows from the pavement outside of shops, or restrict the right of brewery wagons from stopping to make deliveries during certain hours.[17]

Promoting circulation in nineteenth- and early twentieth-century London was not a straightforward issue, and street selling was not as seriously threatened by attempts to address blockages as might be expected, although it was always made precarious by the possibility of action.

As Winter notes, the idea of circulation is a powerful one for those thinking and writing about the city. The cultural historian Ben Highmore points out that 'circulation has perhaps become the most significant trope for writers wanting to understand the condition of urban modernity in both its emergent as well as its more virulent postmodern or hypermodern forms'.[18] Burgeoning writings on movement in the city discuss many categories of circulation and not just that of people and vehicles in the streets. Highmore cites recent works on the circulation of images, for instance, of people within public transport systems, and of objects. His own analysis is based on *Street Life in London*, photographer John Thomson and journalist Adolphe Smith's 1877 response to Mayhew's earlier *London Labour and the London Poor*, which includes photographs of figures such as the 'swag' sellers described in the previous chapter, a sandwich-board man, a street boot-black and homeless 'crawlers'. All these subjects, proposes Highmore, are emblematic of 'stagnation': in a period when modernity was conceptualised as the speeding up of city rhythms, the costermongers, street sellers and homeless people photographed by Thomson typified 'those who move, but who move slowly'.[19] Highmore uses Henri Lefebvre's idea of rhythmanalysis to suggest how the modern city may incorporate both fast *and* slow rhythms, and he advocates 'an approach to modernity that works to grasp its uneven rhythms, its slowing-downs, its torpid circuits as well as faster flows of signs and bodies', countering the emphasis on speeding up in many accounts of modernity, such as those by Georg Simmel or Walter Benjamin.

While Highmore's application of Lefebvre to nineteenth-century London is extremely useful, I suggest one slight adaptation to his analysis: rather than placing the costermongers and street sellers entirely on the side of the slow, the 'torpid', the 'haphazard and wayward', is it possible to see them as embodying both Lefebvre's fast and slow rhythms?[20] If perambulating street sellers moved slowly, and the street markets impeded or even halted the circulation of people and vehicles, they greatly facilitated the circulation of *things*, distributing enormous quantities of goods throughout the city. And although some economic and retail historians have viewed the street market as a traditional form of retailing that was outmoded by the later nineteenth century, the sometimes uneven rhythms of its contribution to urban circulation may perhaps represent an alternative, or overlooked, aspect of modernity, just as the informal economy shadows the development of modern capitalist exchange.

The street markets promoted the flow of foodstuffs and other commodities, and the efficiency with which they did this was noted by many observers. The LCC's 1893 report praises the way the 'necessary and extensive' trade of the street markets took the 'surplus produce' from the authorised markets and retailed it to their working-class customers at low prices.[21] In 1913 J. W. Sullivan compared London's street markets to food retailing in Paris, Berlin and New York, and concluded that London's informal system was the most efficient, with the result that 'American fruit in London streets is cheaper than in New York stores'.[22] Large quantities of goods were being shifted in a repeated daily movement of foodstuffs and other commodities by costermongers and street sellers from the wholesale markets to the mass buying public. George Augustus Sala's 1862 book *Twice Round the Clock* describes the daily round of life for all classes of people in the capital, taking its reader into many representative streets and institutions, and structuring its observations over 24 hours. The book opens at dawn, with 'Four O'clock A.M. – Billingsgate Market', describing how costermongers come to the wholesale fish market to buy their stock.[23] Chapter 3, 'Six O'clock A.M.', takes us to another authorised market, Covent Garden. Sala describes neighbouring Bow Street blocked with costermongers' carts 'drawn by woe-begone donkies' [sic] while 'their masters are in the market purchasing that "sparrergrass" [asparagus] which they will so sonorously cry throughout the suburbs in the afternoon'.[24] Late in the day, at 'Nine O'clock P.M.', Sala describes the costermongers again, still at work selling their goods in the shabby street market in the New Cut, Lambeth, 'the paradise of the lowest of costermongers'.[25]

As is also attested by the Royal Commission on Market Rights and Tolls in 1891, Charles Booth's social survey of the 1890s and many other sources, costermongers started their working day early, buying goods wholesale in the authorised markets in the morning, then preparing these for sale and tramping them around the streets, or taking up their pitches in street markets that could go on until late into the evening. In the process they had the capacity to offer large quantities of goods for sale, at locations that were proximate to the many centres of working-class population, as well as in perambulating trade. They tramped through the city, from wholesale markets to street sites, clocking up miles, sometimes challenged by the police, more often tolerated as a symptom of both the freedom of the streets and free trade, and distributing with some collective agility the goods and provisions necessary for the everyday life of London's masses. They were not fast-moving, but they were efficient, responsive to the fluctuations in their supplies and the changing state of the pockets of their customers. They may have blocked the streets where they set up their stalls, but they facilitated the flow of things.

If street markets both impeded and promoted circulation, there are other similarly contradictory aspects of their situation in time and space that are worth considering. Unlike other forms of retailing, street markets were not constant in their occupation of space. One of their most notable characteristics was that they appeared and disappeared (a characteristic that they shared with other temporary forms of trade and entertainment, the fair and the circus), and as they did so the character of the streets they occupied was regularly, and dramatically, transformed, with movement slowing as selling quickened. Highmore notes how ideal nineteenth-century conceptions of time espoused 'measured rhythms', suggesting 'a metropolitan environment regulated by an almost metronomic tempo', the 'ethics of rhythmicity'.[26] It is certainly the case that the period was wedded to the benefits of regularity, order and habit, in both paid work and domestic life.[27] The rhythms of the street markets, in contrast, were sometimes opaque. They appeared on certain days of the week and not on others, and had a shifting population of stallholders. The costermongers and street sellers were noted for their comings and goings: as befitted their informal nature, some traders resorted to selling on a sporadic basis to supplement income from other sources, and others combined street selling with, for instance, the September exodus to harvest the hop fields of Kent. Although outsiders might view these activities as erratic in a society in which irregularity was a focus of great anxiety and the source of moral judgements, this supple approach to different activities clearly made perfect sense to costermongers and street sellers functioning in the informal economy. Lefebvre suggests that we remember the difference between *repetition* and *rhythm*. The former is 'wearying, exhausting and tiresome', whereas the latter 'has to have strong and weak beats, which recur according to a rule or law – long and short beats, repeated in a recognizable way – pauses, silences, blanks, recommencements and intervals, all with regularity'.[28] To the repetition-preoccupied world of waged labour or domestic routine, the rhythms of the costermongers and street sellers may have been difficult to read, but that does not mean that they did not operate to well-regulated cycles that were responsive to the seasonality of the produce they vended or fluctuations in their customer's buying habits.

There is also the issue of speed: Highmore categorises the street sellers with the slow movers of the city, but they participated in moments of rapid action that would seem to ally them closely with accounts of consumer modernity. The street markets' busiest time was Saturday night: by considering accounts of the Saturday night market, from before it started to after it finished, we can see the appearance and disappearance of the stalls, as well as witnessing the accelerating speed of exchange. Both of these characteristics appear to have been in equal measure perturbing and exciting to outside observers.

Behind every description of a busy street market on a Saturday night is the countervailing idea of what the street is like when the market is not there, and how the transformation occurs to set the scene for the night's selling. In 1867 the journalist James Greenwood described 'Squalors' Market', as he evocatively named the market in Whitecross Street, near Old Street, capturing the preparations for its staging. He arrived early in the evening 'just as it was growing dusk', and the 'gin-palace' at the corner was kindling the gas lamps that lit its exterior. In the market street itself final arrangements were being made for the busy evening's trade: a man selling naphtha for the flaring lights was finishing his round of the stalls, and large quantities of pigs' trotters, 'hot penny puddings' and ham sandwiches were being brought out ready for sale to hungry shoppers. Stallholders made ready their wares:

1 Covent Garden, postcard, *c*. 1890s

2 Chrisp Street market, postcard, *c*. 1910

3 'An East End symphony of salesmanship', *National Geographic*, January 1937

4 John Atkinson Grimshaw, *Blackman Street, London*, 1885

5 Paul Sandby, *A Muffin Man*, c. 1759

6 'The Coster's Mansion', sheet music, c. 1899

7   'The Rise and Fall of the Pearly King', *Picture Post*, 2 August 1947

8   'The Chevalier Quadrilles', sheet music, *c.* 1893

9 'If it Wasn't for the 'Ouses in Between', sheet music, 1894

10 'When the Summer Comes Again', sheet music, c. 1899

11 'When the Stars Are Peeping', sheet music, c. 1899

12 'The Lambeth Walk', sheet music, 1938

> The secondhand shoeseller was busily arranging along the kerb, and in single file, his dissipated regiment of 'wellingtons' and 'bluchers,' administering a little more blacking to this one to make its patches seem less patchy, and solicitously patting and caressing that whose constitution was so fatally undermined that, for all its blooming appearance, it would succumb before a day's wear, and part body and sole; the Hebrew who sold cloth caps and slippers was idly chatting with the Hebrew who, having nicely arranged his brummagem jewellery, had nothing left (but customers) to do.[29]

The account is evocative of a performance about to begin, especially in Greenwood's description of a putative beggar family, preparing for what can only be seen as an act – 'the "unfortunate miner" was, with his afflicted wife, partaking of a final whet of rum at the "Black Boy" before taking their stand, their five sleekly-combed but starving children for the present larking in the gutter'.[30]

In *Living London* (a three-volume work which captured the city in photographs, illustrations and vivid, journalistic description, edited by the journalist and dramatist George Sims) a chapter on 'Saturday Night in London' by A. St John Adcock concentrates on the market streets and the 'great weekly shopping carnival of the poor', building towards a description of Saturday's frenetic late-night buying and selling.[31] Adcock's account takes over from Greenwood's with the market in full swing. Most market traders, and especially fishmongers and butchers, were keen to shift their perishable stock before Saturday evening ended, so that as time wore on prices dropped, as did the quality of what was on offer. Their cries became more insistent, bargains were shouted from the stalls, and the shoppers with least to spend, who had held out in the hope of this fall in prices, were now eager to buy. Late in the evening, says Adcock, butchers were 'goaded to frenzy' by the approach of midnight: he describes how they showed meat to the crowd 'boastfully in both hands, offering it at absurdly high prices, and yet selling it for ever so little a pound to whomsoever will buy'.[32] Greenwood too described such butchers: 'the butcher of Squalors' Market is a madman – a raving lunatic. He unscrews the burners of his gaspipes, and creates great spouts of flame that roar and waver in the wind in front of his shambles-like premises.'[33] The dramatic actions were designed to spur on customers to buy, building towards what Mary Benedetta was still describing in 1936 as 'a frenzied climax of high spirits and quick selling on Saturday night'.[34] At least for one night of the week, the street markets participated in a fast-paced consumer economy, albeit one that sold cheap things to humble customers.

Adcock's chapter concludes as the night's trading reaches a sudden stop, and the market's appearance, described by Greenwood in Whitecross Street at the start of the evening, is reversed into a disappearance:

> Twelve strikes and the public-houses close, not without brawling and a drunken fight or two; but the last stragglers will soon be making for home; the last stall will soon have packed up and gone away; the latest shop will be putting up its shutters, and all the flare and fever and flurry and wrangling and business and

merriment of Saturday night will be quieting down at last under the touch of Sunday morning.[35]

This account echoes a shorter description by George Sims in his 1883 book *How the Poor Live*: 'the crowd thins as closing time comes, and the hawkers pack up what is left of their stock, strike their naphtha-lamps, and wheel off the ground'.[36] These descriptions evoke the idea of the street market as transient, spectacular, fast-paced and performative. In 1926 the journalist H. V. Morton, in a variation upon the theme, described Leather Lane market, which sprang up each weekday lunchtime to serve City workers on their midday break: 'Ting! The luncheon bell! Leather Lane prepares to give its daily *matinée*.' After an hour of rapid exchange, 'the bell rings, the luncheon hour is over ... The men of Leather Lane, having made their short, swift raid on spare pennies, pack up their trifles and depart whistling!'[37] The street markets and their sellers worked to patterns that, while persistent, could be rather opaque to observers, but did not lack dynamism. To understand London's street markets it is necessary to understand blockage and flow, rhythm and movement, regularity and irregularity, speed and slower movement – the complex space-time rhythms of urban modernity.

Flaring lights: illuminating the market

London's street markets were a major site of economic exchange, an important source of provisions, clothing and household goods, especially for the working classes. Their role was not solely an economic one: this section will argue that as a site of exchange they offered their customers both commodities and pleasure, resulting in part from sensory affect. An important source of this pleasure was light, and particularly the artificial light that illuminated the street markets on dark evenings. Saturday night was the busiest time in the street markets because Saturday afternoon was when most workers received their weekly wages. However, as Richard Dennis has noted, 'the attractions of night-time shopping were not just convenience, but related to the *idea* and *experience* of shopping at night'.[38] Many of the most vivid accounts of the street markets describe them on a Saturday night, with the flare and glow of their lights standing metonymously for the excitements of the market as a whole.

There is an established and sophisticated literature on London shops and shopping of the mid-nineteenth- to mid-twentieth-century period. Accounts such as Erica Rappaport's excellent *Shopping for Pleasure* depict the West End as the site of developing, and predominantly female, consumer activities. Bazaars, arcades and department stores increasingly offered bourgeois women the opportunity to engage in consumption practices that provided them not only with goods and services, but also the freedom to experience the city autonomously.[39] This literature is inescapably topographical: it describes *spaces*, *sites* and *routes*. There are the shopping streets of the West End (Regent Street, Oxford Street,

Piccadilly), the premises of individual retailers (Liberty, Selfridge) and the trains, trams and omnibuses that brought women from peripheral suburbs to the city's heart. Mapping analogies abound – and all reveal patterns of light and darkness. Lynda Nead, in *Victorian Babylon*, cites an 1865 account of 'A Night Ascent', a journalist's description of a trip taken over London by night in a hot air balloon, in which the main thoroughfares of the city, gas-lit, appear from above as 'lines of brilliant fire'.[40] Nead notes the particular pleasures of the night-time city in the age of artificial light, a city of 'metropolitan, bourgeois leisure' in which 'gaslit shop windows supplemented public lighting in the city streets', streets which had become 'a glittering gallery of images and goods'.[41] Nead's account and others paint a strong visual image of London spread out map-wise, with the West End's fashionable streets lit up as golden rivers of light, of wealth, of fashionable and pleasurable consumption. Writing nearly seventy years after the 'Night Ascent', Virginia Woolf described Oxford Street (now lit by electricity as well as gas), and her account continues the tradition of the aerial view and the focus on light. The street is described as a 'great rolling ribbon' composed of 'artificial light and mounds of silk and gleaming omnibuses' – 'everything glitters and twinkles'.[42]

Keep in mind this picture of the night-time West End as described in contemporary sources and brought together by Lynda Nead into an extended analogy of light and space.[43] Then add to it another image, again present in many historical sources, predominantly from the earlier part of the 1850–1939 period, and again dissected in a particular body of modern analysis that overlaps to an extent with that already described. In this second view the West End is still lit up and shining, but all around among dimmer areas of the city, and particularly in the east, certain places are intensely *dark*, their impenetrable gloom as thickly black as the dazzling lights of the shopping streets are bright. The literature I am referring to here consists of contemporary accounts that contrast the wealth of the West End with darkness and poverty, and modern scholarship that examines this trope. Judith Walkowitz, for instance, describes the contrast of light and dark as an opposition between 'a West End of glittering leisure and consumption and national spectacle' and 'an East End of obscure destiny, indigence, sinister foreign aliens, and potential crime'.[44] In 1890 William Booth, the founder of the Salvation Army, asked, 'as there is a darkest Africa is there not also a darkest England?' – and he found this darkest England in the poorest streets of London.[45] George Sims also found in London's slums a 'dark continent' that 'lies at our own doors ... within easy walking distance of the General Post Office'.[46] Charles Booth's famous poverty map of London continued the light/dark imagery. In Booth's visualisation of plenty and want, prosperous streets were indicated with bright colours (yellow denoted 'wealthy' and red 'well to do') while the poorest streets were purple, blue and black, the latter described as 'lowest class, vicious, semi-criminal'.[47]

Our map of London now has two, superimposed, schemes. We started with the West End, lit with artificial light and particular showy when viewed by night, and then shaded in areas of contrasting deep black, indicating poverty, to form a visual analogy of light and dark, wealth and want, glittering shopping streets and obscure squalor. The street markets allow us to overlay a third, complicating, set of images: in his social survey Booth described the sights and sounds of the market streets of the 'poor quarters' of London, that is, those areas coloured black, both in his poverty map and in the minds of other concerned social observers. Yet Booth described these markets in terms of light: 'the flaring lights, the piles of cheap comestibles, and the urgent cries of the sellers'.[48] In 1896 the social worker Helen Bosanquet, who worked in the East End, recalled 'the flaring streets where the costers keep their stalls'.[49]

Autobiographical accounts also conjure up the street markets with reference to their lights. The memoir of Grace Foakes describes Watney Street, off the Commercial Road in the East End, in the pre-1914 period:

> There were shops on both sides of the road and stalls lined it from one end to the other. In winter the stalls would be brightly lit with naked naphtha lights, and all the stallholders stood by their wares and shouted and called as you went by, trying to get your custom.[50]

The novelist Ethel Mannin describes the Saturday-night shopping trips of her childhood, again before 1914, as she accompanied her mother to the street market in Lavender Hill, South London:

> the dark tide of humanity, the yellow glare of lights from the shop-fronts, the warm smell of people pressed close together, the dark fire of the market bunches of wallflowers stacked on barrows, the earthy country scent of them, the pungent smell of oranges, and the great glowing blaze of their colour, the bunches of grapes, white and black, suspended like Japanese lanterns from the awnings, the white nakedness of scrubbed celery heads gleaming wantonly in the flicker and shadow, the rhythmic rows of shining apples, and the subtle, acid aroma of them ... And the black-shawled gipsy-looking women who sold these things ... shopkeepers and costers shouting prices, a din of traffic and shouting, a confusion of movement, colour, shadow, flares ... Something deliciously dangerous to my child-mind ... about the wind-blown flares forever threatening the awnings, dipping towards them and then away again, tantalisingly.[51]

If we add these images to our map, the poor quarters previously shaded deepest black are now themselves illuminated by many market streets. They are less bright than the West End but nevertheless bright enough to catch the eye and the imagination of the middle-class social investigators who visited them, and to lodge vividly in the memory of the people who shopped there. But unlike the previous markings on our map, the flickering lights of the market streets, which are widely described in contemporary sources, have as yet made little impact on historians' accounts. Taking notice of the market streets, and focusing on light, alters the geography of London retailing and consumption.

Street markets served a predominantly working-class population. Many descriptions of the goods on sale, the people selling and the people buying stress poverty – the poorest figures in the street markets were ragged children selling a few oranges, or poor women bargaining hard for cut-price, low-quality meat or fish. It wouldn't be difficult to construct a narrative of the London street market that depicts it as a site of destitution and degradation, and indeed many contemporary commentators did just this. Sala, for instance, in *Twice Round the Clock*, described the New Cut (by common consent the poorest and roughest of all the London street markets), thus:

> Women ... brazen, slovenly, dishevelled, brawling, muddled with beer or fractious with gin ... the howling of beaten children and kicked dogs ... the fumes of the vilest tobacco, of stale corduroy suits, of oilskin caps, of mildewed umbrellas, of decaying vegetables ... of deceased cats, of ancient fish, of cagmag meat, of dubious mutton pies, and of unwashed, soddened, unkempt, reckless humanity.[52]

However, this isn't the whole story. The comparative visual analogies that mapped London in the minds of its inhabitants and observers place the market streets on the map lit up like the prosperous streets of the West End. Is it at all appropriate to juxtapose riches and poverty in this way, and to suppose that we might use the same terms of reference or analytical tools to dissect both? In one way the comparison is justified, and that is in the visual pleasure that seems to be common to descriptions of both West End shopping emporia and the market streets. One of the most powerful sources of this visual pleasure was the bright light that contemporaries noted: the autobiographical accounts already cited from Grace Foakes and Ethel Mannin stress the visual stimulus of the brightly lit market streets. Almost without exception, descriptions of these markets describe the naphtha flares that lit them, naked flames that dipped and danced in the wind and that gave a dramatically unsteady light that emphasised colour, shadow and movement, and provoked a shiver of danger in observers. In Mannin's account, the flares impart glow and glitter so that her whole description becomes an extended analogy of light, with bunches of grapes like Japanese lanterns and orange wallflowers transformed into points of fire. The West End streets with their bright gas, and later electric, lights were a source of visual pleasure, particularly at night, when, as Joachim Schlör has noted, the city takes on a different quality in which the potential for both pleasure and threat are heightened.[53] Could the market streets offer a similar experience to the people who visited them?

At Christmas 1872 the *Illustrated London News* ran an illustration of the New Cut market at night (figure 17). This image reveals clearly the naphtha lamps, blazing fiercely and dangerously close to both the hats of the stallholders and the racks of second-hand clothing hung out for sale. Naphtha was the name given to a volatile liquid that resulted from the distillation of coal tar, which was itself a by-product of the burning of coal to produce coal gas, or town gas.[54] In other words, the flaring lights of the street markets were a direct by-product of the gas lights of the prosperous West End, the cut-price spin-off of prosperous

17 'The London poor at their Christmas marketing – a sketch in the New Cut', *Illustrated London News*, 1872

illumination. They were in use from the 1840s onwards, a chronology that fits with the widespread production of coal gas to light towns. Henry Mayhew, writing around 1850, describes stalls in the New Cut lit by the 'intense white light of the new self-generating gas-lamp'. This was clearly a new technology at that point, and Mayhew contrasts it with 'the red smoky flame of the old-fashioned grease lamp'.[55] The 'self-generating gas lamp' terminology that Mayhew used refers to the fact that these lamps heated and vapourised the volatile liquid naphtha before burning it in its gaseous state, giving the 'flaring' quality that the naphtha lights' common name stressed and that was emphasised in so many descriptions.[56] There were a number of different designs of naphtha flare available, including those with a conical reservoir of fuel as depicted in the *Illustrated London News* picture, and another type with a reservoir shaped like a flattened sphere, as shown in the dramatic illustration of a patent medicine seller in figure 18. This was the 'Read Holliday Lamp', made by a Huddersfield manufacturer that specialised in turning the by-products of gas manufacture into profitable commodities, including naphtha and aniline dyes. Read Holliday had a factory in Bromley-by-Bow in the East End of London, where the Imperial

18 Frederick Barnard, 'Why pay a doctor?', in George Sims, *How the Poor Live*, 1883

Gas Light and Coke Company opened a gasworks in 1870.⁵⁷ The naphtha lights constituted a bright and portable form of lighting for market stalls. Each stall had its own light or lights, and each light was self-contained and not dependent upon connection to any commercial or municipal gas supply: the liquid naphtha was bought from vendors who hawked it around the markets, selling it by the measure.⁵⁸

Many historians who have analysed lighting technologies, such as Wolfgang Schivelbusch in his classic account of the industrialisation of light, ally the spread of light to spectacle and consumer modernity.⁵⁹ Chris Otter's 2008 account in *The Victorian Eye* takes issue with this focus, and with another strong historiographical tradition of seeing light in terms of visibility and panoptic regimes of surveillance and control (Schivelbusch sums up the opposition as 'advertising light' versus the 'lighting of a policed order').⁶⁰ Otter suggests instead that, particularly in Britain, it makes sense to pursue 'multiple, overlapping' paradigms, rather than either spectacle or panopticism, seeing the complex history of urban lighting and associated techniques of visuality as formed within the political context of liberalism, where developing technologies interacted in negotiations between the central state, local powers and the self-governing liberal subject.⁶¹ As will be apparent from what I have already said about light, shopping and visual pleasure, I do not follow Otter's dismissal of the light-as-spectacle thesis. Almost every account of a street market that I have read, however brief, mentions the naphtha flares prominently, emphasising their role in visual spectacle. However, without abandoning the idea of light as sensory spectacle, Otter's contribution is useful in foregrounding liberalism. The street markets balanced on the knife-edge where an informal and independent street culture met important but cautiously applied urban mechanisms of control. Such a position is a classically liberal one (and it could also be uncomfortable, both for the costermongers and street sellers themselves, and for those who observed them and didn't quite know whether to admire or despise them). Otter's contention is that the politics of liberalism shaped the space in which lighting technologies and infrastructure emerged: in the case of gas from the early nineteenth century, national government provided the regulating framework (frequently in response to developments that were already happening), and local authorities often took over the gasworks, although in London private ownership 'remained the rule'.⁶² But there were always acknowledged limits to state action and control, and the street markets and their naphtha lights were located at those limits.

Otter doesn't discuss naphtha lighting (as far as I am aware, no historian has paid it any attention), but his focus on liberalism prompts me to suggest that the naphtha lights were as independent and informal as the markets themselves. Their material affect clearly placed them in the category of urban consumer spectacle, but, unlike the gas and then the electric lights of the West End shopping streets, the naphtha flares were a product of the informal economy of small-scale entrepreneurialism, with every costermonger and street seller providing their own light, which nonetheless contributed collectively to the dazzle of the market streets.

Mayhew's 1851 reference to the 'new self-generating gas-lamp' indicates a recent origin at that date for the naphtha flare as market illumination. Writing around a decade later, George Augustus Sala described the market in Whitechapel Road, where different lighting technologies, old and new, still mingled, and some vendors had only 'a rushlight stuck in a lump of clay or a turnip cut in half' while others demonstrate 'a degree of luxury' with 'Holliday's lamps' (naphtha flares).[63] As the mid-nineteenth century saw the naphtha lights arrive, so the interwar years saw them gradually disappear. In 1922 Thomas Burke described how the more prosperous stalls of Chrisp Street in Poplar 'have abandoned the old rowdy naphtha flares and are fitted with electric light', and Mary Benedetta's 1936 book on London's street markets captures the recent end of this lighting technology: 'perhaps they [the street markets] lost a little of their flavour when the naphtha flares disappeared, but the cries and crowds are still the same'.[64] After the demise of naphtha both the fixed shops of the market streets and the stalls too took up electricity on a lavish scale, so that even without the unsteady flare of the naphtha lights the markets remained brightly lit.[65]

'Using fire to express joy is an ancient custom', according to Schivelbusch.[66] As vivid first-hand accounts such as those of Ethel Mannin confirm, the bright lights of the street markets had a particular ability to provoke a sense of pleasure in areas that were otherwise dark, dingy and poor. This is certainly the impression given by George Sims (the traveller who found 'a dark continent' within walking distance of the General Post Office). Sims's 1883 investigation uncovered both darkness and light, metaphorical and physical. He described a typical, though unspecified slum, and the dirty, dingy and decrepit accommodation in which many of its residents lived. And then he went in search of the local market (see figure 19): 'we ... emerge from comparative quiet into a Babel of sound. A sharp turn brings us from a side street into one long thoroughfare ablaze with light and busy as a fair.'[67] The contrast between gloom and dazzle is immediate. As Chris Otter has noted, 'most nineteenth-century Britons still relied largely on oil lamps and candles'; in other words, bright light was a luxury few could afford in their homes.[68] Although the extent of street lighting increased across the nineteenth century (Jerry White cites figures of 30,000 gas street lamps in London in 1850, 91,000 in 1900), poor areas were much less likely to be lit, hence those imaginative maps of the dazzling rich streets and gloomy poor ones, which were material as well as metaphorical.[69] But in those areas of blackness, the street markets enlivened the gloom: in 1868 *Good Words* magazine carried a description of the East End, viewed at night from a train, and described as a 'wilderness of mysterious murk, now thickly, now thinly, sprinkled with withered windfall stars'. But then the train 'rumbles over a bridge' and a market street is revealed below, with 'double avenues of blazing shop burners and street-sellers' flaring lights'.[70] Figure 20 shows what such a street might have looked like close up.

"'ERE Y' ARE; THREE SHOTS A PENNY! NOW'S YER CHARNCE!!!"

19 Frederick Barnard, 'Ere y'are; three shots a penny! Now's yer chance!!!', in George Sims, *How the Poor Live*, 1883

Apart from the spectacular appearance of the lights themselves, what effect did they have upon the goods on sale, and the broader material constitution of the markets as urban sites? Tim Flohr Sørensen and Mikkel Bille, in their 'anthropology of luminosity', examine the effects of various qualities of light upon perception and experience.[71] They discuss the play of light and shadow, the intensification of colour in certain lights, and the way that flickering flames emphasise shininess; all these themes echo the vivid descriptions of the street markets at night. Brightly coloured and shiny objects stand out in the memories of the market customers – highly polished fruit, richly coloured ribbons, the shiny surfaces of polished metal household goods or cheap, highly varnished, wooden furniture.[72] 'Artificial light … helped to make the wares on display look more attractive', contends Schivelbusch, referring to the prosperous streets of London, Paris and other cities, but perhaps we can borrow the analysis and apply it to the market streets as well.[73]

And there is another way in which the flaring naphtha lights contributed to the pleasures offered by the street markets, and that is in defining a bounded sense of place. George Gissing's novel *Workers in the Dawn* (1880) opens with a scene set in a street market, and like so many other accounts, this fictional description includes naphtha lights, 'the flames of which shoot up fiercely at each stronger gust of wind, filling the air around with a sickly odour, and throwing a weird light upon the multitudinous faces'.[74] The bright and dazzling lights have an effect on the ability of the viewer to see what lies outside the immediate

SATURDAY NIGHT IN WHITECHAPEL ROAD.

20 'Saturday Night in Whitechapel Road', in George Sims, *Living London*, 1901

21 'London street scene: costers' stalls in Walworth', *Daily News*, 10 August 1903

area of the stalls, in the comparative darkness beyond, so that there is 'deep blackness overhead' and the alleyways on either side are almost impenetrable, in 'horrible darkness'.[75] Schivelbusch notes that 'any artificially lit area out of doors is experienced as an interior because it is marked off from the surrounding darkness as if by walls',[76] and by the same mechanism the market streets offered those who worked and shopped there after dark a sense of enclosure (as is indicated in figure 21). Gissing's novel (rather like Sala's description of the New Cut) is a gloomy one, depicting the market as a poor and abject place, but an autobiographical account by Elizabeth Flint who grew up in the East End of London is inflected instead with a deep sense of remembered pleasure, as sensory details trigger nostalgia for her childhood outings to Petticoat Lane: 'each stall held its own naphtha flare, and all the flares glowed yellow, and behind every stall was a brazier burning to keep out the cold'. She recalls how 'everyone was half in shadow and half in a fierce glare' and up above, 'the sky was a deep blue darkness', so that 'the Lane' became an almost magical place, separated both from the surrounding streets and the everyday world, a heterotopia.[77] Thomas Burke described the lit street markets as 'arcades of exultant light', comparing their illuminated enclosure with the shopping arcades of the

West End of London, where interiority was achieved architecturally as well as through the effect of light. The cultural geographer Tim Edensor suggests that this effect – when lit space contrasts with surrounding darkness to create a sense of interiority – is a form of 'immaterial architecture'.[78] The street markets as immaterial or 'fragile' architecture will be explored in the next section.

Fragile architecture: market streets and urban place

Is a street market architecture? Is it useful to look at the street market though this particular disciplinary lens? I come to this subject as a historian of design and material culture, with that discipline's natural focus upon objects, yet I am trying to think about how in the street market, objects, cumulatively, might make and define spaces and in turn create places. What can the material culture of the street markets contribute to our understanding of both those markets themselves, but also the city more broadly? How can considering the street markets as a form of architecture contribute to an understanding of this rather overlooked retail environment?

London's street markets were transient: they had no permanent facilities, and barrows and stalls appeared in the morning and were cleared away again at the end of the evening, leaving nothing (apart from rubbish) behind. There were no covered halls or arcaded shelters, no marked pitches, no special provisions for water or waste disposal and no lighting infrastructure (hence the naphtha flares). The markets swelled and contracted from day to day and week to week, as individual costermongers and street sellers chose to attend or not, perhaps dividing their time between a number of different market sites. Sellers either owned, or very commonly hired, the barrows and even the baskets (known as 'shallows') that they traded from. They brought them to the market each day from their homes, which doubled up as store rooms, or from the wholesale markets where they purchased their stock.[79] For those who rented a barrow by the week or even by the day their very presence at the market was dependent on shifting enough goods, at a good enough profit, to allow them to rehire their barrow and restock it.

A market barrow is, essentially, a portable shop counter. Figure 22 shows barrows for hire, and this and other photographic evidence confirms the design – two large wheels at the front, and at the rear legs somewhat shorter than the wheels were high, with a pair of protruding handles to facilitate pushing or pulling. The barrow's floor (set at about waist level or slightly lower) was enclosed at the front and down each side by a rail, at an angle to the floor, to prevent stock from sliding off while the barrow was being moved. When the barrow was parked the rear legs were placed on the ground, sometimes on wooden blocks to level it up. Once in position, many costermongers and street sellers used boards to elongate their barrows to the full dimensions permitted by the Metropolitan Streets (Amendment) Act of 1867, which stated that barrows should be no more than nine feet long by three feet wide, with a gap of four feet between each one.

22 'Barrows for hire', in George Sims, *Living London*, 1901

They also extended them upwards with a framework that held a canvas roof to keep off rain or sun. The slats that supported such a cover are a common visual trope in images of the street markets, although the covers themselves seem to have been commonly left off in dry weather. Other sellers set up stalls not on barrows but on tables composed of trestles and boards, with again a frame above to take the canvas roof.

Once in position in the market, the top of the barrow was transformed

23 'My youngest customer', in Olive Malvery, *The Soul Market*, 1907

into a display of goods, with boxes, crates or baskets used to elevate things at the back. Goods were also hung from the slats of the overhead frame. Thus while the stalls and barrows themselves were small, certainly in comparison to any shop, and the stock they carried was limited, if densely packed and artfully arranged in three dimensions they could make a showy sight that would certainly, at close quarters, fill a customer's field of vision. A photograph of the social explorer Olive Malvery, who worked undercover as a costermonger, shows her next to her barrow in a kerbside position (figure 23). At the back of her stall she has tilted the baskets containing apples and onions to show off their contents, and in front of these there are piles of pears, bananas and more apples, punctuated with cucumbers. Behind, a row of cauliflowers tops off the display. The barrow next door has steeply angled boxes of potatoes, and piles of cauliflowers and cabbages. Malvery's display shows prices clearly marked; the barrow next door has a pair of scales on an upended wooden crate. Both have spare baskets stacked beneath.

A barrow or a stall is not a building. But when a double line of barrows occupied a street, the resulting cumulative sense of enclosure, emphasised at night by the contrast between the flaring lights and the darkness beyond, means that it is perhaps useful to consider the street markets as a form of architecture. There are several interesting currents within architectural history and theory that move beyond buildings per se and consider other ways of contemplating made environments through a wider, though still notably architectural, approach. The architect and architectural theorist Juhani Pallasmaa proposes a mode of building that he calls 'fragile architecture'. Whereas architectural design usually 'proceeds from a guiding conceptual image down to the detail', fragile architecture, he suggests, 'aims solely at qualities arising in the lived experiential situation', 'in opposition to conceptual idealism'. Fragile architecture is thus 'contextual and responsive', flowing from use rather than preceding it.[80] While the examples Pallasmaa gives are all within the realms of professional architectural practice, his definitions are certainly relevant to the street markets.

As well as Pallasmaa's fragile architecture, it is also useful to think about impermanent or temporary architecture. Writing on impermanent architecture in the Democratic Republic of Congo, Z. S. Strother notes how in Western architectural practice and history 'monumental scale and durable materials have been used to justify claims to universal and timeless meaning'.[81] Paying attention to impermanent architecture, on the other hand, 'shifts the subject of analysis from the individual work to its social meaning ... from architect to builder and from builder to issues of reception'. As with Pallasmaa's fragile architecture, this suggests a way to understand the collectively constituted street markets, which had no architect but many 'builders', and which provoked emotive responses from those who 'received' them. Robert Kronenburg, writing on what he calls 'transportable environments', notes how the very temporal uncertainty of non-permanent architectural forms – acts of 'arrival and departure' – can enhance their impact, so that they 'possess a unique quality associated with event and memory that static architecture can never match'.[82] *Event* and *memory* are evocative terms, recalling the appearance and disappearance of the markets that made them as much performances as places.

Carnival, located spatially in the marketplace by Mikhail Bakhtin, is a similarly temporal phenomenon, the festival of becoming – transient, spectacular and transformatory.[83] Bakhtin analysed the carnival at a particular Renaissance moment, but others (most notably Peter Stallybrass and Allon White) have seen how it persisted into the modern period, diffused into many aspects of culture.[84] Did the idea of the carnival have some echoes in London's street markets, which, while primarily places of exchange, carried with them in their impermanent and shifting nature aspects of the 'extraterritoriality' that Bakhtin attributed to the marketplace when it was transformed at the time of carnival?[85] Certainly many commentators on the street markets provide us with descriptions that combine 'commerce' with 'saturnalia' and 'fun, frolic, cheating, almsgiving, thieving and devilry', in George Augustus Sala's evocative formulation,[86] as well as a clear sense of the markets as mutable spaces marked by the tidal flow of occupation and activity. 'At twilight, when the naphtha flares are lit, the line of stalls becomes a fair', notes Thomas Burke.[87] The sense of space and time interlocking in the markets' comings and goings resonates with similar features of the Bakhtinian carnival, as well as the related concept (already discussed) of rhythmanalysis.

The transient and 'light' nature of the markets' occupation of space is revealed more clearly if they are compared with two contrasting categories of retail architecture in the late nineteenth- and early twentieth-century city, market halls and department stores. The market hall is the most direct point of comparison. James Schmiechen, while noting that London did *not* develop covered retail markets, states that 'few buildings in Britain compared in size to the new market halls', listing those built in Newcastle, Aberdeen, Liverpool and Birmingham in the 1820s, 1830s and 1840s as examples.[88] We saw in Chapter 1 how London's only attempt at a monumental retail market hall to rival those of other cities was Angela Burdett Coutts's Columbia Market – a monumental failure. London County Council's plans for local market halls recall Juhani Pallasmaa's notion that 'fragile architecture' functions 'in opposition to conceptual idealism'. The LCC plans were nothing if not idealistic, but they were never built because the council was in the end extremely cautious in imposing architectural form on the informal and organically developed street markets. This prudence was justified: Columbia Market was one reason for caution, and Mary Benedetta reported in 1936 on the market in Chiswick, which had recently been moved from its street location into a new covered building. 'The plan has been a dreadful failure', she notes, with 'the pretentious-looking market' losing the customers who had shopped there before.[89] Thomas Burke observed that the street markets 'lacked the gloss and dignity and brilliance of the shops', but had instead an alluring 'open-air boldness', a component of their informality and a characteristic valued by their customers.[90]

Schmiechen's analysis of market halls stresses scale, as do many dominant narratives of retail history. As Kathryn A. Morrison has noted in her excellent architectural history of English shops and shopping, it is above all department stores which 'dominate the study of nineteenth-century retailing', and they 'grew at a pace, and on a scale, that would have been unimaginable' to earlier generations of retailers.[91] I am not immune to the attractions of scale: one of the basic facts in the history of London's street markets is that they proliferated in number down to the late nineteenth century, and thereafter continued to expand, with many markets growing to include hundreds of stalls. However, it is worth considering in what ways the scale of the street markets differed from that of large market halls and department stores: both qualitative and quantitative comparison is important. A simple demonstration of scale might be a useful starting point: the 131 stalls in Chapel Street market in 1893 (which was large, but by no means the largest at that date) stretched in a double row some 847 feet or 258 metres, if we assume that all complied with the required dimensions of nine feet by three feet with a gap of four feet between each one. In comparison, the Brompton Road frontage of Harrods department store, completed in 1905, is approximately 135 metres in length, little more than half the length of the market.[92] The street markets were thus cumulatively large, but, crucially, no individual stall or barrow could exceed the dimensions established by the Metropolitan Streets (Amendment) Act. Thus, where department stores such as Harrods dominated streets with a luxurious monumentality dressed with architectural elaboration,[93] the street markets were modular, or cellular, with no single unit larger than the nine feet by three feet of the permitted stall. The stalls, with their gaps between, were like beads on a string, in a permeable and impermanent, though persistently recurring, line. And whereas the department stores rose to several storeys in height, the street markets existed solely at street level. They insinuated themselves into the length of the streets they occupied, adding another line of use and occupation that subverted the circulatory purpose of the roadway, returning it to an older, medieval concept of the street as a place to trade, yet doing this within the context of the demands created by the scale of the modern city and the expanding demands of consumer culture.

Another way to think about the scale and the spatial and material characteristics of the street markets is to consider how they were observed and represented. The only way to encounter a street market is to enter it, and the most common way in which the markets were pictured is from a vantage point among the stalls and crowds. To see a department store, the observer can step back across the road to a position that enables a view of the whole building. With a market squeezed into the length of a street, there is nowhere to step back to (and looking end-on allows only a limited understanding, like trying to comprehend the shape of a snake by gazing into its eyes). The majority of the images of street markets that I have found during this research were drawn or photographed from a position among the stalls and the crowds: they are close-up scenes filled to their edges with things and people, and convey above all a sense of crowded and jostling occupation of limited space. Rare exceptions date from 1936, when the Bauhaus refugee Lazslo Moholy-Nagy, commissioned to take photographs for Benedetta's *Street Markets of London*, climbed to upper-floor windows to capture the street markets from above (figure 24). Moholy-Nagy's repertoire of modernist photographic techniques, as Davide Deriu notes, included 'unaccustomed perspectives' and unfamiliar angles to create views that rendered everyday objects and the urban environment as geometric patterns.[94] With the elevated photographs of the London street markets he also achieved a distancing effect and a visual control not available to the artists and photographers who pictured the street markets at ground level from among the crowds, reflecting an impulse towards making 'the city known and therefore governable'.[95] Both approaches are instructive, in immersing the viewer in the crowded scene, or in lifting us above it to see its hidden patterns.

The street markets were both like and unlike the more formal architecture of the consumer city: their flaring lights imparted a visual pleasure that was akin to that experienced by shoppers in the West End's fashionable streets, with these lights providing a sense of enclosure or interiority. The scale of the markets rivalled in some respects the department stores, although they were linear and modular in composition. The impermanent nature of the street markets, at first glance such a contrast to the grand and solid architecture of the department stores and other shop-based retailers, is less different when we take

24   Laszlo Moholy-Nagy, 'Petticoat Lane: "A man who sells a mysterious preparation for making brass fenders look like chromium"', in Mary Benedetta, *The Street Markets of London*, 1936

into account the fact that department stores also traded on ephemerality, creating what Kevin Hetherington describes as a 'phantasmagoric vision' that was 'shifting and uncertain'.[96] Emily Orr notes how the department stores, above all in their display techniques, aimed to foster ever-changing effects within the monumentality of their grand architecture.[97] In this respect, the street markets were less like the department stores than the department stores were somewhat like the street markets – temporary collocations of diverse things, designed for spectacle and affect.

We should consider difference, what the street markets *lacked* in comparison with the prosperous shops of the city, and what they had that the shops did not. The chief lack was the glass of the shop window. Isobel Armstrong, in her history of *Victorian Glassworlds*, describes the visual attraction of glass: 'commercial glass, with its sensuous optical allure, conferred what Trollope called a "double lustre" on goods, giving aura to ordinary objects and multiplying the allure of luxury goods. Glass and scopic desire are bound up with one another.' Yet she also notes that glass distances objects from people, it is experienced as a 'deliberate barrier' with a 'prohibitive aura'.[98] Armstrong contends that the interplay of lustre and prohibitive effect contribute to the intensification of consumer desire: this may well be the case, but nevertheless the immediacy of goods without glass in the street markets had an allure too, and one that was more accessible to poorer consumers for whom shops, with their formal architecture and etiquette, could be intimidating. The absence of glass suggests other absences in the street markets: they did not provide shelter for those who worked there or those who shopped there, and everyone, and all the things, were vulnerable to the weather. They did not provide security (pilfering from stalls seems to have been a common hazard for sellers), and they did not provide facilities to meet the growing demands for hygiene in the sale of food and drink.

Nineteenth-century department stores developed a commercial strategy based on promising to provide what Rappaport calls 'safe, pleasurable and emancipating places for urban women', a convenient base from which to navigate the city.[99] The department stores of the West End were predominantly middle-class spaces (although this was changing towards the end of the 1850–1939 period),[100] while the street markets, although many attracted customers of all classes, drew the majority of their custom from the working classes. They brought the women who shopped there into close proximity with heterodox crowds, especially on Saturday nights when they were the focus of leisure as well as consumption. Thomas Burke describes working-class couples dressing up for Saturday-night shopping that is 'no mere domestic function' but 'a festival, an event'.[101] The women who shopped in the street markets eagerly took the opportunities offered for sociability and the enjoyment of acts of consumption. The memoir of Dolly Scannell, who shopped in Chrisp Street market in Poplar, recalls how her mother 'chatted with friends, for Chrisp Street was the only social outlet mothers had'.[102] Helen Bosanquet noted that 'On Saturday nights especially, the women will often be out until ten or eleven, bringing in the Sunday dinner, and thoroughly enjoying the opportunity for chaffing, bargaining and gossiping', so that shopping was the source of 'an unmixed and never-failing pleasure'.[103]

Whereas accounts of West End shopping stress pleasure that was above all visual, the scopophilic effects of bright light and shiny glass upon luxury goods, descriptions of the street markets evidence the engagement of all the senses, emphasising the immediacy of crowded streets and open stalls, where sights, sounds and smells might be alluring, overwhelming or even alienating, but were anything but distanced. If the street markets lacked glass, shelter, hygiene, amenities and a sense of security for women in the often hostile streets of the city, they did not lack sensory stimulation: in comparison to the formal shops, they perhaps offered a surfeit of it. The visual qualities of the street markets and their goods, the shiny fruit and the flaring lights, have already been described. Many accounts also evidence the overwhelming noise of the markets; for instance, the novelist Thomas Burke described how in Salmon Lane street market, 'the ear becomes deadened by the striving rush of sound. Every stall and shop has its wide-mouthed laureate, singing its present glories and adding lustre to its latest triumphs.'[104] And descriptions of smells are common too: we have already met in the previous section George Augustus Sala, seemingly overwhelmed by the poor and rough New Cut, and describing its mingled odours of 'the vilest tobacco', 'decaying vegetables' and 'dubious' meat pies.[105] Ethel Mannin, entranced rather than repulsed by Lavender Hill market, remarked upon 'the scent of the wet wallflowers' and 'the subtle, acid aroma' of the 'rhythmic rows of shining apples'. Taste is strongly implied in the descriptions of the foodstuffs on sale, and touch too, for instance in accounts of the butchers on Saturday night, whose vigorous selling routines involved not just loud cries and patter but tactile demonstration of the quality of their goods, as Helen Bosanquet described in her account of a typical East End market: 'they proclaim the merits of their fine juicy cuts and slap them about in a succulent way which the poorer shoppers find irresistible'.[106] As Kate Smith has noted in her analysis of the role of touch in eighteenth-century shopping, 'pulling, squeezing, pinching and poking were all necessary skills in assessing the freshness of food'.[107] This was still the case in the street markets a century and more later. Bosanquet described the market in terms of all her senses: 'a walk down one of these streets during the busy hours of the evening bewilders every sense'. She lists the 'uncertain flare' of the naphtha lights, 'the hoarse shouts of costers and shopmen rising above the chatter, laughter, and wrangling of the crowd', and the 'pungent odours' that 'assail the nostrils on every hand'.[108] As Juhani Pallasmaa asserts in his discussion of fragile architecture, modernity has 'favoured the architecture of the eye, with its instantaneous image and distant impact', whereas fragile architecture – the architecture of the street markets – is an architecture of all the senses: 'the feeling of external control and visual effect is replaced by a heightened sense of interiority and tactile intimacy'.[109]

* * *

London's street markets occupied diverse streets across the city, forming shopping spaces that briskly circulated varied goods even as they slowed traffic, and that offered shoppers the pleasures of consumer engagement via the sensory stimulus of bright lights, loud cries and opportunities for social interaction. Once more it was the informality of the street markets that drove these qualities, determining their shifting and impermanent nature. Informality helps us to understand the street markets; understanding the informality of the street markets provides the means to see the consumer geographies of London differently, supplementing accounts dominated by more formal retail spaces.

Notes

1. C. Booth, *Life and Labour of the People in London*, Series I, Vol. I (London: Macmillan, 1902–03), p. 182.
2. Booth, *Life and Labour*, Series I, Vol. I, pp. 182–3.
3. J. White, *London in the Nineteenth Century: 'A Human Awful Wonder of God'* (London: Vintage, 2008 [2007]), p. 16.
4. London County Council Public Control Department, *London Markets, Special Report of the Public Control Committee Relative to Existing Markets and Market Rights and as to the Expediency of Establishing New Markets in or Near the Administrative County of London* (London: London County Council, 1893) (hereafter LCC, *London Markets* 1893), pp. 23–4.
5. LCC, *London Markets* 1893, Appendix B.
6. See, for instance, G. A. Sala, *Twice Round the Clock: Or the Hours of the Day and Night in London* (London: J. and R. Maxwell, 1859), p. 274; M. Benedetta, *The Street Markets of London* (London: John Miles, 1936), pp. 61–3.
7. LCC, *London Markets* 1893, Appendix C; London County Council Public Control Department, *Street markets: report of the chief officer of the public control department as to the street markets in the county of London* (London: London County Council, 1901), p. 3; Lewisham Borough Council minute books, Lewisham Local History and Archives Centre, 4 July 1934.
8. H. Lefebvre and C. Régulier, 'The rhythmanalytical project', in *Henri Lefebvre: Key Writings*, ed. S. Elden, E. Lebas and E. Kofman (London: Continuum, 2003). H. Lefebvre, *Rhythmanalysis: Space, Time and Everyday Life*, trans. S. Elden (London: Bloomsbury, 2013).
9. M. Bakhtin, *Rabelais and his World*, trans. Hélène Iswolsky (Bloomington, IN: Indiana University Press, 1984 [1965]), p. 10.
10. LCC, *London Markets*, Appendix B.
11. Mrs B. Bosanquet [Helen Bosanquet, née Dendy], *Rich and Poor* (London: Macmillan, 1896), p. 128.
12. R. Harding Davis, *Our English Cousins* (New York: Harper and Brothers, 1894), p. 217.
13. J. Winter, *London's Teeming Streets 1830–1914* (London: Routledge, 1993), p. 6.
14. M. Boast, *The Story of Walworth* (London: London Borough of Southwark, 1993), p. 52; LCC, *London Markets* 1893, pp. 23–4.

15 LCC, *London Markets 1893*, p. 21.
16 London County Council General Purposes Committee file, memos, letters and minutes 1924–25, London Metropolitan Archives, LCC/CL/GP/01/210.
17 Winter, *London's Teeming Streets*, p. 10.
18 B. Highmore, 'Street life in London: towards a rhythmanalysis of London in the late nineteenth century', *New Formations*, 47 (2002), 171–93, p. 172.
19 Highmore, 'Street life', pp. 172–3.
20 Highmore, 'Street life', p. 178.
21 LCC, *London Markets 1893*, pp. 23, 26.
22 J. W. Sullivan, *Markets for the People: The Consumer's Part* (New York: Macmillan, 1913), p. 217.
23 Sala, *Twice Round the Clock*, p. 23.
24 Sala, *Twice Round the Clock*, pp. 47–8.
25 Sala, *Twice Round the Clock*, p. 274.
26 Highmore, 'Street life', p. 178.
27 V. Kelley, *Soap and Water: Cleanliness, Dirt and the Working Classes in Victorian and Edwardian Britain* (London: I.B. Tauris, 2010), pp. 60–6.
28 Lefebvre and Régulier, 'The rhythmanalytical project', p. 194.
29 J. Greenwood, 'Squalors' market', in *Unsentimental Journeys, Or Byways of the Modern Babylon* (London: Ward, Lock and Tyler, 1867), p. 8.
30 Greenwood, 'Squalors' market', p. 8.
31 A. St John Adcock, 'Saturday night in London', in G. Sims (ed.), *Living London*, Vol. II (London: Cassell, 1901), pp. 378–84.
32 St John Adcock, 'Saturday night', p. 384.
33 Greenwood, 'Squalors' market', p. 10.
34 Benedetta, *Street Markets*, p. 71.
35 St John Adcock, 'Saturday night', p. 384.
36 G. Sims, *How the Poor Live* (London: Chatto and Windus, 1883), p. 52.
37 H. V. Morton, *The Spell of London* (London: Methuen, 1935 [1926]), pp. 81–3.
38 R. Dennis, *Cities in Modernity: Representations and Productions of Metropolitan Space, 1840–1930* (Cambridge: Cambridge University Press, 2008), p. 129.
39 E. D. Rappaport, *Shopping for Pleasure: Women in the Making of London's West End* (Princeton, NJ: Princeton University Press, 2000).
40 L. Nead, *Victorian Babylon: People, Streets and Images in Nineteenth-century London* (New Haven, CT: Yale University Press, 2000), p. 85.
41 Nead, *Victorian Babylon*, p. 87.
42 V. Woolf, 'The Oxford Street tide', in *The London Scene* (London: Snowbooks, 2004 [1932]), pp. 26–7; K. A. Morrison, *English Shops and Shopping* (New Haven, CT: Yale University Press, 2003), p. 139.
43 In addition to Nead, see D. Epstein Nord, *Walking the Victorian Streets: Women, Representation and the City* (Ithaca, NY: Cornell University Press, 1995), pp. 20–5 on the proliferation of panoramic views of London.
44 J. Walkowitz, *City of Dreadful Delight: Narratives of Sexual Danger in Late-Victorian London* (Chicago: University of Chicago Press, 1992), p. 20.
45 W. Booth, *In Darkest England and the Way Out* (London: Salvation Army, 1890), p. 11.
46 Sims, *How the Poor Live*, p. 5.

47 London School of Economics, Charles Booth Online Archive (http://booth.lse.ac.uk), Poverty Maps of London.
48 Booth, *Life and Labour*, Series I, Vol. I, p. 68.
49 Bosanquet, *Rich and Poor*, p. 127.
50 G. Foakes, *Between High Walls: A London Childhood* (London: Shepheard-Walwyn, 1972), p. 15.
51 E. Mannin, *Confessions and Impressions* (London: Hutchinson, 1936 [1930]), pp. 19–20.
52 Sala, *Twice Round the Clock*, p. 274.
53 J. Schlör, *Nights in the Big City: Paris, Berlin, London 1840–1930*, trans. P. G. Imhof and D. R. Roberts (London: Reaktion, 1998 [1991]), pp. 9–10.
54 The name was also associated with naturally occurring petroleum. *Encyclopaedia Britannica*, 11th edn (1910–11), pp. 595–6.
55 Mayhew, *London Labour*, p. 9; see also L. Hebert, *The Engineer's and Mechanic's Encyclopaedia* (London: Thomas Kelly, 1836), pp. 32–3.
56 *Encyclopaedia Britannica* (1910–11), p. 652; R. Meldola, *Coal and What We Get from It* (London: SPCK, 1891), p. 71; M. Luckiesh, *Artificial Light: Its Influence Upon Civilization* (New York: Century, 1920), p. 56.
57 *Grace's Guide to British Industrial History*; http://www.gracesguide.co.uk/Read_Holliday (accessed 12 April 2017); http://www.gracesguide.co.uk/Imperial_Gas_Light_and_Coke_Co (accessed 12 April 2017); G. A. Sala, *Gaslight and Daylight* (London: Chapman and Hall, 1859), p. 262.
58 Greenwood, 'Squalors' market', p. 8.
59 W. Schivelbusch, *Disenchanted Night: The Industrialisation of Light in the Nineteenth Century* (Oxford: Berg, 1988 [1983]).
60 C. Otter, *The Victorian Eye: A Political History of Light and Vision in Britain, 1800–1910* (Chicago: University of Chicago Press, 2008), pp. 1–8; Schivelbusch, *Disenchanted Night*, pp. 142–3.
61 Otter, *Victorian Eye*, pp. 10, 258–60.
62 Otter, *Victorian Eye*, pp. 153–4.
63 Sala, *Gaslight*, pp. 261–2.
64 Benedetta, *Street Markets*, p. 178; T. Burke, *The London Spy: A Book of Town Travels* (London: Thornton Butterworth, 1922), p. 160.
65 Benedetta, *Street Markets*, p. 55.
66 Schivelbusch, *Disenchanted Night*, p. 137.
67 Sims, *How the Poor Live*, p. 48.
68 Otter, *Victorian Eye*, p. 8.
69 White, *London in the Nineteenth Century*, p. 60.
70 'Saturday night in the East End', *Good Words*, November 1868, p. 693.
71 M. Bille and T. Flohr Sørensen, 'An anthropology of luminosity: the agency of light', *Journal of Material Culture*, 12.3 (2007), 263–84.
72 E. Baillie, *The Shabby Paradise: The Autobiography of a Decade* (London: Hutchinson, 1958), pp. 47–51.
73 Schivelbusch, *Disenchanted Night*, p. 147.
74 G. Gissing, *Workers in the Dawn*, Vol. I (London: Remington, 1880), pp. 1–2.
75 Gissing, *Workers in the Dawn*, Vol. I, p. 2.
76 Schivelbusch, *Disenchanted Night*, p. 149; see also Schlör, *Nights in the Big City*, p. 63.

77 E. Flint, *Hot Bread and Chips* (London: Museum Press, 1963), p. 42.
78 T. Edensor, 'Light design and atmosphere', *Visual Communication*, 14.3 (2015), 331–50, pp. 332, 341.
79 Booth, *Life and Labour*, Series I, Vol. II, p. 50.
80 J. Pallasmaa, 'Hapticity and time: notes on fragile architecture', *Architectural Review*, 207 (May 2000), 78–84, pp. 80–1.
81 Z. S. Strother, 'Architecture against the state: the virtues of impermanence in the kibulu of Easter Pende chiefs in Central Africa', *Journal of the Society of Architectural Historians*, 63.3 (2004), 272–95, p. 272.
82 R. Kronenburg, *Transportable Environments: Theory, Context, Design, and Technology* (London: Spon Press, 1999), p. 1.
83 Bakhtin, *Rabelais*, p. 10.
84 Stallybrass and White, *Politics and Poetics*, pp. 6–7.
85 Bakhtin, *Rabelais*, pp. 153–4.
86 Sala, *Gaslight*, p. 262; further examples include Burke, *London Spy*, p. 170; T. Burke, *Nights in London* (New York: Henry Holt, 1918), p. 145.
87 Burke, *London Spy*, p. 165.
88 J. Schmiechen and K. Carls, *The British Market Hall: A Social and Architectural History* (New Haven, CT: Yale University Press, 1999), p. 34.
89 Benedetta, *Street Markets*, p. 129.
90 Burke, *London Spy*, p. 149.
91 Morrison, *English Shops*, p. 125.
92 Morrison, *English Shops*, p. 164; Harrods frontage measured using measuring tool on Google maps, 26 March 2015.
93 Morrison, *English Shops*, p. 162.
94 D. Deriu, '"Don't look down!": a short history of rooftopping photography', *Journal of Architecture*, 21.7 (2016), 1033–61, p. 1040. See also D. Deriu, 'The photogenic city: aerial photography and urban visions in Europe, 1914–1945', unpublished PhD thesis, Bartlett School of Architecture, University of London, 2004.
95 Dennis, *Cities in Modernity*, p. 55.
96 K. Hetherington, *Capitalism's Eye: Cultural Spaces of the Commodity* (London: Routledge, 2007), p. 120.
97 E. Orr, 'Designing display in the department store', PhD dissertation, Royal College of Art, 2017.
98 I. Armstrong, *Victorian Glassworlds: Glass, Culture and the Imagination 1830–1860* (Oxford: Oxford University Press, 2008), pp. 121–2.
99 Rappaport, *Shopping for Pleasure*, p. 10.
100 B. Lancaster, *The Department Store: A Social History* (Leicester: Leicester University Press, 1995), p. 101.
101 Burke, *Nights in London*, p. 145.
102 D. Scannell, *Mother Knew Best: An East-End Childhood* (London: Pan, 1975), p. 34.
103 Bosanquet, *Rich and Poor*, pp. 130, 127.
104 Burke, *Nights in London*, p. 148.
105 Sala, *Twice Round the Clock*, p. 274.
106 Bosanquet, *Rich and Poor*, p. 129.

107 K. Smith, 'Sensing design and workmanship: the haptic skills of shoppers in eighteenth-century London', *Journal of Design History*, 25.1 (2012), 1–10, p. 4.
108 Bosanquet, *Rich and Poor*, p. 128.
109 Pallasmaa, 'Hapticity and time', p. 80.

4

People

One way of understanding London's street markets is to know about the people who ran them: with a retail form as light on the ground and as impermanent as a street market, its character is determined as much by its people as by barrows, stalls and goods on sale. As elsewhere in this book, Henry Mayhew's *London Labour and the London Poor* is a natural starting point. Mayhew famously (notoriously) commenced his investigation with an anthropologically inflected description of 'Wandering Tribes', citing various ethnographic sources, and several examples – 'Bushmen', 'Lappes' and 'Bedouins' – to assert that 'there are two distinct races of men, viz.: – the wandering and the civilized tribes', each having characteristic physical features.[1] This eye-catching opening leads Mayhew into an analysis of 'The Wandering Tribes of This Country', in which group he includes the 'London Street Folk', including the costermongers. The costermongers, says Mayhew, 'appear to be a distinct race', marked by physiognomic traits including 'high cheek bones and protruding jaws', as well as by violence, lack of education, and a love of gambling and low entertainments.[2] Mayhew is clear from the outset that the costermongers were *other* and *strange*, suggesting that, at the start of our period, they operated on the very margins of the economy, society and culture.

This chapter investigates the costermongers and street sellers (as throughout, using the former term to denote the core of London's street sellers who sold the most commonly vended classes of produce, that is fish, fruit and vegetables, and the latter to indicate street traders more widely, including those who sold various non-perishable goods). Who were the costermongers and street sellers? How and why were they marked out by Mayhew as distinct and different, a 'race'? Did the sense of difference derive from or determine the informality of street trade, with its chief site in the market patterned by alternative city rhythms? How might the characteristics and experiences of the street markets' people have changed across the period of this study? How did the presence of many immigrants among London's street sellers – most influentially Irish and Jewish newcomers to the city – affect their identity? What was the role of women as sellers in the markets? The aim is to understand the economic function of those who traded on the streets, their social position, and the cultural formation of their distinctive identity. Those who kept stalls in regular markets overlapped to an extent with those who did a perambulating trade, especially in the earlier part of the period, so that in this chapter, with its focus upon people, it is not always useful to attempt to distinguish too rigidly between these two groups.

It is important to remember that accounts of the urban poor and working classes in the nineteenth and early twentieth centuries frequently stress neediness, degradation and abjection. Much of the evidence at the historian's disposal was generated by people located outside the communities they described, and there is a tendency for such accounts to be marked by discomfort, anxiety and even disgust, which enhances the perception of degradation and abjection. Similarly, a considerable amount of analysis by historians focuses not just on poverty and the poor, but on the attitudes of social investigators, campaigners and politicians. Both contemporary sources and modern works of history, therefore, reflect both lived experience and the layers of ideological inflection that overlay it, so that this chapter will investigate the *rhetoric* around the people of the street markets almost as much as the people themselves, using evidence that contains a messy entanglement of economic and social description and cultural representation. This suggests one further question: to what extent did representations overtake the reality of the street market during this period, transforming its people, by the early twentieth century, into a potent myth of the character of the Londoner?

The first section commences with Henry Mayhew's 1850s description of the 'street folk' of London as the main source for a baseline description of the people of the street markets, and section two takes up a number of themes, including the immigrant's role, the informal structures of self-regulation that shaped street selling, and the economic status of those who sold on the streets, tracing them into the later nineteenth and early twentieth centuries. The third section engages with the problematic figure of the pearly king to examine the complex interplay of myth and reality in cultural representation, particularly in the later decades covered by this study. Although myths might sometimes be simple, the people who traded in London's street markets were not, and nor were they homogeneous: the picture is a complex one, not easily reduced to analytical simplicity.

Urban nomads: street sellers as other

Henry Mayhew's opening description of the London costermongers as 'wandering tribes' is an example of how some nineteenth-century observers understood aspects of working-class life by analogy with the 'primitive' other. While Mayhew commences with this racialised, proto-anthropological discourse, he goes on to provide very extensive empirical description of London's costermongers and street sellers, including valuable accounts of the street markets that were developing strongly in the mid-nineteenth century, with the New Cut in Southwark and the Brill in Somers Town among his examples.[3] Mayhew stands at the chronological starting point of this book, and this, with his concentrated focus on London's street sellers, means that he is an essential source, especially for the people of the street markets. However, he is also a difficult one, and the variable quality of his analysis, which is prone to inconsistencies of fact and tone, is matched by the uncontrolled abundance of his evidence.[4] Mayhew's work was controversial when first published, and has divided opinion since it was rediscovered by historians in the latter decades of the twentieth century.[5] It originated in a commission for the *Morning Chronicle* newspaper to which Mayhew contributed material on London's industries to a series of articles on labour and poverty across the nation, published between October 1849 and December 1850. At this date, Mayhew split from the *Morning Chronicle*, continuing his investigation independently for serial publication, and giving particular prominence to the plentiful material he had gathered on the street trades. He brought together his articles into a book, *London Labour and the London Poor*, the first volume of which was published in the summer of 1851; the most commonly read version is the collected edition of 1861.[6]

Mayhew is often judged on the basis of his methodology: can he be seen as a true social scientist, one of the first in a long line of investigators who critically analysed poverty? In this respect, *London Labour and the London Poor* is judged to be problematic in comparison to the more intellectually disciplined and profound critique of political economy that Mayhew was developing in his *Morning Chronicle* work. E. P. Thompson and Eileen Yeo, authors of one of the first accounts to resurrect Mayhew's reputation, do so on the basis of the *Morning Chronicle*, arguing that once Mayhew had split from the newspaper, he was channelled into publishing on the street sellers by commercial pressures. He thus retreated to become the 'somewhat quainter – but also more dramatic and more readable – Mayhew of the London street folk', with *London Labour* representing 'the most unsatisfactory remnant of an unfinished venture'.[7] For the purposes of this study it would be perverse to regret Mayhew's concentration on the street folk: this is precisely what makes his work so rich a source on the London street markets. It is, however, useful to ask *why* he decided to concentrate on these people, as well as what can be learned from the abundant evidence that he presented. One reason Mayhew directed his focus as he did, apart from the journalistic motive of exploiting a potentially sensational subject, may have been that he saw something interesting in this aspect of the informal economy in terms of his broader economic critique. He had already investigated related themes in his *Morning Chronicle* work on the contrast between 'honourable and dishonourable trades' – artisan versus sweated labour – in various manufacturing sectors.[8]

The historian Karel Williams, echoing Thompson and Yeo, notes that 'historians have usually been thoroughly condescending about *London Labour*', and not just for the perceived over-emphasis on the street folk. Williams singles out for critique Mayhew's undisciplined use of statistics, passages of sensational disapprobation, and the many internal contradictions of the work.[9] Mayhew could switch tone in the space of a few lines, from describing the costermongers as 'the principal purveyors of food to the poor' and 'as important a body of people as they are numerous', to condemning them roundly: 'the consciences of the London costermongers, generally speaking, are as little developed as their intellects'.[10] I argue that both contradiction and condemnation seem less notable in a reading of Mayhew that contextualises his analysis in a wider history of the London street markets and street selling: these themes are present in other sources too. As we saw in Chapter 1, for instance, London County Council's 1893 report on London's street markets incorporated a similar mixture of praise and disapprobation, as do many other sources describing the street markets from across the 1850–1939 period. This says much about the struggle of many observers, and not just Mayhew, to grasp the informal nature of street trade, which was variously condemned as chaotic, or tolerated as necessary, or even celebrated for its efficiency in bringing cheap food to the people and light and pleasure to London's drearier quarters – but which was as troubling as it was useful.

When Mayhew deals with the generalised and the quasi-anthropological he poses one view of the costermongers and their 'barbarism'. Yet much of *London Labour* is based upon his extensive interviews, and when he allows his respondents to tell their experiences the picture that emerges is rather different. Mayhew's voice steadies, with the words of his subjects grounding his account in the details, however chaotically told, of everyday life.[11] It would be naive to assume that Mayhew recorded the voices of his subjects without leaving his trace upon them – it has been shown that he sometimes edited together two or more respondents, so that what appear to be individuals were in fact composites.[12] But neither should we assume the voices of the costermongers to have been so weak that nothing authentic was left of their experiences, values and self-fashioned narratives once Mayhew had transcribed them. *London Labour* is a complex mixture of reportage and ideology: there is a disjuncture between moralising general descriptions and the accounts in the interviews, with multiple voices, and not just Mayhew's, found within. For this reason – and notwithstanding the debates around Mayhew's handling of his evidence – *London Labour and the London Poor* stands as an essential resource in understanding costermongers and street sellers.

In the passages based upon his interviews, Mayhew gives us much that is neither sensational nor lurid: we have brief life stories, accounts of where street sellers buy their stock, where they sell it, who their customers are, how much profit or loss they make, their relations with the police, and all the factors that determine their success or failure in the constant struggle to make a living on the streets – in other words, we are introduced to many of the people of the London street markets of the mid-nineteenth century, a period when the London economy was becoming ever more complex, particularly in its deployment of labour. The growth of casual labour in the capital was an economic issue that provoked considerable anxiety, although, as has been discussed in Chapter 2, recent economic historians have noted the economic dynamism that could accompany worker insecurity.[13] Many historians have concentrated on the docks and manufacturing industry as the locus of casualisation, but insecurity fed into retail and distribution too, and this is the context for the costermongers and street sellers: they existed in a casual and competitive labour market in which informal entrepreneurialism of the most humble sort existed alongside chronic insecurity in many areas of waged labour.

Mayhew described men, women and children who made their living on the streets selling all sorts of goods, and providing a bewildering range of services, among whom the costermongers, those who sold fish, fruit and vegetables, were most fully described (see figure 25 for Mayhew's generalised depiction of the 'The London Costermonger'). Although *London Labour*'s opening analysis depicted the costermongers as a hereditary 'distinct race', it is immediately clear that even within the category of costermongers, let alone the many other street sellers that Mayhew described, he found all sorts of people, some of whom had been 'born' to the street and others who had taken to it for a variety of reasons. He also found varying fortunes.

At the bottom of the heap were a 'poor shoeless urchin', enabled to deal in sprats by the loan of a shilling for stock from Mayhew himself, and an old woman selling oysters who was reluctant to disclose her past life, but had fallen from 'better days'.[14] A young male sprat seller, 'dressed in a newish fustian-jacket, buttoned close up his chest, but showing a portion of clean cotton shirt at the neck, with a bright-coloured coarse handkerchief around it', falls into the category of those who had taken to the streets because of failure or bad luck in another calling. This man had been a servant, but when he found himself out of work he borrowed a small amount of money from an old acquaintance and learned how to deal in fish, guided by a costermonger who took pity on him: 'so I started in the costermonger line, with the advice of my friend, and I've made from 5s. to 10s., sometimes more, a week, at it ever since'.[15] Other costermongers were 'hereditary', such as the woman selling shrimps who tells Mayhew: 'I was in the s'rimp trade since I was a girl … My husband sells fish in the street; so did father.'[16] Although the majority of the costermongers Mayhew reports on were men, he also includes many women working alongside their husbands or running their trade in their own right, as with the shrimp seller described above, or the keeper of a fruit stall in a street market in Marylebone who had traded in this location for thirty-eight years.[17] Street selling could be a viable informal mode of labour for women with young children for whom waged employment was not possible. Mayhew describes how in 'hereditary' costermonger families children were drawn into their parents' trade, either helping with the stall or barrow or sent out on their own with a basket at an early age. An 18-year-old

THE LONDON COSTERMONGER.
"Here Pertaters! Kearots and Turnups! fine Brockello-o-o!"

25   'The London Costermonger', in Henry Mayhew, *London Labour and the London Poor*, Vol. I, 1861

seller of apples reported, 'my mother has been in the streets selling all her lifetime. Her uncle learned her the markets and she learned me.'[18] At the top of the economic pile, one of the better-off costermongers Mayhew interviewed was a seller of winkles working in New Cut market. This man could take between three and four pounds on a Sunday afternoon, although considerably less on other days of the week.[19]

London's street sellers were not homogeneous, ranging in economic status from those who made a modest living and were reasonably prosperous within the ranks of the working classes, to the desperate and almost destitute. The latter, little more than beggars, feature prominently in Mayhew's account, and among them children, the old and the disabled are well represented. Even the most well-off, however, stressed in their conversations with Mayhew the precarity of their trade, with seasonal interruptions in supply or fluctuations in the buying power of their customers meaning that hard times were only ever a few slack days or weeks away. The costermongers and street sellers were clearly working-class in terms of their income, living conditions and identity, yet they were somewhat anomalous in that they worked for no master, and drew their income not from wages but from the profits of their own enterprise. Few historians have paid much attention to these 'penny capitalists' since John Benson analysed them in 1983, yet as the economic historians Ball and Sunderland point out, they were a key component of the distributive trades within London's economy (and have some parallels with similar low-wage service activities in today's global cities).[20] They were at the extreme end of the scale of casual labour in London, and even those who made a reasonably steady living were regarded by others, and sometimes by themselves, as being less respectable for plying their trade upon the streets. 'It was reckoned degrading to go into the streets', remarked one of Mayhew's respondents, a costermonger who sold shellfish and had made a decent, although variable, living for twenty years since losing his trade as a boot-maker when rheumatic fever affected his hands – 'it was just a choice between street-selling and starving, so I didn't prefer the last'.[21]

Despite the fact that Mayhew's account of the London street folk commences with that assertion of their character as 'wandering tribes', street 'nomads' to be contrasted with settled, 'civilized races', and 'moving from place to place preying upon the earnings of the more industrious portion of the community', the day-to-day activities of the individuals he describes are patterned by hard work, long hours and considerable entrepreneurial ingenuity in adapting to seasonal fluctuations in trade.[22] They arrived at the wholesale markets around six or seven in the morning to pick up bargains among the goods not already sold to shopkeepers and dealers, and this involved considerable judgement in, for instance, 'the calculation as to what a bushel of apples ... will make in half or quarter pecks'.[23] The aim was always to buy decent stock at a rate that would allow it to be sold at a price to suit the pockets of the costermongers' customers and still turn a profit. Almost every costermonger Mayhew reports on discusses the complexity and uncertainty of this calculation, which was clearly the subject of one of his standard interview questions. Most also show anxiety over the risk of having perishable goods left unsold. As one respondent reported:

> I buy my lettuces by the score ... at 1s. 6d., and sell them at 1½d. each, which is one shilling profit on a score. I have sold twenty, and I once sold thirty score, that way in a day. The profit on the thirty was 2l. 5s., but out of that I had to pay three boys, for I took three with me, and our expenses was 7s. But you must consider, sir, that this is a precarious trade. Such goods are delicate.[24]

Unsold lettuces quickly 'spoil' he notes: the costermonger's unsold stock could become worthless in just a few hours, which was why, especially late on Saturday nights, prices were reduced and a frenzy of quick selling ensued. A costermonger who sold fish described to Mayhew his efforts to clear his stock late on Saturday evenings in the nervy game of cat and mouse between poor customers holding out for a bargain and poor costermongers holding out for a decent price: 'At about quarter to twelve I begin to halloo away as hard as I can, and there's plenty of customers that lay out never a farthing till that time, and then they can't be served fast enough, so they get their fish cheaper than I do ... Anything rather than keep fish over a warm Sunday.'[25]

If the costermongers were in fierce competition with each other, Mayhew also presents evidence of their mutual support. The sprat seller, for instance, who was taught his trade by an established costermonger, evidences informal aid, as does the rheumatic shellfish seller who was laid low by a recurrence of his illness: when he recovered, a fellow costermonger loaned him a few shillings to buy new stock and resume his business. This also indicates the tiny sums involved in the 'penny capitalism' of the streets, which was often dependent on borrowed money to fund the purchase of stock, or to hire a barrow or even a basket. Both mutual aid and petty credit were a corollary of the self-reliance and independence necessary for life as a street seller, which went along also with an uneasy attitude to authority, including the police. Mayhew was writing before the Metropolitan Streets Act of 1867 and the introduction of discretionary powers for the police to allow the placing of barrows and stalls on the 'nine by three by four between' rule. In the 1850s and 1860s the legal framework around street trading was open and unpredictable, and no costermonger could be sure that they wouldn't be moved on by the police, although often they were not, as noted by the sprat seller when he remarked that 'the police don't trouble me much. They is civil to me in 'portion [proportion] as I am civil to them.'[26]

Mayhew devoted a whole section of *London Labour and the London Poor* to Irish street sellers, claiming that there were 10,000 or more when he carried out his research.[27] The Irish were a well-established migrant group in London centuries before Mayhew, but their presence increased from early in the nineteenth century, and was further amplified in the late 1840s by the tragedy of the Great Famine. As the historian Jacqueline Turton notes, 'famine was a catalyst, which reinforced a pre-existing trend', driving emigrants out of Ireland and into the mainland United Kingdom following the failure of the Irish potato crop between 1846 and 1848 and the lack of an effective response by successive British governments to alleviate the catastrophic food shortages that ensued.[28] By 1851 the census recorded that 4.6 per cent of London residents, or nearly 109,000 people, were Irish: the real figure was probably much higher than this official total.[29] Most Irish migrants of this period came from farming communities and lacked the skills necessary to thrive in an urban industrial economy. They became disproportionately concentrated in informal labour, working in the docks, for instance, or in railway construction, or as street sellers.[30] Mayhew was adamant that they sat right at the bottom of the hierarchy of street sellers and costermongers, dealing in 'such articles as are easy of sale, like apples, nuts, or oranges, for they are rarely masters of purchasing to advantage'. The Irish 'seldom prosper', Mayhew noted, and quite frequently turned to begging as 'a more profitable calling' than selling.[31]

Keith Hart's 1973 study of Accra, which is one of the foundations of economic and anthropological concepts of informality, focused on a particular area of that city that was home to many internal migrants from rural districts of Ghana, and he drew a link between immigrants and the informal economy of casually paid labour and small-scale street trading.[32] Informality is frequently the recourse of newly arrived immigrants who find it difficult to access formal labour markets because of a lack of relevant skills or local connections. Mayhew observed many immigrants more or less precariously employed on the streets, and although the Irish were most prominent, there were also 'Italian organ boys, French singing women, the German brass bands, the Dutch buy-a-broom girls, the Highland bagpipe players, and the Indian crossing-sweepers'. He also describes the 'Jew clothesmen'.[33] Like the Irish, Jewish immigrants to London had a firmly established presence dating back many years, and they also had a long association with street trading. The historian Adam D. Mendelsohn describes how Irish immigrants fleeing famine in the late 1840s came into competition with Jewish dealers already established in the more marginal street trades and particularly in selling old clothes, oranges and nuts.[34]

The Jewish old clothes dealer buying and selling second-hand garments and rags on the streets was a well-established character in the London Cries, series of cheap prints or illustrated books depicting street sellers and captioned with the traditional phrases they used to advertise their goods. Sean Shesgreen, in his history of the Cries, shows an example from 1804, depicted with the racial stereotyping common in nineteenth-century representations of Jewish people, carrying a sack of garments slung over his shoulder as he calls out 'Old clothes!' Mayhew's picture of a Jewish old clothes man in *London Labour* half a century later – who cries 'clo,' clo,' clo'' – bears a striking resemblance to this image, although it is based on a daguerreotype (figure 26).[35] The Irish were also depicted in racialised images: cartoons from the 1860s (a period of Fenian nationalist unrest and terrorism) show the Irish as almost simian – short in stature with heavy brows, large jaws, flat skulls and short, broad noses.[36] As figures 27 and 28 show, satirical depictions of costermongers from a similar date

THE JEW OLD CLOTHES-MAN.
"Clo', Clo', Clo'."

26 'The Jew Old Clothes-Man', in Henry Mayhew, *London Labour and the London Poor*, Vol. II, 1861

are markedly similar, visually conflating Mayhew's notion of them as a distinct 'race' with a stereotyped version of Irishness, and demonstrating how London's street sellers were hybridised, in representation at least, with various migrant influences. In figure 29 in particular the costermongers are contrasted with the

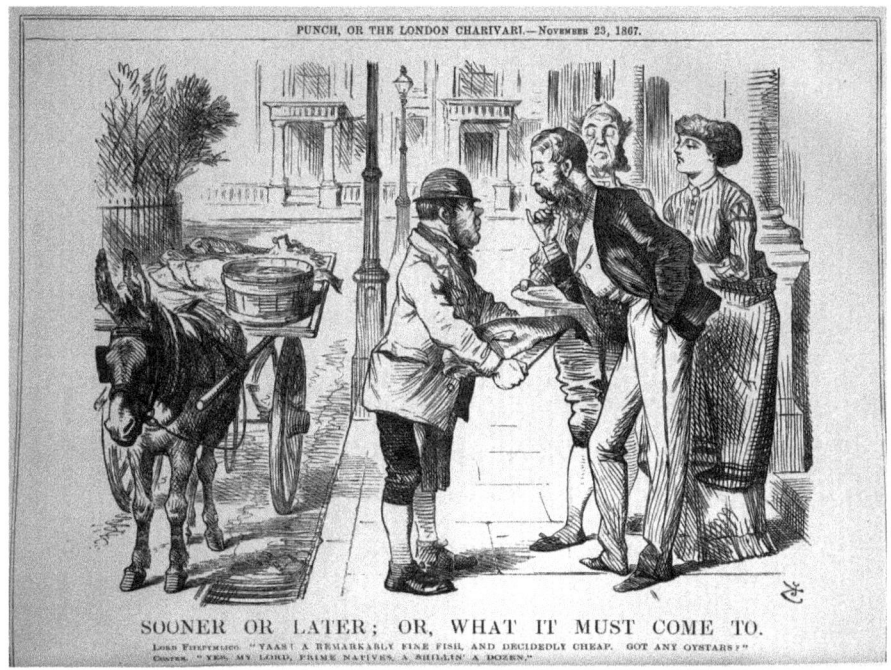

27 'Sooner or later; or, what it must come to', *Punch*, 23 November 1867

tall and upright figure of Gathorne Hardy, the Home Secretary, who they thank for his role in the amendment of the Metropolitan Streets Act, which allowed street selling to continue.

While Mayhew's interviews provide valuable detailed evidence on the nature of street trade and costermongers' lives, some of his commentary, as we have seen, sits uneasily with this interview material, in particular his insistence on the costermongers as nomadic, alien and even degenerate. The nomad analogy is both striking but also misleading: many of the street sellers did indeed ply their business nomadically, but by the mid-nineteenth century they were already well into the process of settling into fixed, although strictly informal, street market sites. And even if they wandered as they sold, they could hardly be categorised as nomads in the usual sense of the term: most were not migratory or homeless (although some of the poorest did live in common lodging houses), and Mayhew describes in detail several costermonger homes, two at least of which were the epitome of settled domesticity in poor circumstances.[37] The costermongers' presence on the streets was nonetheless both unsettled and unsettling, and this was reflected in their cultural identity beyond the pages of *London Labour*.

It is easy to read Mayhew as the originator of a certain way of depicting the costermongers, but as Christopher Herbert has pointed out in his history of

28 'A civil deputation to the Home Office', *Punch*, 7 December 1867

People

29   'Returning from the Derby', in Richard Harding Davis, *Our English Cousins*, 1894

the nineteenth-century ethnographic imagination, Mayhew drew the ideological material for his 'fictive processes' from sources to hand. He proceeded by 'stamping upon his subjects ... the lineaments of a fabricated conception of his own', but he did not 'invent the London poor out of whole cloth ... but out of existing ethnographies of primitive peoples, themselves highly prejudicial, ideologically and textually saturated inventions'.[38] And apart from this ethnographic material, Mayhew continued a long tradition of the depiction of the street folk of London in the London Cries.

The Cries had originated in continental Europe in the mid-sixteenth century and by the 1590s versions local to London began to appear.[39] New Cries were still being created in the nineteenth century, so that when Mayhew was writing he had recent antecedents in the depiction of the street sellers of London as other and alien.[40] John Thomas Smith's Cries from 1839 was peopled by street folk marked by national, racial or physical difference – an Italian seller of artificial flowers, several black traders noted for their wit and humour, and numerous examples of the dis- or differently abled, including a 'dwarf' of great strength, a beggar without legs, a 'noisy bow-legged ballad singer' known for his songs about Dick Whittington and his cat, and an old soldier with only one arm and one leg.[41] The wonderfully titled and relentlessly comic *Streetology of London* from 1837 ('being a graphic description of extraordinary individuals who exercise professions or callings in the streets of the great metropolis') included the crossing sweeper Sam Springer ('A Full Length Modern Giant, in Indian Ink') and Don Diego de los Santos (the 'Black Dwarf').⁴² As Sean Shesgreen has noted, the Cries commenced by 'picturing hawkers as representative and typical', and ended in showing them as 'bizarre, deformed, freakish and mad'.⁴³ Mayhew took up both of these tendencies simultaneously. Many of his illustrations, despite being engraved from daguerreotypes, show a marked similarity to earlier depictions in the Cries, as we have seen with the picture of the Jewish old clothes man. Shesgreen identifies Mayhew as both inheritor of the tradition of the Cries, and as the bridge that carried it forward into later, more sociologically inflected investigation.⁴⁴

The representation of the costermonger and street trader as exotic and transgressive stands as a cultural fact, reflecting and reinforcing the marginal and precarious position of the street market and street trade. In many of the Cries the seller is depicted in a doorstep encounter with a customer that juxtaposes the street with an interior scene: an example is Paul Sandby's 1759 illustration of a ragged muffin seller crossing in front of an open window that reveals fashionable women inside taking tea (plate 5). The world of the street meets domesticity, the disreputable meets the respectable, and poverty meets wealth: the result, while often picturesque, was also uneasy, an uneasiness that was strongly present in Mayhew's work.

Sitting close to Mayhew in date, and following shortly after the later examples of the London Cries, Christina Rossetti's poem *Goblin Market* (written in 1859, published in 1862) is, I propose, a further powerful example of the othering of street sellers. The poem tells the fantastical story of two sisters, Lizzie and Laura, and how Laura falls under near-fatal enchantment after eating fruit bought for a lock of hair from goblin traders who tramp along the glen near the sisters' home. Laura is saved by Lizzie, who goes to purchase more fruit from the goblins as an antidote to the wasting Laura suffers after she first eats the goblins' wares. Lizzie refuses to eat the fruit herself and the angry goblins attempt to force her to consume, pressing ripe berries to her lips and smearing her face with sticky juice. Lizzie runs home to Laura, who, licking and sucking the crushed fruit from her sister's skin, is cured.

The poem is one of the strangest cultural artefacts of the Victorian era: many critics have identified its underlying sexual and religious allusions to ecstasy, sacrifice and forbidden fruit, and some have read into it themes of addiction and anorexia. Others have focused on gendered consumption and the 'market' (in the broader economic meaning of the term).⁴⁵ Clayton Carlyle Tarr offers an interesting link to a specific market site, proposing that the wholesale fruit and vegetable market at Covent Garden was the model used by Rossetti (who lived in London all her life) for her goblin market.⁴⁶ However, this identification of Covent Garden with its large market hall as the origin of the imagery misses the *mobility* of the goblins, who appear and disappear sporadically, like the street markets. Surely they are costermongers, even if Rossetti transposes them to a rural fairy-world where they sell their goods by the brook where the sisters go to draw water and hear their vocal advertisements: 'Come buy our orchard fruits,/ Come buy, come buy:/ Apples and quinces,/ Lemons and oranges,/ Plump unpecked cherries,/ Melons and raspberries.' Rossetti's goblins are very strange, alien and animalistic: 'One had a cat's face,/ One whisked a tail,/ One tramped at a rat's pace,/ One crawled like a snail,/ One like a wombat prowled obtuse and furry,/ One like a ratel tumbled hurry-scurry.'[47] Their otherness reflects the disquieting presence of London's street sellers, the 'distinct race' described by Mayhew thus: 'there is a greater development of the animal than of the intellectual or moral nature ... and ... they are all more or less distinguished for their high cheek-bones and protruding jaws'. Mayhew's descriptions of the costermongers' character is also framed in terms that are not inconsistent with Rossetti's goblins and their rough and capricious dealings with Lizzie and Laura: 'their use of slang language', 'their lax ideas of property', 'their general improvidence', 'their repugnance to continuous labour', 'their disregard of female honour', 'their love of cruelty – their pugnacity – and their utter want of religion'.[48]

It is clear that the more sensational parts of Mayhew's analysis borrowed from existing ethnographic description, from the tradition of the London Cries, and from a widespread mid-nineteenth-century cultural distrust of the poor and the (apparently) vagrant, the unregulated world of the informal economy on the streets. As Lynda Nead has pointed out, the 1850s and 1860s in particular was a period when Londoners were conscious of modernity and striving for progress, battling for clean water, sewerage systems, street lighting, new roads and bridges, and a unified city government to replace the medieval sway of the City of London's Corporation and the ancient parishes: 'London in the 1860s was the centre of a highly focused set of representations concerning modernity and urbanisation, but it was a present haunted by the image of ruin. The past threatened constantly to obstruct the project of improvement.'[49] The many people who made a living from street selling were all the more perturbing in light of this striving for a certain sort of modernity and order. They were a continuation of older traditions of street trade that may indeed have been in some cases 'hereditary', as Mayhew indicates, passed down within families within the capital. Street selling was also the recourse of those who had no other means to make a living – the old, the unsupported young, the sick and disabled, the recently arrived immigrant. And if Mayhew's more sensational commentary depicts these people as shiftless and threatening, the detailed evidence of his interviews could equally well support the view that the costermongers and street sellers were characterised by the long hours of their work and the careful calculation necessary for them to turn a small profit and eke out a living from the streets.

On the edge of the street: cultural and economic marginality

How does Mayhew's account of the mid-nineteenth-century costermongers and street sellers compare with the work of later observers? One obvious comparison is with Charles Booth's social survey, *Life and Labour of the People in London*, evidence from which has already been discussed alongside that from Mayhew in earlier chapters. Booth's research commenced in 1886, and between 1889 and 1903 he and his team of researchers and writers published multiple works that eventually ran to three series (*Poverty*, *Industry* and *Religious Influences*), and seventeen volumes, documenting in huge detail the social and economic lives of Londoners, and concentrating on the poor and working classes.[50] This section will use evidence from Booth and from other social observers and journalists to continue the analysis of the people of the street markets.

For those historians who see Mayhew as an early social scientist, Charles Booth stands as the best-known example of the more sophisticated late Victorian development of the discipline. His methods, like Mayhew's, have not been immune to criticism, and like Mayhew's his analysis was 'firmly grounded in the class anxieties of Victorian England'.[51] Nevertheless, *Life and Labour* rests on a stronger analytical system than Mayhew's *London Labour*: compare Mayhew's repeated quasi-anthropological identification of street sellers as nomads and 'wandering tribes' with Booth's efforts to position them in his system of classes, ranging from very poor to wealthy and coded from black to red on his famous poverty map of London. Many commentators have questioned the basis of Booth's ascriptions, but they are nevertheless systematically articulated.[52]

Booth describes in detail costermongers, street sellers and street markets. In the first volume of the *Poverty* series he analyses a variety of working-class occupational groups in East London that include costermongers and street sellers.[53] The east was the most homogeneously working-class area of the capital, and by the later nineteenth century it contained the greatest concentration of street markets. The total number of people employed in street selling in this district was 15,000 (mostly male heads of households), and Booth divided these according to his classification of poverty. Small numbers sat in class A, the lowest class ('occasional labourers, loafers and semi-criminals') and class F, the highest working-class category ('higher class labour'). Most were divided between the intervening classes: B, casual earnings ('very poor'); C, intermittent earnings; D, small regular earnings; and E, regular standard earnings ('above the line of poverty').[54] The economic condition of the street sellers and costermongers clearly encompassed large variations, extending from the bottom to the top of the working classes in Booth's scheme. Booth thus found a situation similar to that Mayhew had observed four decades earlier. He also, like Mayhew, noted that many street sellers depended upon borrowed money to hire their equipment and purchase stock: many were still both poor and precarious, and the key for the small numbers who achieved greater prosperity was the accumulation of a small amount of capital and its careful management:

The man who has wit to get together a little money, and resolution enough to keep his capital sacred, spending only his profits, and saving out of them against the loss of a donkey, or the need of a new barrow, will surely prosper. Those who have to borrow pay dear for the accommodation, and besides are probably the men whose character or necessities make saving impossible to them.[55]

As Mayhew had also found, Booth noted that costermongers' days could be long: 'they buy in the early morning at Covent Garden, bring home what they buy, sort it over, and then turn out to sell; work very hard early and late and for the most part drink hard'.[56]

Booth's methods did not produce detailed personal narratives equivalent to Mayhew's. Nevertheless, the fine grain of lives lived does emerge with some clarity when *Life and Labour* analyses examples of representative streets, described in detail to demonstrate the methods used to generate the poverty map.[57] Many of these streets had costermonger residents, located in notable clusters. As the site of their trade was the street, the only place for costermongers to store the tools and stock of their trade was at home. They needed landlords and neighbours who would tolerate them cluttering streets and alleys with barrows, carts and the refuse discarded as they prepared their stock for sale, and tended to live together where they found such conditions. 'In such streets as these a pony or donkey entering or leaving by the front door of a house is no uncommon sight', reported Booth.[58] Costermongers were notorious for stabling their donkeys in backyards, or even front rooms, a practice that, while often dictated by necessity, was nonetheless powerfully disruptive of the symbolic boundaries of home, which by the mid-nineteenth century was firmly ordered around its separation from the world of work (see plate 6 for a humorous depiction of a costermonger home, with donkey). Street selling, and the concomitant use of the home as warehouse and stable, blurred boundaries in the home as much as it did in the street, where spaces of circulation became sites of trade: the costermongers and street sellers did not fit easily into categories. One of the facilities provided by Baroness Burdett Coutts's ill-fated Columbia Market was stabling for donkeys, but this scheme did not find favour with the people of the street markets or their customers.[59]

Life and Labour's observations of the streets inhabited by costermongers, for all their classificatory zeal, still carry echoes of Mayhew's description of the costermongers as a 'distinct race'. The costermonger inhabitants of a street described as 'an excellent specimen of a casual and coster street' are reported as having 'a rough look, almost savage'.[60] If Mayhew had popularised a quasi-anthropological view of the costermongers, eliding ethnographic language with a view of those who worked the streets as strange and alien, a distinct and hereditary 'tribe', the idea had not ended with him, and was repeated many times between Mayhew and Booth by many other commentators. In 1867 the journalist James Greenwood described how 'the genuine costermonger is bred and born to the business', and in 1877 Adolphe Smith, in *Street Life in London*, commented that 'costermongers ... are almost a race apart, and differ both in their habits and even physically'.[61] 'The genuine costermongers form a race apart', echoed the social worker Helen Bosanquet in her 1896 book *Rich and Poor*. Recounting her observations of Shoreditch in East London, Bosanquet classified the costermongers as the

> really 'old inhabitants,' whose families have been in this or similar neighbourhoods for generations ... You may know them by their personal appearance, when you are once used to the type, though it is difficult to convey the exact impression in words. Generally speaking they are shortish thick-set men, with big jaws and diminutive skulls, retreating rapidly from the brow.[62]

The description is reminiscent of the *Punch* cartoons discussed earlier that blurred a costermonger ethnicity with a stereotyped Irishness.

The American journalist Richard Harding Davis described the costermongers he saw dressed in their best on Derby Day, when Londoners of all classes made a trip to the races at Epsom in Surrey into a festive outing (see figure 29):

> The London coster is quite as typical in his way as the London policeman. He wears a white and blue dotted kerchief as the badge of all his race, and a high-cut waistcoat and a full long-tailed coat, both strung with pearl buttons as closely as they can be sewed together. If he is very smart he has his trousers slashed like a Mexican vaquero's, with a triangle of black velvet and more pearl buttons. This is his unofficial uniform. Many of the gypsies wear it too, and it is all the more picturesque because it is unofficial.[63]

And he provided an equivalent description of a typical female costermonger – this was an occupational and social category that included both men and women, and Harding Davis's 'coster girl' is as showy as her male counterpart, wearing a large silver locket and chain, and a flamboyant hat:

> Her bonnet is as broad as a sombrero, slanting down in front over her eyes and hair, and towering at the back above her head, covered with colored feathers and ribbons and velvet. This bonnet is as characteristic and local to the coster girls of the east of London as are the gold head-dresses to the women of Scheveningen.[64]

With his references to the Mexican *vaquero* (cowboy) and Scheveningen in the Netherlands, famous for its women's elaborate traditional head ornaments,[65] Harding Davis makes explicit ethnographic connections that recall Mayhew's opening comparison of the costermongers to Bedouins and Lappes. Harding Davis's emphasis is on clothing more than physiognomy, but Mayhew too discussed the costermongers' distinctive dress, and in 1869 John Hotten's *Slang Dictionary* described the 'kingsman', the brightly coloured neckerchief said to be favoured by costermongers: 'with both sexes they are more valued than any other article of clothing. A coster's caste, or position, is at stake, he imagines, if his KINGSMAN is not of the most approved pattern.'[66]

One of the most straightforward definitions of informality is that it sidesteps regulation. Street sellers and costermongers, as we have seen from multiple sources, disliked rules and restrictions that were too onerous: this was one of the reasons why Columbia Market failed so utterly. The street markets might not have been heavily regulated by law, or by the rules imposed in authorised market buildings, but were they governed by mutually observed common conventions of behaviour? If street sellers and costermongers had a sometimes antagonistic relationship with authority, did that also mean that they were antagonistic to each other, atomised and wholly individualistic in their small-scale entrepreneurialism? There is plentiful evidence to the contrary, including Mayhew's descriptions, already discussed, of mutual support between costermongers in the form of small loans and the sharing of expertise. Later sources provide quite detailed accounts of the accepted systems by which pitches in the markets were claimed and retained in the period between 1867 and 1927, when the street markets' legal position was governed by the status quo of the Metropolitan Streets (Amendment) Act and the power it gave to the police to tolerate street stalls within given dimensions. In her 1909 book *The Soul Market*, the social explorer Olive Malvery went undercover in a series of working-class occupations, and one of the roles she adopted was that of a 'coster-girl'. She observed that regular street market pitches were looked upon as 'freeholds': 'only in rare instances is it necessary for the costermonger to worry about his regular place in the street where he always sells', as interlopers were expelled by the trading community.[67] The evidence on this point can be contradictory: as we saw in Chapter 1, for instance, John Denton told the Royal Commission on Market Rights and Tolls that his pitch was only his by right of daily occupation. However, on the whole there do seem to have been commonly agreed procedures for the allocation of pitches. These varied somewhat from market to market as perambulating street sellers settled into regular, if informal, market sites and geographically based codes of behaviour emerged.[68]

Towards the end of the nineteenth century, the costermongers developed more formal trade organisations – costermongers' unions. The historian Marc Brodie points out that political historians have tended to categorise costermongers as 'jaunty individualists' whose politics followed their occupational identity as small-scale entrepreneurs pursuing 'a middle-class occupation at a working-class level of life'.[69] Brodie suggests that this view may be inaccurate: he interprets the growth of costermongers' unions as an impulse towards collectivism. The costermongers' unions were trade associations that, as Brodie points out, were locally focused on certain markets or areas, and did not have negotiation or contest with employers as their aim (as the costermongers were all self-employed) but rather represented the costermongers and street sellers in disputes with local authorities. Brodie may somewhat overstate the significance of these unions. Evidence to the Royal Commission on Alien Immigration of 1902–03 indicates that many were fragile and dependent upon the energy of a single individual.[70] The listings in Marsh and Smethurst's *Historical Directory of Trade Unions* suggest that most originated in the 1890s and 1900s (in the aftermath of the new unionism), that they had small and fluctuating membership, and tended to last just a few years.[71] Costermongers are necessarily ruled out of some dominant narratives of labour history by their independent and entrepreneurial nature, despite their indisputably working-class identity. Brodie's attempt to bring them back into these narratives usefully points to the fact of their mutual organisation, but I suggest that it makes more sense to think about these mutual impulses as social rather than political, focused on ordering their own community in the street markets, and on mutual support. Mayhew, as we have seen, presented instances of this mutuality going back to the 1850s, and the tradition seems to have continued. Malvery was one of several observers who described 'a friendly lead' or benefit night, a gathering of costermongers in the private room of a public house with the purpose of raising money for a fellow costermonger whose wife had died. The 'lead' was publicised with a printed card calling on the market people to 'rally round one who has always been the first to drop to others'. Donations were collected discreetly, and at the bidding of the chairman those present rose in turn to sing a song for the entertainment of the group.[72] George Sims's *Living London* (1901–03) describes a similar 'friendly lead' for the family of a deceased comrade, as well as support for a man who has no money to replenish his stock: his fellows 'strip their barrows' with 'one here giving a bushel of apples, one there a box of grapes'.[73]

If mutual support and self-regulation were consistent themes in the history of the street markets from Mayhew to Booth and beyond, then what of the migrant presence, dominated in Mayhew's account by Irish street sellers? Mayhew mentioned many other smaller immigrant groups, and gave the Jews considerable attention, second only to his detailed account of the Irish. From 1881 a large new influx of Jewish immigrants began to arrive from Russia, Russian-ruled Poland and Romania, in response to economic upheaval and state persecution in those countries. By 1900, according to Sunderland and Ball's economic history of London, the city had around 120,000 Jewish residents; the historian David Englander puts the figure at 140–150,000.[74] By this date, Englander notes, the Irish communities established in mid-century were beginning to scatter and integrate, so that they were 'geographically more dispersed and socially less visible' than they had been, and fears previously aroused by Irish immigration subsided somewhat, to be replaced by anxiety around Jewish migrants.[75] A Jewish community had long been present in the East End of London, and the new migrants of the late nineteenth century almost all settled in the East End too, in the borough of Stepney, making them very prominent in this area. Historians have debated the experiences of these Jewish immigrants: what was the extent of the anti-semitism to which they were subjected? What was the nature of their economic and cultural contribution in their newly adopted home? Opinion of the late nineteenth and early twentieth centuries was concentrated on the effects of the migrants upon local employment and housing, with commentators questioning whether the new arrivals constituted an alien presence (a 'ghetto') or were open to interchange (social, cultural and economic) with their non-Jewish neighbours. This opposition is present in Sims's *Living London*, where two essays by different authors asserted contradictory opinions: the author of 'Sweated London' claimed that 'the Ghetto is a fragment of Poland torn off from Central Europe and dropped haphazard in the heart of Britain', whereas the author of 'Russia in East London' insisted that 'race and creed are forgotten' in the 'busy beehive' of the East End.[76] The historian Tony Kushner suggests that the street was a 'meeting place for peoples of different cultures'.[77] What role did the street markets play in this process, and how were they affected by the Jewish migrants?

The Jewish newcomers who arrived in the late nineteenth century were characterised, according to Englander, as 'a peculiar people', in terms of both racial characteristics and distinct social and economic traits. They were believed to have business and entrepreneurial skills fostered by their discriminatory exclusion from many areas of paid employment in their homelands, and intellectual capacities developed by study of the Talmud, and although Englander describes this characterisation of the Jewish immigrants as nothing more than the 'intellectual baggage' of the period, other historians (notably William J. Fishman) present it as having some element of truth.[78] Whatever was the case, it was certain that many Jewish immigrants (and not just in London) worked for themselves, engaging in small-scale entrepreneurialism rather than entering paid employment. Nancy L. Green, in her comparative study of Jewish immigrants in Paris, London and New York, identifies 'what could be called ... "Jewish" trades, in small-scale commerce and small-scale industry', noting that these trades might more accurately be classified as 'immigrant' pursuits and not necessarily exclusively Jewish ones.[79] We have already seen how street selling was and is the recourse of newly arrived migrants, and Jewish migrants in London in the 1880s and 1890s were no different. A proportion set up as street sellers, integrating the informal economy of the streets with the flexible specialisation of ready-made clothing manufacture (Henry Feldman) or using it as a stepping stone to business success in shop-based retailing (Jack Cohen).

Because of the extremely concentrated nature of Jewish settlement in the East End, the street markets of this area, always densely packed and already marked with a Jewish flavour through the long-established old clothes trade, grew in scale and became more Jewish in nature. Petticoat Lane was at the heart of this development, which transformed the East End into a network of busy market streets providing not just goods, but selling-as-entertainment and the mixing of cultures. A press report of 1877, some years before the intense immigration of the last two decades of the century, described Petticoat Lane as 'the narrow lane where Hebrews most do congregate'.[80] By the 1890s this Jewish character was heavily reinforced, and the market was emerging as a distinct destination for Sunday morning leisure as well as functional buying. A press report from 1895 described how on Sundays Petticoat Lane attracted visitors from 'far and near to listen to the patter of the quacks and dealers and idle away their Sunday holiday'.[81] On weekdays Petticoat Lane's character was more determined by everyday shopping, and 'buyers and sellers both are children of Judah, and the voices rise in broken English, Yiddish, German, and Hebrew, turning this corner of Whitechapel into a Babel of strange sounds'.[82] In 1909

Olive Malvery (some of whose writings were marked by notable anti-semitism) remarked tersely of Petticoat Lane that 'the prevailing note of the place is frankly foreign'.[83] The Baedeker travel guide to London, which gave detailed listings of West End and City shops and shopping, made its first mention of any street market in its 1915 edition with an entry on Petticoat Lane – 'Middlesex Street (formerly Petticoat Lane), noted for its Jews market on Sun. morning (beware of pickpockets)'.[84] Dolly Scannell's memoir of East End life recalls a visit in the 1920s from a cousin who lived in rural Dorset, whose 'lifelong ambition was to visit Petticoat Lane'.[85] Bishopsgate Institute has in its collection a postcard of Petticoat Lane from around 1900, obviously purchased by an American visitor to London. The written message reads 'This is the Jewish section, something like the East Side of N.Y. Am going down there some Sunday morning.'[86] Clearly by this date London's street markets were acknowledged as a distinct part of the city's urban character, and Petticoat Lane was a destination for tourists, at the same time as it was a site of contestation between those who welcomed the Jewish migrants and those who saw them as a threat.[87]

On the streets, and in the street markets, the presence of large numbers of migrants caused friction, but also led to the development of diverse and spectacular sites of consumption, and even to some signs of the hybridising of the culture of the 'hereditary' costermongers with the immigrant Jews, as had been the case with the Irish several decades earlier. In 1894 the illustrator Phil May provided drawings for an article in St Paul's magazine (figure 30), depicting a crowded street scene (surveyed from the margins by a police officer) with market traders standing on stepladders showing garments (which by this date were more likely to be cheap new clothes than second-hand ones) to their audience of shoppers. Petticoat Lane's Jewish traders were famous for their inventive and assertive sales patter, which included comic exaggeration of the merits of their own goods, and scurrilous humour directed against their rivals. May's drawing is explicit about the Jewish nature of the scene: several figures are racially stereotyped in ways that make for uncomfortable viewing. The largest figure in the foreground is one of those stereotyped – a young woman with notably 'Jewish' features, according to the racial tropes of the day. But she is also notably similar to contemporary descriptions of costermongers, wearing a showy feathered scarf and a large and elaborate hat that is clearly akin to those described by Richard Harding Davis. Several years later May produced a more elaborate drawing that developed some of the characters and motifs from the 1894 cartoon (figure 31). A female figure, identified in the caption as 'the beauteous Rebecca', is clearly reminiscent of the earlier image. Rebecca's hat is even larger and more eye-catching than that in the 1894 drawing, topped with a huge bow and artificial flowers that explode from its crown.

Just as the 'wandering tribe' of the costermongers in the 1850s and 1860s was seen as both a 'distinct race' but also confused and conflated with stereotyped Irishness, so the costermongers of the 1890s and 1900s were viewed as a 'race apart', but were tangled in the popular imagination with the Jewish community

30 Phil May, 'The Londoner's Sunday – 1. Petticoat Lane', *St Paul's* magazine, 9 June 1894

with which, especially in the East End, they rubbed shoulders in the everyday life of the streets and markets, and not just in the cartoons of Phil May. Tony Kushner has noted in his historical 'anthropology' of the East End that although home life might be strictly segregated, in the crowded conditions 'so much of ... life took place outside the home ... that the two communities were forced to make contact whether at work or in leisure'.[88] The street markets were a key site of such mixing. Ethel Brilliana wrote a magazine account of a visit to Petticoat

31 Phil May, 'From Petticoat Lane to the Lane of the Park', *Punch*, 1898

Lane in 1895, describing a 'stout Jewess' selling pudding basins from a barrow in a noisy auction, and wearing a hat that sounds much like Rebecca's – 'a wondrous bonnet of flowers and feathers'.[89] Brilliana was happy to acknowledge this woman and her fellow Jewish street sellers as 'a living, breathing part of this great metropolis', suggesting the cultural fertility of the informal economy of the streets with its lively entrepreneurial independence which was to develop further into the early twentieth century. At the same time it took a turn into wider popular culture, with the people of the street markets emerging as an ever more recognisable type in the representation of London's working classes.

The costers' carnival: representation and myth

In Mayhew's day the street folk were mostly poor, often desperate, and represented as both strange and other. Although many remained poor and in some respects marginal, they soon began to be depicted in ways that suggest how the popular imagination was finding means to tame them, in the process entangling their social identity with a set of cultural representations that may not have aligned directly with life as it was lived in the market streets. We can see the origins of these representations as early as the late 1860s and 1870s, in the work of James Greenwood, a journalist best known for his account of 'A Night in the Workhouse' (1866), one of the earliest examples of undercover social investigation. Greenwood produced many accounts of London street folk and the street markets: four of these, read in series and in parallel, provide an early case study of the construction of the costermonger as a picturesque type. In December 1867 Greenwood gave evidence to the Food Committee of the Society of Arts, based upon research in Whitecross Street market.[90] This evidence was sober and restrained, underpinned with statistics on the scale and nature of the market's trade, and following a pattern by now familiar, that is, to praise the street sellers' utility in the efficient distribution of food while at the same time concluding that they were ignorant and degraded, troubling and low. Greenwood used the same evidence presented to the Society of Arts as the basis for a newspaper article, 'Squalors' Market', anthologised in his 1867 book, *Unsentimental Journeys*.[91] Here the raw material was turned into a much more vivid description, with statistics supplanted by colourful reportage. For instance, a detailed discussion in the Society of Arts evidence of the price and quality of meat is not duplicated in 'Squalors' Market', but there *is* an eye-catching description of a butcher, who 'wears on his head a cap made of the hairy hide of the bison or some other savage beast; his red arms are bare to the elbows, and he roars continuously … clashing his broad knife against his steel to keep time'.[92]

Elsewhere in *Unsentimental Journeys* Greenwood gives a lively account of a trip to Barnet Fair, one of London's few surviving periodic fairs, and a festivity that was popular among costermongers who came to eat, drink, socialise, enjoy the sideshows and trade donkeys and ponies. The article is titled 'The Costers' Carnival', and it is similar in its descriptive strategies to 'Squalors' Market'. The people converging on the fair are described as 'costermongerish in the extreme', packed into donkey carts also loaded with plentiful food and drink.[93] As Greenwood used his observations of Whitecross Street to drive both his evidence to the Society of Arts and his more colourful account of 'Squalors'

Market', so he used his research on Barnet Fair to produce both 'The Costers' Carnival' and a later piece, published in *Low-Life Deeps* in 1876.[94] This goes one step further still than the lively descriptions of 'Squalors' Market' and 'The Costers' Carnival'. Greenwood moves beyond reporting, instead ventriloquising the costermonger to produce a first-person fictionalised narrative, and claiming that his article is written by 'one ... among the confraternity' of costermongers. The idiom Greenwood gives his protagonist is worth quoting at length:

> There's two ways of going to Barnet, like there's two ways of doing everything. You may take the rail for it – but that's not my way. I ain't a proud cove, but, cert'ny I *should* look down on any one that I knowed as was capable of keeping up the anniwersary in that shabby kind o' way. Mind you, I don't hold with extrawagance; and though it was all right havin' them four new spokes put in the barrer wheels (Joe Simmon's wife being a hounce or two heavier than a hinfant, and my old gal rapidly growin' out o' that silf-like figger she had when we was courtin'), there's no denying, as it was werry much like pomp and wanity, havin' the vehicle painted yeller with a picking out of green. But her mind was bent on havin' every thing to match her shawl and bonnet, and, as she tenderly remarked, bless her hard workin' 'art: 'We don't kill a pig every day, Samuel:' wich so touched me that I went the whole annimal, and had it warnished as well.[95]

This is an identifiable example of the transition from the costermonger of the street market to that of the popular imagination. A humorous fictionalised type emerges who is garrulous, good-natured, fond of leisure and pleasure, wedded to tradition, sentimentally attached to his wife and keen on a showy display of plebeian prosperity. Greenwood was drawing upon antecedents in the broader stereotype of the cockney, or working-class Londoner, and particularly Charles Dickens's most famous cockney character, Sam Weller of *The Pickwick Papers*, in whose distinctive accent 'v' and 'w' sounds are transposed, and 'h' sounds dropped in some places to pop up unexpectedly in others.[96] Weller was by profession a servant and odd-job man; Greenwood's 'Barnet Fair' prefigures a process that gathered pace into the later nineteenth century by which the centre of the broad category of 'cockney' was increasingly filled by a specific occupational group, the costermongers.[97] In this regard, even if informal street selling may have existed beyond London, it is with London that it is most closely associated.

More specific yet than either cockney or costermonger were the 'pearly kings' and 'pearly queens', who emerged – somewhat mysteriously – in the later nineteenth century. The pearly kings and queens were strongly identified with the street markets, as can be seen in the postcard in figure 32, in which a man dressed in the distinctive pearly costume (a suit heavily decorated with mother-of-pearl buttons) calls out to invite visitors to Petticoat Lane. An edition of *Picture Post* magazine from August 1947 provides a retrospective view of the mature development of the pearly king and queen, illustrated with photographs of the 'Pearly monarch of Hampstead' (Bert Matthews) and his family, who are shown dressed in costumes with some elements cut in the style of

32 'Petticoat Lane on Sunday morning', postcard c. 1900

the late nineteenth century, and sewn densely with mother of pearl buttons in elaborate motifs (see plate 7). [98] The pearly kings and queens, says *Picture Post*, are 'costermonger royalty', and it supplies them with a history confected from various folkloric elements. Their origins are complex and uncertain – and worth pursuing because of what they can tell us about the representation and self-presentation of the costermongers and street sellers, and how the perceived cultural identity of the people of the street markets changed across time.

Apart from journalistic accounts such as that in *Picture Post*, the first attempts to give the pearly kings and queens a history date from the 1970s. The most solid of several not very substantial narratives from this period is illustrator Pearl Binder's book *The Pearlies: A Social Record*. There are also pamphlets by the journalists Peter F. Brooks and Adam Joseph, both of which are more speculative again than *Picture Post*'s account and do not cite any documentary evidence.[99] Attempts by professional historians to write a history of the pearly kings and queens are limited to Gareth Stedman Jones's chapter on 'The "cockney" and the nation' (1989), and a further chapter by Stedman Jones and Raphael Samuel.[100] The first of these is an important and substantial piece of scholarship, despite being based, by Stedman Jones's own admission, on 'preliminary' and incomplete research. Stedman Jones surveys the history of the 'cockney', analysing how in literary representation this London type shifted radically over time, moving across classes and occupations. By the end of the nineteenth century it had settled on the costermonger as the carrier of an identity that was both mythic and nostalgic, and reached its culmination in the pearly kings and queens, whose antecedents lay in comic singers performing a version of the street market costermonger and singing songs that humorously dramatised life on the streets for music hall audiences. Among the earliest of these performers were Hyram Travers, described in the press simply as 'the Pearly King', whose career commenced around 1865, and Alfred Vance ('the Great Vance') whose broad repertoire of 'swells' featured a number of working-class characters including, in his 1870 song 'The Chickaleary Cove', a costermonger.[101]

All these sources, in different ways, suggest that the pearly kings and queens were, as Stedman Jones claims, an 'invented tradition', created during that period of three or four decades before the First World War when, according to Eric Hobsbawm 'the creation of traditions was enthusiastically practised' both 'officially and unofficially' across a Europe being shaken by modernity.[102] *Picture Post*, Binder, Brooks and Joseph all uncritically recount (and elaborate) orally transmitted origin stories only shakily supported with evidence. Stedman Jones explains this invention by suggesting that it was from stage performances that what we might call the 'costermonger-cockney' (and the pearly king and queen as the most flamboyantly performative iteration of that type) stepped on to the streets. 'Pearly dress' was 'the invention of the music hall' and the pearly kings and queens were generated exclusively by representation, dreamed into life on the stage, and only tenuously based on any real costermonger characteristics.[103]

The transition of the 'pearlies' from stage to street (and not the other way around) was initially driven by the efforts of a street sweeper from Somers Town in north London, Henry Croft. In the mid-1880s Croft decorated his suit with pearl buttons in imitation of Travers et al. in the music halls (according to Stedman Jones) and set out to collect donations for hospital charities.[104] The key impetus in the ongoing popularity of the comic music hall costermonger-cockney was the career of Albert Chevalier, a middle-class theatre actor who took to the music halls as the 'coster laureate' in 1891, performing in costume a string of hit 'coster' songs (see figure 33). Chevalier's sentimentalised performances expunged the previous association of the costermongers (and costermonger-cockney acts such as Travers and Vance) with unruliness, marginality and incipient violence, and with the disquieting world of Mayhew's streets. He was hugely popular with audiences of all classes, and his version of the costermonger was taken up enthusiastically (and with agency) by London's working classes, not just as entertainment, but as something to be imitated. As Stedman Jones asserts, working-class audiences received Chevalier's act

> not simply as consumers of a representation bestowed upon them, but at least as much on their own terms. The 'cockney' was no doubt a very partial representation of their lives … but in so far as they lived out this representation, it was as much their own creation as Chevalier's and shaped to their own purposes.[105]

33 Albert Chevalier in costume as a costermonger

From as early as the first decade of the twentieth century, this stage-generated version of the costermonger-cockney was self-consciously replicated on the streets within certain London working-class communities, with pearly kings and queens claiming hereditary, if informal, right to their titles, which were linked to specific localities (as with Bert Matthews and his claim to be Pearly Monarch of Hampstead). In a newspaper interview in 1911 Henry Croft called himself the 'original Pearly King of Somers-Town', and laid claim to the title of 'Button King of the World', on the basis of the superlative number of buttons sewn on his suit.[106] His fame, and that of other pearly kings and queens, was propagated by newspaper reports and appearances at events such as the International Horse Show at Olympia, which by 1907 held a competition for the best-turned-out pearly king with donkey and cart.[107]

Derek B. Scott has traced the history of the costermonger-cockney on the music hall stage, concluding even more firmly than Gareth Stedman Jones that the figure was quite removed from any resemblance to life on the streets, becoming by stages a 'replicant', an 'imagined real' that may have had an impact upon how cockneys saw themselves, but that was in origin little more than a confection of representations, a Baudrillardian, 'third-order simulation', which 'substitutes signs of the real for the real itself', an 'image created by the music hall and perpetuated by the music hall's feeding upon itself rather than by drawing ideas from, or representing, the world outside'.[108] This then, was the origin of the costermonger-cockney of the early twentieth century – not in the street markets, but rather on the stage, formulated by songwriters and performers who were often, like Chevalier, middle-class in background, and who invented a version of working-class life for humorous and sentimental effect. The people of the street markets and the wider working-class community took back this representation and used it as the basis for the pearly kings and queens, but it did not come to them in direct line from Mayhew's street folk and Booth's costermongers, but rather via the stage, in an exaggerated detour rather akin to that through which Hollywood wrested the cowboy from history and made him instead a figure of myth.

Stedman Jones is uncomfortable with aspects of the myth of the cockney in general and the pearly kings and queens in particular: 'The "cockney" is traditional and "English", and the community is of a *Fings Ain't What They Used to Be* world, of the singsong and the knees-up, of an old-fashioned Saturday night, or of the atmosphere conjured up in faded photographs of street parties festooned with Union Jacks.'[109] Such discomfort with the role of the pearly king and queen in a particular identity-myth of working-class London, with its belligerent nostalgia and incipient conservatism, is to some extent understandable. Stedman Jones and Raphael Samuel have noted that the pearly king is a carnivalesque figure, reminiscent of folkloric traditions.[110] For all its apparent disruption of the social hierarchy, carnival can be 'a strategy of containment' or 'recuperation', licensing disruptive figures and in doing so rendering them safe.[111] What the pearly kings and queens became was very safe indeed, associated with 'a gorblimey London of "knees up Mother Brown", where times were rough but the spirit of the people indomitable'.[112] To explain them away as a myth, therefore, a fabricated representation, satisfactorily resolves both their troubling nostalgia and the obvious invention that sits behind accounts such as that in *Picture Post*.

All written history wrestles with the problems posed by the space between historical events and people and the evidence by which we know them, which is always only a representation. Cultural history makes the story of the representation a legitimate object of study in itself. The mythic construction of the pearly kings and queens and what that tells us about the climate of ideas and opinions is what Stedman Jones and Scott pursue in analysing the costermonger-cockney's links with the music hall. The following chapter, which considers the street markets as a source of performances, will pursue this line of enquiry in more detail, but for now I am not quite ready to let history collapse entirely on to representation, and will consider further some of the more disparate evidence that lay behind the 'invention' of the pearly kings and queens (as do Stedman Jones and Samuel, briefly, at the end of their chapter on the pearly kings).[113] Were they really summoned out of thin air by performers such as Albert Chevalier, or are there some traces that connect them, however uncertainly, with the evidence considered in the previous sections of this chapter? The French historian Pierre Nora talks critically of 'running a knife between the tree of memory and the bark of history'.[114] The historically demonstrable facts of the careers of Vance, Travers and above all Chevalier perhaps allow this operation to be performed with too surgical a precision. In doing so they displace other claims, and the 'folk memory' of origins that lies, however mistily, behind the pearly kings and queens' own conception of their genealogy. This traces their beginnings back not to Chevalier and other music hall performers who influenced street-market street sweeper Henry Croft, but rather to Croft himself and the costermongers with whom he associated in Somers Town's Chalton Street market, and it links to the memory of an established tradition of informal authority within street market communities. Peter Brooks, in his rather flimsy 1970s account, explains this authority, claiming that the costermongers 'banded together, generally on a borough or street or market basis, to form self-protective groups. These "clans", as they were called, elected a leader and he became known as the Coster King, and his wife as the Coster Queen.'[115]

Similar stories feature in Binder's and Joseph's accounts, and are still told today on the websites of many pearly king and queen families and associations.[116] While there is little historical evidence to support them (at least in such a neat and tidy form), they should not perhaps be entirely dismissed. This book is after all a history of an informal institution and it is appropriate that it recognises what Raphael Samuel calls 'unofficial knowledge' and 'popular memory', and Patrick Wright an 'informal sense of history'.[117] This is not to uncritically accept accounts that have no documented evidence to support them, but rather to supplement Stedman Jones's and Scott's explanation of the performed genesis of a representation with consideration of a few, tantalisingly fragmentary remnants of evidence that suggest that, however influential the music hall costermonger-cockneys, there may have been some legacy that passed from the 'street folk' of the 1850s to the pearly kings and queens of the early twentieth century without first processing across the music hall stage.

The obvious starting point is dress. The suit covered with mother-of-pearl buttons worn by Henry Croft from the 1880s, and which seems to have spread to many other pearly or 'button' kings by the first decade of the twentieth century, was certainly influenced by music hall performers. One newspaper reported on Albert Chevalier's costume, describing how he wore:

> a rag of coloured cloth where the rest of us wear a collar; a check-patterned jacket on the meagre body, turned up with velveteen; trousers trumpet-shaped, like those of a Mexican vaquero ... et puis, des boutons, des boutons, des boutons ... everywhere rows of pearl buttons. It is all very ugly, very quaint – and very interesting.[118]

Why did Chevalier wear pearl buttons in his costermonger performances? Perhaps it was because some costermongers themselves favoured the decorative use of buttons on their clothes. Henry Mayhew noted the flamboyant dress of the costermongers, using it (alongside other evidence such as their distinctive 'back slang' dialect) in his ethnographic construction of them as a distinct 'race'.[119] His analysis includes mention of fancy buttons on the costermongers' corduroy waistcoats: 'if the corduroy be of a light sandy colour, then plain brass, or sporting buttons, with raised fox's or stag's heads upon them – or else black bone buttons, with a flower-pattern – ornament the front; but if the cord be of dark rat-skin hue, then mother-of-pearl buttons are preferred'.[120] If these mother-of-pearl buttons were not placed purely for the sake of decorative profusion, like those of the later pearly kings and queens, they nevertheless suggest a distinct and showy costermonger style of dress. The costermongers (or at least the better off among them), Mayhew asserts, were served by particular tailors who provided 'flash togs', including brightly patterned kingsman scarves, flaring trousers, and coats and waistcoats trimmed with the generous application of buttons.[121]

The mention of the *'vaquero'* (or Mexican cowboy) in the early review of Albert Chevalier's onstage persona is duplicated in Richard Harding Davis's 1894 description of costermongers on Derby Day (see figure 29). This postdates Chevalier's 1891 debut,[122] and it is quite possible that either Davis's account or the costermongers he observed were heavily indebted to Chevalier and the publicity around his acclaimed performances. Yet it is also possible that Davis depicted something like a genuine costermonger 'type'. Certainly the costermongers in his account are not sentimentalised, the central characteristic that Stedman Jones attributes to Chevalier as the key to his success in widening the appeal of the costermonger on stage. The depiction of their faces owes something to Mayhew's idea of a distinct race, and they appear to be riotously drunk.

Then there is the issue of the pearly kings and queens' 'royal' status.

Such claims are at the very least a marked oversimplification, an attempt to justify retrospectively the ceremonial position that pearly kings and queens claimed. However, the notion of costermonger 'royalty' is foreshadowed in the self-regulating customs of the street markets discussed earlier. A few historical sources give tantalising glimpses of authority figures within the markets who are described in terms of royal status. Charles Booth's *Life and Labour* describes one costermonger as 'a leader among these people ... known as the King of the Costers'.[123] And an article in the *St James's Gazette* from 1884 describes the funeral of Mary Robinson, a street trader from Somers Town known as 'the Queen of the Costermongers'. Robinson had accrued a significant fortune: her authority seems to have been based on making weekly loans at the rate of a shilling in the pound to poorer costermongers to enable them to buy their stock, a position quite consistent with well-documented accounts of the business model of many penny capitalists.[124] Neither of these accounts links informal authority figures to mother-of-pearl buttons or any sort of distinctive costume. It may have been the case that a particular costermonger style of dress existed separately from costermonger customs of informal regulation by authority figures within the street market community. If the two were brought together later by the pearly kings and queens, this does not mean that they were wholly fictitious in origin.

Perhaps the most interesting teller of the history of the pearly kings and queens is Pearl Binder. Her account was produced at the same 1970s moment as those slim pamphlets by Brooks and Joseph, but whereas they seem merely to recount the invention of a tradition, she had some experience of its origin. Long before she wrote her book, Binder lived in the East End of London, working as an illustrator and producing lithographs to accompany a book called *The Real East End* (1932) by Thomas Burke.[125] Gareth Stedman Jones declares ambivalence about the continued relevance of the cockney to contemporary Britain, partly because of the exclusive whiteness of the cockney in a multi-ethnic world.[126] I have suggested that even in the 1890s Phil May's pictures of the 'beauteous Rebecca', with her clear links to Richard Harding Davis's costermongers, show that the cockney (at least in the street markets) need not be entirely monocultural: in Rebecca we have a female Jewish costermonger-cockney. Binder's contribution to the story reinforces this: she was the child of a Jewish immigrant, and she retold and retailed her cockney interlude over her whole life. In 1977, the year of Queen Elizabeth II's Silver Jubilee, she designed a 'pearly king' mug for Wedgwood, maker of traditional ceramics, including a good many objects commemorating 'royalty' conventionally defined. On its base it tells the 'story' of the pearly kings and queens, describing them as:

> a hereditary group of working cockneys who collect money for charity. Their distinctive uniform, covered with hand-sewn patterns in pearl buttons, was devised by Henry Croft whose election as the first Pearly King of Somerstown c.1880 marked the birth of Pearly Royalty.[127]

The story may not be wholly accurate, but it is not perhaps wholly fictitious either; the very fact of its existence shows the power and tenacity of the tradition well into the later twentieth century.

* * *

This chapter started with Mayhew, and his multi-volume, mid-century study of *London Labour and the London Poor*, moving on to Charles Booth's even more extensive survey. The *New Survey of London Life and Labour* (1932) was an attempt by the London School of Economics to replicate Booth's inquiry and to ascertain if the 'conditions of life and labour' were becoming better or worse. Its optimistic conclusion was that, economic fluctuations notwithstanding, the overall trend had been markedly upwards since Booth's day. The *New Survey* allows us to step back from representations and return to lives lived, with a final attempt to capture the people of the street markets in all their diversity, and at the other end of the period from the vivid, if troublesome, descriptions of Henry Mayhew. The *New Survey* addressed the street markets in some detail, in a chapter focused on East London which declares surprise at the continued flourishing of the street markets in light of that overall increase in the standard of life:

> Since it is chiefly the poor who are to be found in the street markets, and since the number of those living in poverty has been shown elsewhere in this volume to have largely decreased since Charles Booth's time, it might be expected that the street markets would also show a tendency to decline. In fact, however, they have shown a very substantial increase.[128]

As discussed in Chapter 1, the number of street markets grew considerably right across the 1850–1939 period. They continued to flourish as an informal retail site, with new recruits taking to street selling, including unemployed ex-servicemen after the end of the First World War and the economic downturn of 1920–22, and the unemployed more generally as the Depression began to bite from 1929 (although unemployment in London was considerably lower than in many industrial areas).[129]

The poorest of the street sellers in 1932 were no longer as absolutely destitute as, for instance, Mayhew's 'poor shoeless urchin' discussed earlier in this chapter, although many markets continued to include sellers who operated on their fringes, selling from a basket or tray or even their hands, rather than from a barrow or stall, and engaging in perambulating as well as stationary trade.[130] At the top end of the scale, a few sellers were 'very profitable', and again this upper echelon appear to have been elevated above the level of prosperity achieved by, for instance, the seller of shellfish in the New Cut market described by Mayhew as an example of the most successful costermongers of his day. Jewish sellers of 'cloth, clothing, hosiery and trinkets' are noted as being among those who flourished, many becoming small shopkeepers.[131] The *New Survey* contains many themes already familiar from both Mayhew and Booth, most notably the varying fortunes of different traders, the skill, tenacity and hard work needed to flourish, and the economic uncertainty to which they were subject:

> It may be said that practically all the stallholders in the markets seem to be assured of a reasonable living, though some of the hangers on, selling from baskets and trays, may lead a very precarious existence. Some stallholders are prosperous and even wealthy. All have to work very long hours and are subject to fluctuations of trade ... The long hours and the alternations of good trade and bad tend to induce the stall holder to spend recklessly when the money's there, and struggle through as best he may when times are bad.[132]

Many sources used in this chapter on the people of the street markets have tended to towards ideological inflection, if not downright myth-making: it is a feature of the informal economy that the more sober records of business and the state don't always capture it, and those documents there are may be inclined to romanticise or sensationalise their subjects. But in 1927, when licensing was introduced, the street markets *were* recorded in the bureaucratic record. The new legislation made London's borough councils responsible for licensing the street markets in their areas, and at this point the people of the markets are laid out in the minute books of council market committees that list the traders who were granted licences in each street market. This information may be terse and business-like, but it gives a snapshot of the markets and their people. In Stepney, for instance, the council granted around 430 licences to trade in the street in Petticoat Lane and a tangled network of side streets, describing the locations of the various stalls by the simple expedient of noting which shop they operated in front of, a curious doubling of the formal and informal, with the stallholder's details inserted tenuously into the formal system of numbered premises, just as the stalls themselves were inserted into the length of the street.[133] In Lambeth, licences were issued for street markets including Lambeth Walk, Lower Marsh and the New Cut.[134] In Lewisham, where the borough council had been attempting to get rid of the street market in the High Street almost since it first appeared in the 1890s, the council hesitated over the licensing process, but in 1934 it issued fifty-four licences to street sellers in the market.[135]

In 1936 Mary Benedetta published her book on the street markets of London. She lifted her quantitative analysis and overview of the markets' history more or less wholesale from the *New Survey*, but added lively reports of her visits to the market streets and interviews with many of the street sellers (figure 34 shows an engraver in Petticoat Lane market, described by Benedetta as 'Mr J. Park, who will engrave your dog collar for you on the spot').[136] It is possible to sort through Benedetta's text, in which she identifies, describes and quotes many of her subjects, and link these people to borough council minute books where applicants for licences are listed. In Petticoat Lane, for instance, Benedetta describes her meeting with 'Isidore Michael', who runs a musical instrument stall. He can play half a dozen different instruments, and 'can sell you a really lovely old fiddle for 5s'. 'He speaks in a quiet, rather educated voice', and 'picks up an

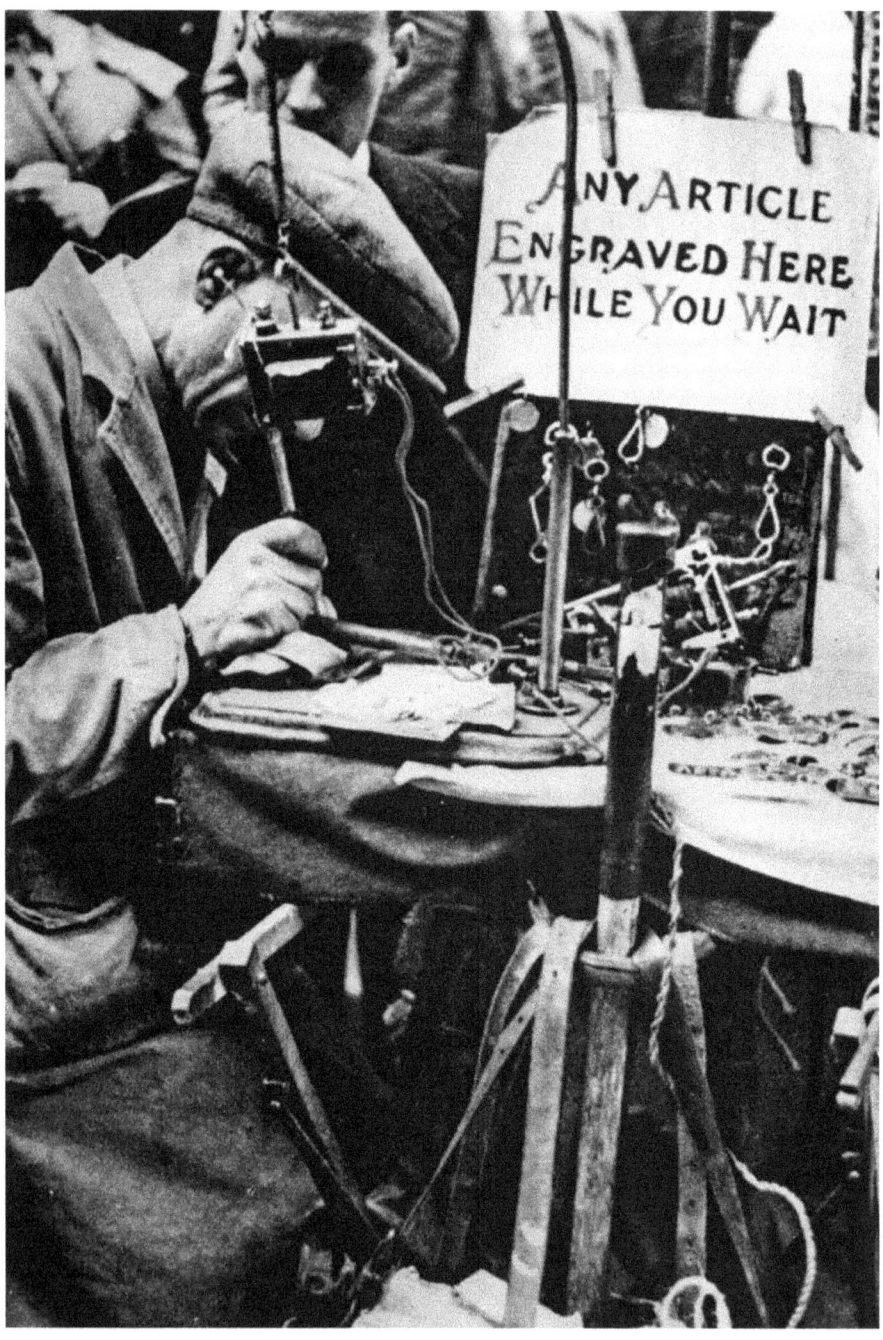

34 Laszlo Moholy-Nagy, 'Petticoat Lane: an engraver', in Mary Benedetta, *The Street Markets of London*, 1936

instrument now and again and plays a few bars of some haunting melody.'[137] An Isadore Michaels is entered in the Stepney minute books, and, despite the slight inconsistency of spelling, this is clearly the same person; Michaels is given a licence for the sale of musical instruments from a stall opposite 15–17 Middlesex Street which he has occupied for eighteen years.[138] Charles Hayday is listed in the council minute books as selling rubber stamps and stencils in Petticoat Lane on Sundays.[139] Benedetta has him as 'old Heyday': 'I asked him what he did the rest of the week. "I go round other markets," he said, "and in harvest-time I go to the village markets all round Norwich and various parts of Norfolk."'[140]

In Lewisham the sellers Benedetta describes include Alice Hillyard, the self-proclaimed 'oldest street trader in Lewisham'; a man known as 'Mush' (Herbert Reeves) who sold a variety of mushrooms grown locally; and, most memorably, 'Mad Ginger' (Frank Alford), who kept a fruit and vegetable stall and was well known for his inventive patter ('Mrs. Russell, come an' eat yer nobby brussel ... Mrs. Baker, step this way for yer old tater ...').[141] Hillyard, Reeves, Alford and a number of other traders described by Benedetta are all found in Lewisham Council's list of street sellers licensed in 1934.

What then can be said in summary of people such as Michaels, Hayday, Hillyard, Reeves and Alford, and their predecessors in the London street markets? Their numbers across the period encompassed both rich and poor, although the overall standard of life had edged upwards, in line with that for society as a whole. Migrants such as Michaels were always important in the London street markets, but whereas in the 1850s the Irish were prominent, alongside an established Jewish minority in the old clothes and a few other trades, by the 1930s a new wave of Jewish immigration had stamped a particular character and vibrancy on the street markets of the East End in particular, making these a space of cultural mingling, as well as a paradise of cheap consumer products. Perhaps it was in the cultural identity of the market people that we can see the greatest change: in Mayhew's time the people of the markets were seen as urban nomads, strange, unsettling, even threatening. By the 1930s these currents remained, especially in some views of the 'alien' Jewish immigrants. But parallel to this was a move to cultural incorporation, as the costermongers and street sellers stepped into the centre of a myth of the London working classes, a myth that was conservative, nostalgic and powerful. The performance of this myth, in the street markets and beyond, is the subject of the next chapter.

Notes

1 Henry Mayhew, *London Labour and the London Poor*, Vol. I (London: Griffin, Bohn and Co., 1861 [1851]), pp. 1–4. All subsequent references to Mayhew in this chapter are to this volume unless otherwise stated.
2 Mayhew, *London Labour*, pp. 2–3, 11–42.
3 Mayhew, *London Labour*, pp. 9–11.
4 See S. Roddy, J.-M. Strange and B. Taithe, 'Henry Mayhew at 200: the "other

Victorian bicentenary"', *Journal of Victorian Culture*, 19.4 (2014), 482–96, for a recent overview of the problems with Mayhew as a historical source.

5 See, for instance, *The Economist*, quoted in E. P. Thompson and E. Yeo (eds), *Unknown Mayhew: Selections from the Morning Chronicle, 1849–50* (London: Merlin, 1971), pp. 43, 57.

6 Roddy et al., 'Henry Mayhew at 200', pp. 481, 488–9. Throughout, Mayhew drew on the work of a team of collaborators; Karel Williams, *From Pauperism to Poverty* (London: Routledge and Kegan Paul, 1981), pp. 238–9. The 1861 edition has been used in this research.

7 Thompson and Yeo (eds), *Unknown Mayhew*, pp. 49, 580.

8 Williams, *Pauperism*, pp. 248–50.

9 Williams, *Pauperism*, pp. 267–70. See also Roddy et al., pp. 489–90.

10 Mayhew, *London Labour*, p. 101.

11 J. Seed, 'Did the subaltern speak? Mayhew and the coster-girl', *Journal of Victorian Culture*, 19.4 (2014), 538.

12 C. Steedman, 'Mayhew: on reading, about writing', *Journal of Victorian Culture*, 19.4 (2014), 550.

13 G. Stedman Jones, *Outcast London: A Study of the Relation Between Classes in Victorian Society* (London: Penguin, 1984 [1971]), is the classic account. D. Green, 'The nineteenth-century metropolitan economy: a revisionist interpretation', *London Journal*, 21.1 (1996), 9–26, is a balanced overview of more recent thinking on this issue.

14 Mayhew, *London Labour*, pp. 70, 75. The shilling came out of charitable funds entrusted to Mayhew, not from his own pocket.

15 Mayhew, *London Labour*, pp. 69–70.

16 Mayhew, *London Labour*, p. 72.

17 Mayhew, *London Labour*, p. 99.

18 Mayhew, *London Labour*, p. 45.

19 Mayhew, *London Labour*, p. 76.

20 J. Benson, *The Penny Capitalists: A Study of Nineteenth-century Working-class Entrepreneurs* (Dublin: Gill and Macmillan, 1983); M. Ball and D. Sunderland, *An Economic History of London 1800–1914* (Abingdon: Routledge, 2001), pp. 67–8.

21 Mayhew, *London Labour*, p. 71.

22 Mayhew, *London Labour*, p. 2.

23 Mayhew, *London Labour*, pp. 64, 81, 84.

24 Mayhew, *London Labour*, p. 93.

25 Mayhew, *London Labour*, p. 68.

26 Mayhew, *London Labour*, p. 70.

27 Mayhew, *London Labour*, p. 104.

28 J. Turton, 'Mayhew's Irish: the Irish poor in mid nineteenth-century London', in R. Swift and S. Gilley (eds), *The Irish in Victorian Britain: The Local Dimension* (Dublin: Four Courts Press, 1999), p. 127; D. MacRaild, *The Irish Diaspora in Britain, 1750–1939* (Basingstoke: Palgrave Macmillan, 2011 [1999]), pp. 22–6.

29 R. Swift, *Irish Migrants in Britain 1815–1914: A Documentary History* (Cork: Cork University Press, 2002), pp. 35, 27.

30 Swift, *Irish Migrants*, p. 49; Turton, 'Mayhew's Irish', pp. 131–2.

31 Mayhew, *London Labour*, pp. 104, 116.

32 K. Hart, 'Informal income opportunities and urban employment in Ghana', *Journal of Modern African Studies*, 11.1 (1973), 61–89.
33 Mayhew, *London Labour*, p. 7.
34 A. D. Mendelsohn, *The Rag Race: How Jews Sewed Their Way to Success in America and the British Empire* (New York: New York University Press, 2015), p. 24.
35 S. Shesgreen, *Images of the Outcast: The Urban Poor in the Cries of London* (Manchester: Manchester University Press, 2002), p. 168; Mayhew, *London Labour*, Vol. II, image opposite p. 118.
36 See L. Perry Curtis, Jr, *Apes and Angels: The Irishman in Victorian Caricature* (Washington, DC: Smithsonian Institution Press, 1997).
37 Mayhew, *London Labour*, pp. 47–8.
38 C. Herbert, *Culture and Anomie: Ethnographic Imagination in the Nineteenth Century* (Chicago: University of Chicago Press, 1991), pp. 201–8.
39 Shesgreen, *Images of the Outcast*, p. 2.
40 See the excellent London Sound Survey website for a chronological 'Street Cries Bibliography for Researchers', drawn from the British Library catalogue and compiled by Adam Tovell. This lists *Cries* from 1646 onwards, with the most recent from 1929; http://www.soundsurvey.org.uk/index.php/history/street_cries (accessed July 2017).
41 J. T. Smith, *The Cries of London: Itinerant Traders of Antient and Modern Times* (London: John Bowyer Nichols, 1839), pp. 50, 52, 89, 97–9.
42 Jack Rag, *Streetology of London* (London: James S. Hodson, 1837), Frontispiece and pp. 10, 47. Rag was a fictional name, as was Richard Tynt, the man on whose papers the book claims to be based. According the catalogue of the Bishopsgate Institute Library, the real name of the author was Harcourt Brown.
43 Shesgreen, *Images of the Outcast*, p. 6.
44 Shesgreen, *Images of the Outcast*, pp. 167–9.
45 See H. F. Tucker, 'Rossetti's goblin marketing: sweet to tongue and sound to eye', *Representations*, 82 (2003), 117–33 for a brief round-up of different approaches to the poem. See also Mendelsohn, *Rag Race*, p. 29, and K. Lysack, 'Goblin markets: Victorian women shoppers at Liberty's oriental bazaar', *Nineteenth-Century Contexts*, 27.2 (2005), 139–65.
46 C. Carlyle Tarr, 'Covent goblin market', *Victorian Poetry*, 50.3 (2012), 297–316.
47 C. Rossetti, 'Goblin Market', in *Goblin Market and Other Poems* (London: Macmillan, 1862).
48 Mayhew, *London Labour*, pp. 2–3.
49 L. Nead, *Victorian Babylon: People, Streets and Images in Nineteenth-century London* (New Haven, CT: Yale University Press, 2000), p. 10.
50 D. Englander and R. O'Day (eds), *Retrieved Riches: Social Investigation in Britain 1840–1914* (Aldershot: Ashgate, 1998), 'Introduction'. For brevity I refer to Booth as the author of the investigation, although many chapters were written by his assistants.
51 Englander and O'Day, *Retrieved Riches*, 'Introduction'.
52 D. Englander, 'Comparisons and contrasts: Henry Mayhew and Charles Booth as social investigators', in D. Englander and R. O'Day (eds), *Retrieved Riches: Social Investigation in Britain 1840–1914* (Aldershot: Ashgate, 1998), pp. 123–4.

53 C. Booth, *Life and Labour of the People in London* (London: Macmillan, 1903), Series I, Vol. I, pp. 57–8.
54 Booth, *Life and Labour*, Series I, Vol. I, pp. 33, 7.
55 Booth, *Life and Labour*, Series I, Vol. I, pp. 57–8.
56 Booth, *Life and Labour*, Series I, Vol. II, p. 50.
57 Example streets are given false names, and are classified by the nature of their inhabitants, using as evidence the reports of middle-class observers such as School Board visitors and clergy.
58 Booth, *Life and Labour*, Series I, Vol. II, p. 116.
59 'Stables and stores for costermongers; near Columbia Market, Hackney Road', *Builder*, 10 November 1877.
60 Booth, *Life and Labour*, Series I, Vol. II, p. 112.
61 J. Greenwood, 'Evidence to Food Committee', *Journal of the Society of Arts*, 27 December 1867, p. 94; J. Thomson and A. Smith, *Street Life in London* (London: Sampson Low, Marston, Searle and Rivington, 1877), p. 100.
62 Mrs B. Bosanquet [Helen Bosanquet, née Dendy], *Rich and Poor* (London: Macmillan, 1896), p. 57.
63 R. Harding Davis, *Our English Cousins* (New York: Harper and Brothers, 1894), pp. 3–4.
64 Davis, *Our English Cousins*, pp. 6–7.
65 See examples at http://metmuseum.org/art/collection/search/157060.
66 Mayhew, *London Labour*, pp. 51–2; J. C. Hotten, *The Slang Dictionary* (London: John Camden Hotten, 1869), p. 166.
67 O. Malvery, *The Soul Market* (London: Hutchinson, 1907), pp. 144–5.
68 M. Brodie, '"Jaunty individualists" or Labour activists? Costermongers, trade unions and the politics of the poor', *Labour History Review*, 66.2 (2001), 147–64, pp. 150–1.
69 Brodie, 'Jaunty individualists', p. 147, quoting H. Pelling.
70 Royal Commission on Alien Immigration, 1903, Report and Evidence, evidence of Henry Weston, minute 7704, p. 259.
71 A. Marsh and J. B. Smethurst, *Historical Directory of Trade Unions*, Vol. 5 (Aldershot: Ashgate, 2006), pp. 142–9.
72 Malvery, *Soul Market*, pp. 148–9.
73 C. Duncan Lucas, 'Coster-land in London', in G. Sims (ed.), *Living London: Its Work and Its Play, Its Humour and Its Pathos, Its Sights and Its Scenes*, Vol. II (London: Cassell, 1901), pp. 75, 78.
74 Ball and Sunderland, *Economic History*, p. 52; D. Englander, 'Booth's Jews: the presentation of Jews and Judaism in *Life and Labour of the People in London*', *Victorian Studies*, 32 (1989), 551–71, p. 552.
75 Englander, 'Booth's Jews', p. 552.
76 S. Gelberg, 'Jewish London', in Sims (ed.), *Living London*, Vol. II, p. 29; Count E. Armfeld, 'Russia in East London', in Sims (ed.), *Living London*, Vol. I, p. 26.
77 T. Kushner, 'Jew and non-Jew in the East End of London: towards an anthropology of "everyday" relations', in G. Alderman and C. Holmes (eds), *Outsiders and Outcasts: Essays in Honour of William J. Fishman* (London: Duckworth, 1993), p. 39.
78 Englander, 'Booth's Jews', pp. 554–8; W. J. Fishman, *The Streets of East London* (London: Five Leaves, 2006 [1979]), p. 88.

79 N. L. Green, 'Immigrant Jews in Paris, London and New York: a comparative approach', *Judaism*, 49.3 (2000), 280–91, p. 281.
80 'London as it is', press cutting, Tower Hamlets Local History Library and Archives, 652.1, 1877.
81 'Pictures of Living London', press cutting, Tower Hamlets Local History Library and Archives, 652.1, 1895.
82 'Pictures of Living London'.
83 Malvery, *Soul Market*, p. 219.
84 Anon., *London and its Environs* (Leipzig, London and New York: K. Baedeker, 1915), p. 159.
85 D. Scannell, *Mother Knew Best: An East End Childhood* (London: Macmillan, 1974), p. 114.
86 Postcard of Petticoat Lane, Bishopsgate Institute photographic collection, Box 2 D31–21, *c.* 1900.
87 Royal Commission on Alien Immigration, evidence of John B. Lyons, minutes 19857 and 19921, pp. 717, 719; evidence of Henry Weston Blake, minute 7704, p. 259; A. Kershen, 'The 1905 Aliens Act', *History Today*, 55.3 (2005), 13–19, p. 13.
88 Kushner, 'Jew and non-Jew', p. 35.
89 E. Brilliana, 'Petticoat-lane' (1895), in E. Ross, *Slum Travelers: Ladies and London Poverty 1860–1920* (Berkeley, CA: University of California Press, 2007), pp. 254–5.
90 Greenwood, 'Evidence to Food Committee', pp. 91–5.
91 J. Greenwood, 'Squalors' market', in *Unsentimental Journeys, or Byways of the Modern Babylon* (London: Ward, Lock and Tyler, 1867).
92 Greenwood, 'Squalors' market', p. 10.
93 J. Greenwood, 'The costers' carnival', in *Unsentimental Journeys*, p. 197.
94 J. Greenwood, 'Barnet Fair', in *Low-Life Deeps: An Account of the Strange Fish to be Found There* (London: Chatto and Windus, 1876).
95 Greenwood, 'Barnet Fair', pp. 306–7.
96 D. B. Scott, 'The music-hall cockney: flesh and blood, or replicant?', *Music & Letters*, 83.2 (2002), 237–58, pp. 237–9; P. J. Keating, *The Working Classes in Victorian Fiction* (London: Routledge and Kegan Paul, 1971), pp. 261–2.
97 G. Stedman Jones, 'The "cockney" and the nation, 1780–1988', in D. Feldman and G. Stedman Jones (eds), *Metropolis London: Histories and Representations since 1800* (London: Routledge, 1989), p. 294.
98 'The rise and fall of the pearly king', *Picture Post*, 2 August 1947, pp. 12–14.
99 P. Binder, *The Pearlies: A Social Record* (London: Jupiter Books, 1975); P. F. Brooks, *Pearly Kings and Queens in Britain* (Chichester: Barry Rose, 1974); A. Joseph, *King of the Pearly Kings: The Story of Henry Croft* (London: Cockney Museum, n. d.). The latter two sources are slight indeed, but they are worth mentioning as both are cited by later historians.
100 Stedman Jones, 'The "cockney" and the nation'; G. Stedman Jones and R. Samuel, 'Pearly kings and queens', in R. Samuel (ed.), *Patriotism: The Making and Unmaking of British National Identity*, Vol. 3 (London: Routledge, 1989).
101 'A chat with Hyram Travers', *Era*, 19 October 1895, p. 17; H. G. Hibbert, *Fifty Years of a Londoner's Life* (London: Grant Richards, 1916), p. 93.
102 E. Hobsbawm and T. Ranger (eds), *The Invention of Tradition* (Cambridge: Cambridge University Press, 1992 [1983]), p. 108.

103 Stedman Jones, 'The "cockney" and the nation', p. 306.
104 'The pearly king', *London Daily News*, 15 April 1911, p. 2; Stedman Jones, 'The "cockney" and the nation', pp. 277, 306.
105 Stedman Jones, 'The "cockney" and the nation', p. 305.
106 'The pearly king', p. 2.
107 'The pearly king and his prize moke', *Penny Illustrated Paper*, 22 June 1907, p. 390; 'Pearly kings', *London Daily News*, 7 April 1911, p. 7; 'Donkeys' day', *Illustrated Police News*, 22 May 1913, p. 7.
108 Scott, 'The music-hall cockney', pp. 247–8, quoting J. Baudrillard.
109 Stedman Jones, 'The "cockney" and the nation', p. 278.
110 Stedman Jones and Samuel, 'Pearly kings'.
111 J. Fiske, *Understanding Popular Culture* (London: Routledge, 2011 [1989]), p. 81.
112 Stedman Jones and Samuel, 'Pearly kings', p. 70.
113 Stedman Jones and Samuel, 'Pearly kings'.
114 P. Nora, 'Between memory and history: les lieux de mémoire', *Representations*, 26 (1989), 7–24, p. 10.
115 Brooks, *Pearly Kings*, p. 5.
116 See, for instance, www.thepearlies.co.uk, or www.pearlykingsandqueens.com.
117 P. Wright, *On Living in an Old Country: The National Past in Contemporary Britain* (London: Verso, 1985), p. 5; R. Samuel, *Theatres of Memory: Past and Present in Contemporary Culture* (London: Verso, 1994), 'Introduction'.
118 A. Chevalier (with Brian Daly), *Albert Chevalier, A Record by Himself* (London: John MacQueen, 1895), pp. 116–17.
119 Mayhew, *London Labour*, pp. 23–4.
120 Mayhew, *London Labour*, p. 51.
121 Mayhew, *London Labour*, pp. 51–2.
122 Chevalier, *Albert Chevalier: A Record*, p. 115.
123 Booth, *Life and Labour*, Series I, Vol. II, p. 140.
124 'Funeral of "the Queen of the Costermongers"', *St James's Gazette*, 15 January 1884, p. 10.
125 The Gentle Author, 'Pearl Binder, artist and writer', *Spitalfields Life*, 1 May 2010, http://spitalfieldslife.com/2010/05/01/pearl-binder-artist-writer/ (accessed 3 May 2017).
126 Stedman Jones, 'The "cockney" and the nation', p. 273.
127 Wedgwood 'Pearly King' mug (correspondence between Wedgwood Museum, Barlaston, and the author, April 2017).
128 London School of Economics, *New Survey of London Life and Labour*, Vol. III (London: P.S. King, 1932), pp. 290–1.
129 T. J. Hatton, 'Unemployment and the labour market', in R. Floud and P. Johnson (eds), *The Cambridge Economic History of Modern Britain*, Vol. II (Cambridge: Cambridge University Press, 2004), pp. 348–53.
130 M. Benedetta, *The Street Markets of London* (London: John Miles, 1936), p. 175.
131 LSE, *New Survey*, Vol. III, p. 302.
132 LSE, *New Survey*, Vol. III, p. 307.
133 Stepney Borough Council Markets Committee minutes, Tower Hamlets Local History Library and Archive, L/SMB/A/15/1, 15 February 1928.
134 Appendix to Report on the Regulation of Street Trading, Lambeth Borough Council

Town Clerk's Department Street Trading files, Lambeth Archives, MBL/TC/R/268, 1928.
135 Lewisham Borough Council minute books, Lewisham Local History and Archives Centre, 4 July 1934.
136 Benedetta, *Street Markets*, p. 5.
137 Benedetta, *Street Markets*, p. 6.
138 Stepney Borough Council Markets Committee minutes, Tower Hamlets Local History Library and Archive, L/SMB/A/15/1, 15 February 1928.
139 Stepney Borough Council Markets Committee minutes, Tower Hamlets Local History Library and Archive, L/SMB/A/15/1, 15 February 1928.
140 Benedetta, *Street Markets*, p. 2.
141 Benedetta, *Street Markets*, p. 69.

5

Street markets, informality and the performance of London

In the view of the French sociologist Michel de Certeau, the market has a dual function: 'at the same time as it is place of business, it is a place of festival'.[1] Other writers have also identified the overlap in the market between commerce and festivity; in her 1936 book on London's street markets Mary Benedetta claimed that 'the tradition of the [London] street markets ... forms a colourful link with the past that goes back to before the days of Bartholomew Fair'.[2] One of a number of annual or periodic fairs in London, Bartholomew Fair was medieval in origin, with its roots in the Christian calendar when saints' days were marked by prayer and celebrated with feasting. The coming together of people for both religious observance and revelry at set points of the liturgical calendar enabled a further double function, as sociability and entertainment overlapped with trade and business.[3] 'Festival', 'feast' and 'fair' are linked in their etymological origins, and 'fair' has a dual meaning in modern usage, indicating a site of both leisure and celebration and economic transaction.[4] Many of the sources on the London street markets describe them as 'fairs', conflating the traditional characteristics of the everyday market and the periodic fair. In 1883 George Sims visited an unnamed market in a poor district of London where 'side by side with the meat-stalls, the fish-stalls, the fruit and vegetable-stalls, and the cheap finery stalls' there were 'shooting galleries, try-your-strength machines, weighing chairs [and] raffling boards', so that the whole constituted 'a complete picture of an old-fashioned fair'.[5] And close to the start of our period, in 1862 George Augustus Sala noted how in the shabby street market in the New Cut, 'the broad pavement presents a mixture of Vanity Fair and Rag Fair' – two examples that together associate the market with morally questionable entertainments and the economic transactions of the poorest sections of society.[6]

One aspect of the long-standing mingling of commerce and festivity was that the marketplace was the original site of the theatre, the first realm of secular theatrical performance. In the medieval period Church rites developed into mystery plays that were then taken over by guilds, moving out of the precincts of the church and into the marketplace at times of festival. As Jean Christophe Agnew has shown, by the later middle ages market and theatre were 'closely identified ... as if they shared a common anatomy or frame that occasion might dress out differently according to the needs of the ecclesiastical and commercial calendars'.[7] Still in the mid-nineteenth century there was some affinity between the market and the theatre, even though the latter had long since moved on from the marketplace. This chapter will examine that affinity, focusing in the first section on how and why contemporary observers saw in the street markets an urban space that was about both rough and ready commerce and cheap and cheerful entertainment – a combination that can be understood by bringing together the idea of economic informality with Bakhtin's notion of the carnival.

Several aspects of the material and sensory qualities of the street markets have been examined in previous chapters: in section two this chapter will further explore the soundscape that was created when crowds gathered, costermongers used their voices to attract custom, and sideshows and musicians offered entertainment. Consideration of this soundscape reinforces how the mingling of commerce and festivity in London's street markets contained strong performative elements. The street markets were not solely a *site* of performance, but also a *source* of performance: the third section will pick up again the cultural turn that was broached in relation to the people of the street markets in the previous chapter, before the difficult issue of the pearly kings and queens left us balanced uncomfortably on the wavering line that divides reality and myth. This chapter will move across this line, from noisy performance in the street markets to the performance of the street markets: what happened when they were not just represented but also performed into popular culture, finding a place in one type of theatre in particular, the burgeoning urban entertainment of the music halls. The activity of the market was performed on the stage as a subject matter for drama and humour, and in the process the costermonger became a music-hall type, and one that stood for certain aspects of London and its people. In the previous chapter we saw how some accounts of the costermonger on the stage wrestle with the (more or less) invented tradition of the pearly king, resolving it by concluding that the stage costermonger had little or nothing to do with the street costermonger. The final section of this chapter will question further whether this was always the case, or whether stage performances of costermonger characters retained some recognisable traces of the street markets. Do any of the themes we have pursued through the previous chapters manifest themselves, in however attenuated a form, in the performance of market characters on the stage?

Market, fair and carnival: exchange and informality

The Russian literary critic Mikhail Bakhtin identified the marketplace as both the site of trade and the site of festivity, giving rise to the cultural forms that he describes with the adjective *carnivalesque*. Bakhtin does not distinguish rigorously between marketplace, fair and festival, and describes a world in which economic exchange and entertainment are closely linked in cultural interaction.[8] Bakhtin was a Russian scholar of literature whose best-known work, *Rabelais and his World*, is an account of the sixteenth-century French writer François Rabelais and his ribald and fantastical novels telling the story of the giants Gargantua and Pantagruel. Bakhtin identified in Rabelais a particular Renaissance moment in which the 'grotesque realism' of popular culture was written into literature. He was concerned with 'folk humour' – ritual spectacles, comic linguistic forms and humorous obscenities, often based on bodily processes or the 'lower bodily stratum' – the chief site of which was the marketplace, the traditional open space of exchange at the centre of the medieval and Renaissance town, which periodically housed carnival. This marketplace is the source of what Bakhtin describes as 'various genres of billingsgate', obscene, rough or abusive language.[9] It is a space apart within the city, in which, at times of festivity, hierarchies are reversed, authority is challenged and even language is inverted, with obscenities as well as the exaggerated claims of publicity and advertising displacing polite speech. The marketplace is 'the center of all that is unofficial; it enjoyed a certain extraterritoriality in a world of official order and official ideology, it always remained "with the people"'. In the marketplace 'the exalted and the lowly, the sacred and the profane are levelled and are all drawn into the same dance'.[10]

Bakhtin's work on Rabelais has been taken up by many cultural theorists, including the historians of literature Peter Stallybrass and Allon White, who have used it to analyse a range of subjects including the markets (although not the *street* markets) of London.[11] Stallybrass and White investigate both the history and the literary representation of the London fair and marketplace (as with Bakhtin, and other sources, fair and market are not strictly distinguished in their work). They focus on the period immediately before that covered in this book, depicting the pre-1850 chartered London fairs and markets as, despite their official sanction, places of disorder and chaotic exchange. They analyse in particular Bartholomew Fair, which was co-located with the livestock market at Smithfield. When it was established in the medieval period Smithfield was on the periphery of the city, but by the nineteenth century it had long been engulfed by urban growth, and frightened animals were driven to the market through congested urban streets. Once at Smithfield they were traded, slaughtered and butchered in public view in the open square in which the market took place, so that the gutters ran with blood and the air rang with the sounds of animals in distress.[12] As the historian Patrick Joyce has commented, Smithfield was a liminal place characterised by transition, exchange and the breaking of boundaries. Country was imported into city, and live animal was translated into dead meat.[13]

Stallybrass and White find the nostalgia-tinged focus upon folkloric subject matter in Bakhtin's notion of the carnival problematic. They note, as have many other critics, that the festivities associated with carnival, which Bakhtin saw as a liberating challenge to political control, may ultimately have quite the opposite effect because, in expressing licensed dissent within limited parameters, carnival takes challenge and incorporates it into the system it ostensibly threatens, which is thereby strengthened rather than undermined. Carnival is nothing more than 'a permissible rupture of hegemony'.[14] Stallybrass and White do not, however, surrender the notion of carnival, instead widening its application to a broader notion of 'symbolic inversion' and 'transgression', using this to analyse the formation of hierarchies around 'high' and 'low' in culture, and particularly 'the processes through which the low troubles the high'. Their attention thus turns to an enormously fruitful application of these concepts across a spectrum of cultural forms, from sewers to servants.[15]

But what of the marketplace? Stallybrass and White describe how the more transgressive aspects of the periodic fairs and traditional markets of London (and other towns and cities) were reformed in the mid-nineteenth century. London's surviving medieval fairs were suppressed, including, in 1855, Bartholomew Fair. Likewise in 1857 Greenwich Fair was ended: it had been described by Charles Dickens in the late 1830s as an occasion for uncontrolled drunken festivity, or what the journalist James Greenwood designated, in comic-cockney mode, as 'orful goings on'.[16] The mid-nineteenth century was also the moment when the Corporation of London and several of London's private market owners rehoused and modernised the authorised markets, as discussed in Chapter 1. In Stallybrass and White's analysis this is the end of the story of the marketplace as a site of transgression: the fairs were gone, and the reformed authorised markets lacked their previous associations with category confusion and hierarchy inversion. The carnival seeped away into other cultural sites and practices in a process of displacement.[17] Yet the mid-nineteenth-century period when reform took place was also the moment when many of the street markets began to spring up, in a process of vigorous growth that continued into the early twentieth century. What if we keep our focus on markets, but switch from the authorised to the unauthorised (street) markets? As they resisted or dodged regulatory control, did they have an ongoing trajectory as Bakhtin's 'centre of all that is unofficial'? Did they inherit any of the transgressive potential of Smithfield prior to its reform, or of Bartholomew Fair, even if that transgression was restricted to the realm of performance?

This book is founded upon the notion that the most productive lens through which to conduct an analysis of London's street markets is their informality; how does Bakhtin's idea of the marketplace as the site of carnivalesque activities, and Stallybrass and White's application of the principle of symbolic inversion to broader culture, relate to the idea of informality? Bakhtin defines the marketplace as a space (and carnival as a time) in which usual systems of control and hierarchies of authority do not pertain. He stresses repeatedly that the world in which the carnivalesque forms of the marketplace are located is one ordered by political, and above all religious, regulation, yet within this world the playful folk humour and popular grotesque activities that occur in the marketplace at certain times are unequivocally 'nonofficial, extraecclesiastical and extrapolitical', marking 'the suspension of all ... norms and prohibitions'.[18] Stallybrass and White contend that Bakhtin's characterisation of the fair or festival as a site beyond the reach of authority is weakened by his concentration on the culturally performative and playful aspects of marketplace activity, and his failure to fully analyse the economic and trading functions of fairs and markets, which were part of the official order.[19] In the case of the London street markets, I would argue that both their leisure and their economic functions were marked by the sidestepping of authority, and that this is a clear link between Bakhtin's ideas and the informal economy of the London street markets.

As we have seen throughout, and particularly in Chapter 1, street markets operated on the margins of the law, outside developing systems for the regulation of the streets. Attempts to incorporate them into authorised market provision, most notably the Columbia Market scheme, were utterly unsuccessful. Costermongers and street sellers simply did not recognise the systems of regulation around them, and were known for their truculent independence in the face of authority. Their relationship to the law was, however, rather delicately balanced: 1867 and the Metropolitan Streets Act marked a moment when street selling might have been cleared off the streets of London, for good or ill. In fact national government and local authorities, including the Metropolitan Police, preferred to let it persist, and in this respect the informal street markets were in similar relationship to authority as Bakhtin's folk-humorous rituals: they rejected normative structures, but were nonetheless quietly tolerated – perhaps because, in both cases, they offered an element of economic and cultural utility.

If we consider not just the trading functions of the street markets, but also their culturally performative aspects – the sideshows and attractions, as well as the entertainment incorporated into the very 'act' of selling – there are many more parallels between these informal sites and the 'non-official' world described by Bakhtin and by Stallybrass and White in their analysis of the troubling relationship of high and low culture. I have noted previously that the street markets were to some extent invisible to official eyes in the nineteenth and early twentieth centuries, in that many of the bureaucratic processes of the developing modern state were unable to overcome the fact of the markets' legal marginality and economic informality in order to recognise them in processes of data gathering. Yet in other respects the street markets were as spectacularly visible as the medieval and Renaissance marketplace culture that interested Bakhtin in Rabelais. In drama, literature and popular journalism the representation of the street market as a site of trade, entertainment, unruly encounter and the clash of cultures was an established trope. Stallybrass and White may have queried the political efficacy of carnival as a challenge to authority, but Bakhtin himself saw the challenge as a symbolic one, opening up space for dialogic speech and playful, joyful, mockery *within* the context of an existing order, and marking a 'temporary liberation' from norms and the 'suspension' of hierarchies – but not their permanent overturning.[20] The London street markets share some of these characteristics.

There are many examples of popular press illustrations of the street markets that bring together as many social types as possible in crowded street scenes, depicting hybridity and the clash of cultures (see figures 1, 2, 17, 20, 30 and 31). Such images, as we have seen, very frequently have a police officer observing from the periphery as an indication of the troubled relationship of this site to established authority, not quite under control, but not entirely beyond its purview either. In the texts that accompany these images, there is a marked tendency to capture both commerce and performance, and to bring high and low into uncomfortable but fascinating juxtaposition. George Augustus Sala, for instance, described the street market in the New Cut with the full prurient eloquence of Victorian sensation journalism:

> I wish that I had a more savoury locality to take you to than the New Cut. I acknowledge frankly that I don't like it ... It isn't picturesque, it isn't quaint, it isn't curious. It has not even the questionable merit of being old. It is simply Low. It is sordid, squalid, and, the truth must out, disreputable.[21]

Yet the delight with which Sala lavishes elaborate description on this street leaves the distinct impression that he does, in fact, rather like the New Cut and its 'flaunting, idle, vagabond, beggarly-fine don't-care-a-centishness'. In his analysis, the market and its people jostle for space with a sparklingly new 'gin-palace' and the Victoria Theatre, whose mawkish, dramatic and violent productions Sala nonetheless describes with reference to Italian opera and West End theatre, in a playful collision of high and low.[22] Sala's treatment of the market is a clear demonstration of the clash of revulsion and desire which Stallybrass and White identify as a central feature of those cultural impulses that ostensibly aimed simply to eliminate the 'low', but which in fact embodied the transgressive potential that is the modern legacy of the carnivalesque mode, as the low is brought into troubling dialogue with high culture.[23]

The pattern set by Sala was followed many times, by many writers. Journalists short of inspiration or editors in search of copy engaged in a specialist form of the class tourism known as slumming, taking a trip to a street market on a Saturday night or a Sunday morning. The resulting accounts always stress how fascinatingly horrid it all was, utterly nasty and repulsive – and yet there is a strong frisson of allure and excitement too. As George Bernard Shaw has Professor Higgins say of the street flower seller Eliza Doolitle in *Pygmalion*, 'she's so deliciously low – so horribly dirty', 'almost irresistible'.[24] The American journalist Richard Harding Davis prefaced his account of street markets in the East End with a warning that the district was 'entirely too awful' for description – yet describe it he did, with some literary enthusiasm.[25] A lengthy account of 'Saturday Night in the East End' in *Good Words* magazine tells how the author engaged a police constable to be his guide, to take him up and down market streets, into the haunts of thieves and beggars, and to a music hall where prostitutes ('female corsairs') picked up sailors with business-like efficiency.[26] The author quotes his policeman guide's response to the investigation, and critique of the slightly timid efforts made by some seekers after low culture:

> What do you say to a peep at the Spitalfields Thieves Nest? You've been there before, have you? Oh, by day ... I expect you didn't look about you much – didn't go up any of the courts – just walked through Flower-and-Dean-street, or something of that sort. Some folks fancy they can see London life that way, and what they don't see they can make up.[27]

'You gents have a gift for making a precious lot out of a little', he concludes, indicating the journalistic propensity to write up low encounters for dramatic effect, evidencing the play of distaste and delight that structures many accounts of 'low' scenes and people, including those in the street markets. The prurience expressed in such late nineteenth-century accounts is new, the product of the process by which 'low domains, apparently expelled as "Other", return as the object of ... fascination'.[28] Yet the underlying impulse is clearly linked to the juxtaposition of high and low that is the ruling spirit of Bakhtin's grotesque realism.

Stallybrass and White assert that as markets and fairs were reformed in the mid-nineteenth century, one motivation was to end 'the deep conceptual confusion entailed by the fair's inmixing of work and pleasure, trade and play', separating 'rational, commercial trading' from 'popular pleasure-ground'.[29] But in fact retail development from the mid-nineteenth century onwards continued this mixing: even in the formal world of West End shopping the department stores were sites of both great economic rationality (the rapid turnover of goods rendered cheap by economies of scale) and spectacular entertainment. The street markets contained a similar admixture, albeit of a less luxurious nature, and were marked by complexity and contradiction. Stallybrass and White sum up this hybrid nature of the market:

> How does one 'think' a marketplace? At once a bounded enclosure and a site of open commerce, it is both the imagined centre of an urban community and its structural interconnection with the network of goods, commodities, markets, sites of commerce and places of production which sustain it. A marketplace is the epitome of local identity (often indeed it is what defined a place as more significant than surrounding communities) and the unsettling of that identity by the trade and traffic of goods from elsewhere. At the market centre of the polis we discover a commingling of categories usually kept separate and opposed: centre and periphery, inside and outside, stranger and local, commerce and festivity, high and low.[30]

Both Bakhtin's analysis of the marketplace's potential for symbolic contest, and Stallybrass and White's development of his ideas to describe the market as a place of radical hybridity, reconfirm the informal nature of the street markets, which extended from their economic and legal status to their social composition and cultural ramifications. The following section will pursue this analysis with a look at performance within the market, with a focus on soundscapes, and expanding on Bakhtin's ideas of dialogic speech and humour in noise, cries and vocal advertising.

Performance in the street market: the sound of informality

Dolly Scannell's childhood memoir of Poplar recalls vividly the market in Chrisp Street. The stalls excited Dolly, with their varied merchandise and the sensory stimulation they provided.[31] And to supplement the appeal of their goods, the stallholders generated entertainment as a means to win custom, making the act of selling into a dramatic interaction, as with the vendor of a patent medicine that 'cured every illness known to mankind', who would 'talk non-stop about all the places in the world where he had cured people after doctors had given them up; even royalty'.[32] In his memoir of his Hoxton childhood, Bryan Magee talks of the 'sheer multiplicity of life' in the local street market, an 'enlivening' place of stimulation, crowds, colour, movement – and noise.[33]

Charles Booth discusses one particular, and particularly noisy, aspect of the street markets that made them such a lively source of entertainment, the Dutch auction that was a frequent mode of selling, especially on busy Saturday nights. This was an auction in reverse, commencing with the seller crying out an exaggeratedly high price for a piece of fish, joint of meat or any other commodity, holding the goods aloft for shoppers to see. When enough potential customers had gathered, the seller would begin to reduce the price in increments: '"Eightpence?" "Sevenpence?" "Sixpence?" "Fivepence?" – Say "Fourpence?" – well, then, "Threepence halfpenny?"' The gathered customers held out until the price seemed good, and one among them signalled her willingness to buy. At this point,

> the fish, or whatever it is passes from the right hand of the seller on which it has been raised to view, on to the square of newspaper, resting on his left hand, is bundled up and quick as thought takes its place in the buyer's basket in exchange for the 3½ d, which finds its place in the seller's apron or on the board beside the fish – and then begins again the same routine, "Eightpence?" "Sevenpence?" "Sixpence?" &c.[34]

The trick for sellers was to start high and make much of the falling price to create the impression of an irresistible bargain; for buyers the objective was to hold out until the price seemed reasonable, and then get a bid in quickly before anyone else could secure the deal. By this means shopping became a noisy game, although a deadly serious one in which the skilful deployment of limited budgets collided with the necessity of wringing profit from cut-price goods.

Bryan Magee also describes Dutch auctions, run by a man selling confectionery who was 'so quick and amusing in his banter with the crowd that he always had a laughing audience round his stall'.[35] One of the approaches I have taken in trying to understand the informal nature and material culture of the street markets is to pay attention to the evidence available to all the senses. Western culture has in the modern period been over-committed to the idea that vision is pre-eminent in the hierarchy of the senses, but the street markets need a more rounded approach in order to understand their material constitution and the culture that flowed from it. As discussed in Chapter 3, of the 'other' senses that are frequently marginalised by the prioritisation of vision, sound, taste, smell and touch are all represented in descriptions of the street markets.[36] Sound, however, is the most dominant sense-quality, alongside the glare and sputter of the naphtha lights that contributed so much to the markets' distinctive visual atmosphere. Magee recalls this sound as 'multi-layered', with 'a background noise of hundreds of people talking at once' and, 'overriding everything else, the air-splitting cries of the stall-keepers ... each trying to draw attention to his particular goods by shouting either his wares or his prices, the jokers also joshing with the passers-by or with neighbouring stall-keepers'.[37]

As with the flaring lights, the sounds of selling played a part in identifying and demarcating the space of the market, differentiating it from surrounding streets. The French historian Alain Corbin has investigated the link between sound and space in his inquiry into church bells in the villages of France. The auditory reach of the bells 'helped to create a territorial identity' and the sense of 'an enclosed space structured by sound emanating from its center'.[38] Many observers described the approach to the street market through the city streets in terms of a sudden flowering of the distinctive flaring lights, and just as sudden an upsurge in the noises of the market. George Gissing, in a fictional account, described arriving at Whitecross Street market as a contrast between the surrounding 'dim and quiet regions' and the market's 'glare of lights and ... hubbub of cries'.[39]

There has been a notable recent upsurge in sensory studies and sensory history, with the work of writers such as Corbin, who has written on smell as well as sound, at the forefront. Corbin's essay 'Charting the Cultural History of the Senses' is a clear methodological guide.[40] His first insight is the necessity of being aware of the different values within which sensory perception operates in any given place or time – sense values are formed in culture, or as Mark Paterson puts it, 'the sensory order is always simultaneously a moral order and a social order'.[41] Different classes of evidence may betray the relationship between sense perception and value, so that, for instance, prescriptive texts such as medical manuals and advice literature report normative standards, whereas memoirs and diaries may be more reflective of experience. We have already heard from various autobiographical accounts that describe the street markets, retrospectively written descriptions in which the warmth of nostalgia is stoked by vivid recall of sensory details by adult authors recalling childhood experiences. Normative accounts are less celebratory; as the historian James Winter describes, nineteenth-century reformers were perturbed by the vigour and liveliness of life on some of London's streets (of which the market streets were among the most lively) and the effects on children (especially boys) who grew up with 'quick wits' among the clamour of the streets, but who might be better served by more time 'indoors and in a quiet, ordered environment'.[42] Winter describes the music that was a frequent component of the street market soundscape, and was reluctantly tolerated by authorities wedded to the idea of freedom of the streets. It was vigorously contested by campaigners. An 1869 pamphlet titled 'The Nuisance of Street Music', by 'A London Physician', contrasted the quiet and orderly interior of a hospital with an adjacent street 'densely peopled by a low population with a large Irish and criminal element', and where 'ragged urchins .. are dancing with delight' to the music of a barrel organ.[43] Excessive noise, and particularly street noise, was a sign of class difference, disorder and the 'unofficial' world allied to Bakhtin's marketplace as a space apart from authority and hierarchy. As Peter Bailey notes, vision is the 'prime medium of official regulation, commercial enthralment and masculine hegemony' and the 'sound of authority' is in fact 'silence'.[44] The tumultuous sounds that they generated marked the noisy street markets as informal spaces, belonging to an independent culture of the streets.

If, as Bailey suggests, vision is associated with official order, and noise with the unofficial, one way of thinking about sound in the street market is to consider how it was in some respects in contest with vision. Street trading had a well-established and distinct auditory quality, pre-dating the mid-nineteenth-century growth of the street markets, and imparted by the cries of perambulating sellers. Bakhtin emphasises heavily the Prologues with which Rabelais commenced each of his books, and their humorous appropriation of the language of the Paris Cries, street sellers' verbal advertising: 'the culture of the common folk idiom was to a great extent a culture of the loud word spoken in the open, in the street and marketplace'.[45] These vocal methods were the dominant mode of commercial selling in France in the time of Rabelais, and the tradition of crying wares for sale in the streets of London was also an old one. As with the Paris Cries, the London Cries (illustrations of street sellers captioned with their traditional shouted advertisements, discussed in the previous chapter) document a long history of noisy selling. They record the habitual Cries that could become stylised over time, and which were impenetrably exotic to outsiders. An 1866 French-language edition of the Baedeker travel guide to London gives phonetic renderings of some of the Cries which, it said, were 'incomprehensible to the foreigner, and even to those perfectly acquainted with the English language'.[46] Milk was advertised with a cry of *'milkóo!'* or *'kióo!'* or even *'low!'* (an abbreviation of 'below', to capture the attention of servants in basement kitchens). Sellers of periwinkles called *'Wink! wink! periwink! penny wink!'* indicating to those in the know both the goods and the price. Baked potatoes were advertised with *'all ot! all ot!'* (*'tout chaud'* or 'all hot') and butchers called out simply *'Buy! buy! buy! buy! buy!'*, explained as *'très-vite, comme baï-baï-baï-baï-baï!'*[47]

In the mid-nineteenth century, as perambulatory selling came under some pressure and the street markets grew and proliferated, the tradition of the Cries was perpetuated and developed in performative sales practices in the markets characterised by vocal display and patter, humorous or persuasive. Yet at the same time, retailing more broadly began to spawn ever more spectacular visual cultures, particularly in the proliferating texts and images of paper-based advertising. The urban environment began to be filled with posters, while pictorial advertising infiltrated the pages of the newspapers and magazines of the rapidly growing popular press, and shops were stocked with branded products that were brightly packaged and promoted on the shelf and counter by colourful printed ephemera.[48] Window displays (at their most lavish in the huge plate-glass windows of the department stores) expanded the visual allure of the commodity.[49] The street markets were not excluded from most of these developments; together with the shops that bounded the market streets, the stalls were visually stimulating. They were the source of the consumer staples that provisioned working-class families, and by the later nineteenth century these included not just unbranded commodities (apples by the pound or plain yellow soap sold in brown paper) but branded products that came wrapped in colour and imagery for added visual impact (Edward's dessicated soup, Sunlight and Lifebuoy soap, Worcestershire sauce).[50] Figure 35 shows East Street market in Walworth in 1939, with advertisements for branded goods, including Sunlight, amid the stalls. But as well as these developments in the growth of visual consumer culture, the street markets also kept hold of the older auditory cultures of selling. Writing of the 1930s, Bryan Magee gives numerous examples of street

35   East Street market, Walworth, 1939

sellers and costermongers crying their wares – 'Lovely carpets, nice rugs!', 'Any hat you like for sixpence!', 'Tuppence a pound pears!'[51] The street markets adapted to the new visual cultures of selling at the same time as being the place in which auditory techniques persisted.

One aspect of retailing, that of the taking and handling of cash, provides a clear example of a distinct auditory gradient between types of selling space, including the markets and different sorts of shop. The cash register ('a mechanical genius in brass and steel') was invented in the late 1870s in the United States. By recording, visualising and sounding out with ringing bells the passage of cash from customer to sales clerk it both generated a record of transactions and prevented dishonest employees from diverting money into their own pockets. The cash register soon became a common feature of pubs, bars, restaurants and more everyday shops, in Britain as well as the USA.[52] It had a rival, however, in cash railways and pneumatic cash-handling systems, which were common in department stores. These whisked money and bills of sale away from the shop counter in networks of vacuum tubes, taking them unobtrusively to an accounts office, before quickly returning change and receipts.[53] The difference between the two systems, emphasised in the way in which they were promoted, lay in sound: the cash register made the transaction assertively audible, whereas the pneumatic tube kept it silent and discreet, and was associated with higher-class retailers.

In the street markets, the only cash-handling equipment was the time-honoured wooden block with curved indentations to accommodate different denominations of coin. However, here the noisy Dutch auction made the act of selling that much louder than even the cash register, with vocal fanfares that spoke the price of the transaction, and the public exchange of coins. This was a culture of selling that noisily celebrated the purchase of food and drink and the humblest of luxuries, in which bargains were a source of delight in communities where many people lived hand to mouth. Alain Corbin, in his advice for the writing of sensory history, advises that moments of crisis can reveal tensions that are otherwise hidden.[54] The contrast between spectacular visual cultures of consumption that were relatively quiet and the persistent vocal cries of the markets, and between cash-handling systems that minimised or maximised the sound of the transaction, suggests that noise was a contested issue in retailing. One specific crisis confirms this: Columbia Market, Baroness Angela Burdett Coutts's disastrous attempt to provide formal, off-street market premises for the retailing done in street markets, had at number two in its list of 20 bye-laws a prohibition on the 'crying' of goods in the market, punishable with a fine of five shillings.[55] Burdett Coutts attempted to outlaw excessive noise from her market, but the attempt failed with the market itself.

Bakhtin saw the Paris cries as one aspect of the dialogic speech of a marketplace filled with humour; another aspect was the closely related abuses, curses, oaths and profanities of 'billingsgate' speech, which refused 'to conform to conventions, to etiquette, civility, respectability'.[56] Columbia Market's list of prohibitions included, alongside its ban on the crying of goods, the use of 'profane cursing and swearing'.[57] This was a further attempt to outlaw the street markets' noise, a good deal of which carried echoes of Bakhtin's low speech, breaking through in the loud and lively auctions, the humorous patter and jokes, the repartee and insults between rival sellers. This vocal duelling was particularly pronounced in Petticoat Lane, where Jewish street sellers offering cheap, mass-market fashions were famous for the entertainment value of their selling techniques. Richard Harding Davis recorded the insults flung around in Petticoat Lane, describing a stallholder who declared loudly that the clothes his rival sold, 'ain't fit for nothink but to bury folks in, 'cos if yer moves in 'em they falls ter pieces and leaves you naked ... moth-eaten cholera blankets, robbed from 'ospitals and made over'.[58] These abuses deploy disease, death and the naked human body, subjects of humour that resonate with Bakhtin's view that 'the theme of mockery and abuse is almost entirely bodily and grotesque', concerned with 'the body that gives birth and is born, devours and is devoured, drinks, defecates, is sick and dying'.[59] The Petticoat Lane patter recorded by Harding Davis falls very far short of the exaggerated and joyful obscenity that Bakhtin finds in Rabelais, which would have been quite unprintable in the public media in Harding Davis's day. In his advice for the writing of sensory history, Corbin warns of the necessity of considering what is not said because it is either too commonplace to merit comment or too delicate to be broached.[60] It may have been that what Harding Davis heard, in contrast to what he wrote, contained a stronger echo of the grotesque. His description of Petticoat Lane contains the warning that 'I cannot quote in print the incidents or repeat the stories which go to prove what I say', clearly suggesting the removal of at least some obscene words or scatological or sexual references in an account that was bowdlerised for polite consumption.[61]

Dolly Scannell also recalls the humour of insults traded between street sellers, describing 'Sweet Harry', the keeper of a confectionery stall in Chrisp Street in Poplar. On Saturday nights, Scannell recalls, Sweet Harry was as good as a 'music hall turn', with innuendo-laden sexual humour to match:

> He would gather up whipped cream walnuts, candy and toffee and sell them all in one parcel amid screams of laughter, but everyone waited for the punch line. On one side of the sweet man was the large flower lady, enormously breasted, bright faced ... On the other side of Sweet Harry was a gentle blind man. With eye-lids closed he would sell matches and bootlaces from a little tray suspended round his neck. He always wore a bowler hat and every few seconds he would say gently, 'Is there anyone else, is there anyone else?' Sweet Harry with perfect timing would tell the crowd, 'Last night the flower woman was in bed and she said ...' and then came the blind man's, 'Is there anyone else, is there anyone else?'[62]

Scannell's autobiography described the early twentieth century, but was written retrospectively, in the changed *moeurs* of the 1970s. Even so the sexual references that are so overt in Rabelais are present here in much gentler form, shrouded (though not heavily) behind *double entendre*. The 1963 autobiography of the writer Ralph Finn, born in 1912, includes a similar example of less-than-innocent meaning imputed to ostensibly blameless words, this time by a trader selling underwear ('lucky knickers') in Petticoat Lane.[63]

To claim the London street markets as the direct descendant of Bakhtin's Renaissance marketplace would be too simple, ignoring the development of the modern bureaucratic state and capitalistic economy, the regulations that hemmed the markets about (without managing to suppress them), and the spectacular cultures of modern consumerism to which the markets certainly made some contribution. Yet strong evidence suggests that older traditions of selling persisted in the street markets even as they adapted to modernity, especially in the soundscapes that were generated by the performance of public selling. The words and sounds of the markets, together with their distinct visual culture and atmosphere, are amenable to Bakhtinian interpretation. Stallybrass and White, and many others, pursue the carnivalesque ingeniously through diverse cultural forms, to the extent, as Peter Bailey noted as long ago as 1986, that the idea of carnival can be 'more cliché than tool' (although this criticism certainly does not apply to Stallybrass and White's work).[64] One way to engage with carnival constructively might be to find it hiding in plain sight in exactly the place where Bakhtin originally located it, in the (street) marketplace, where many of its constituent elements still offer considerable analytical utility. The carnival is in sympathy with (and to some extent maps on to) the informal; I argue that certain characteristics of informality drove the flow of culture from the street market into wider culture and performance, channelled primarily through the music halls.

Performing the street market: costermongers on the stage

In the previous chapter we saw how the pearly kings and queens emerged as a peculiar crystallisation of the identity of the costermonger-cockney, a mythic figure that pinned the central point of London working-class character to an origin in the street markets. Those few historians who have investigated the pearly kings and queens identify them as an almost purely *invented* tradition, generated not in the markets themselves, but on the stage of the music halls, from whence they found their way to the streets, carrying with them a fictive origin story. I cautiously dispute this analysis, contending that while the pearly kings and queens certainly owed a great deal to the music hall stage, they may also have had some links to more 'real' origins. Pearly royalty is a difficult subject of historical analysis, with the main difficulty located in the uncertain and barely documented transition from street to stage or stage to street in the meeting of social life and cultural representation (which may shade into myth). This section will tell a slightly more straightforward story of the tangling of the street markets' performativity and performance on the stage. The markets – with their vigorously performative culture of cries and humour – provided a cast of costermonger-cockney characters that were recreated again and again as archetypes and then stereotypes of the working-class Londoner, and the informality of the street markets drove this process. What was it about the informal street markets that made them such a temptingly rich source of characters through which to depict London and its people?

If the pearly kings and queens with their distinctive pearl-button decorated dress originated at least in part in the music halls of the 1880s and 1890s, and from there stepped into the working-class communities that were the locale of the street markets, that was not the limit of cross-fertilisation between street market and stage. The distinct pearly dress may have owed as much to stage as to street, but the broader characteristics of the stage costermonger-cockney flowed, at least in general origin, from the street markets on to the stage. The street markets were performative spaces; Dolly Scannell described 'Sweet Harry' by comparing him to a music hall turn, and she listed too the many sideshows and entertainments that were interspersed between the market stalls, including a tattooed escape artist who was believed to be a cousin of the great escapologist and music hall sensation Harry Houdini.[65] This sort of performer on the street was idiomatically related to acts in the halls, even if Scannell's Houdini does not seem likely to have been related by blood to his more famous 'cousin'. These performers' presence made Scannell's visits to Chrisp Street market rather like the enjoyment of a variety show, albeit one in which the acts, strung out along the street, all performed at once and repeatedly, rather than in temporal succession.

The chief dividing line between street and stage performers was that of success, and not any categorical difference in the nature of the performance. This was the case for those who sold their performance itself in the market: what of costermongers and street sellers whose performances were used to sell other, more tangible, commodities as part of the patter of a sales routine? In the 1890s the cartoonist Phil May created in a single illustration a compact narrative of the meeting point between selling in the street market and performance on the stage, in his depiction of a Jewish Petticoat Lane street seller, 'Ike Levi' (figure 31). Levi is described in the cartoon's caption as:

> The merriest, cleverest, loudest and most versatile clothes-seller in the world. He bombards his customers with shouts, and wheedles them with song ... The gent in the top hat is a music-hall agent from South Africa. He sees money in Ike, and engages him on the spot.

May's narrative was a fictional one, but it nonetheless documents the perceived similarity between performance in the street market and on the stage. Thomas Burke, in a 1918 description of Salmon Lane street market, suggested a direct overlap in personnel between street market and stage, with stallholders paying 'decayed music hall men' to cry their wares for them (although these men moved in the opposite direction to Ike Levi, stepping down from rather than up to the stage).[66] Although my research into music hall performers has uncovered few examples of costermongers or street sellers who moved into a career 'on the halls', the style and manner of music hall performance owed a great deal to the street. The character, cries, patter and style of the costermongers provided the inspiration for some of the most successful music hall performers, whose 'costermonger' acts kept the street market and stage linked within a wider culture of leisure and entertainment.

The historian Peter Bailey describes the development of the music halls out of the frenzy of urbanisation of the 1830s and 1840s, originating in public house back-room singing events ('free-and-easies'), where amateurs performed for enthusiastic audiences and the division between audience and singer was shifting and porous.[67] James Ewing Ritchie describes such a free-and-easy in London in the 1850s: in a pub upstairs room in 'a very low neighbourhood', around a hundred people (many of them costermongers) gathered to drink, to listen, and to take their turn at singing.

> The pots of heavy and the quarterns of juniper are freely quaffed, and the world and its cares are forgotten, and the company becomes hourly more noisy and hilarious ... Anybody sings who likes; sometimes a man, sometimes a female, volunteers a performance, and I am sorry to say it is not the girls who sing the most delicate songs.[68]

The nascent pub entertainment of early to mid-century developed into larger and more organised singing saloons, where some at least of the performers were paid. Purpose-built music halls with increasingly lavish premises were built by theatrical entrepreneurs from the 1860s, in London led by venues such as the Canterbury music hall in Lambeth and the Oxford in the West End.[69] Music hall remained fundamentally different from the mainstream theatre. Rather than extended dramatic narratives, it presented variety shows that featured a succession of disparate performers, the most successful of whom were often contracted to appear at several halls in one night, and whose acts were shaped to quick entrances, maximum impact and the rapid climax of a triumphant exit.[70] The music hall singer Albert Chevalier described his audiences, somewhat defiantly, as 'people who dare to avow their preference for a Variety Entertainment over a three hours' spell of Shakespeare'.[71] The theatre critic William Archer condemned music hall's typical productions as 'scrap shows', undemanding of sustained attention from their audiences.[72] The similarity of these 'scrap shows' to the fragmented street performances viewed by Dolly Scannell was clear to many commentators: critics, including Archer, traced music hall back to the medieval marketplace roots of theatre more broadly, describing its acts as 'wares'.[73]

Both the street markets and the music halls occupied a position on the margins of broader categories, the street markets on the informal edge of retailing, the music halls in subaltern relationship with the established theatre. Both were categorised by observers with reference to their lack of official sanction or cultural status, the street markets as 'unauthorised' and the music halls as 'illegitimate' or 'irregular'.[74] Chevalier talked of the 'regular' theatre versus the 'irregular' music hall, and contrasted the halls with 'theatre proper (?)', although the question mark in parenthesis signals his scepticism regarding this widely accepted division.[75] The music halls perpetuated a vestige of the free-and-easy's fluid interchange between singer and audience (unlike the formal theatre with its 'fourth wall'), and impromptu exchanges between stage and gallery formed an important part of the entertainment. Bailey contends that this back and forth aspect of music hall performance owed something to street cries and market patter: on the music hall stage, as in the street, the relationship between performer and audience was 'very much one of give as well as take'.[76] It is notable that the free-and-easy described by Ritchie was populated chiefly by costermongers, who appeared to take particular delight in this sort of entertainment, and in the exchange between performers and listeners. Henry Mayhew around 1850 described similar interactions in a 'penny gaff' or informal theatre, again from an audience largely made up of costermongers, in this case adolescents and young adults who took raucous delight in sexual humour.[77]

Gareth Stedman Jones, in an influential analysis, has described the late nineteenth-century music halls as providing a 'culture of consolation', the distraction of the working classes from larger political discontents by mass entertainment and the provision of 'small pleasures'.[78] Stedman Jones posits a process of corporatisation (and incorporation): as music halls became larger in scale towards the end of the nineteenth century, owners and managers, under threat of having their licences removed, policed their acts for content likely to invite the disapproval of vocal, middle-class, 'rational recreation' campaigners. At the same time, more socially mixed audiences began to enjoy at least the more metropolitan halls. Stedman Jones thus suggests that authentically working-class forms of entertainment were replaced by business enterprises in which a version of working-class culture was sold back both to those it represented and to wider audiences by predominantly bourgeois proprietors, songwriters and performers.

Peter Bailey's riposte to Stedman Jones is to propose the development of 'knowingness' among both audiences and performers, defining this knowingness as 'what everybody knows, but some know better than others'.[79] He suggests a culture not of 'consolation' but of 'competence', as the double-coded lyrics of songs and the interactions of performer and audience kept open a space for discourse that questioned official cultures without directly challenging them, in ways reminiscent of the symbolically subversive power of Bakhtin's carnival: 'the counter discourse of music hall knowingness was limited to the infraction rather than the negation of the dominant power relationships'.[80] Knowingness allowed playfully subversive humour to flourish, so that, for instance, Marie Lloyd's most famous song, 'A Little of What You Fancy Does You Good', could signal small consolatory and innocent pleasures, or something much more suggestive. The words were as innocuous or as saucy as the audience (or different people within it) chose to make them, although their reception was undoubtedly steered by Miss Lloyd's delivery and gestures, which hinted broadly at a cheerfully bawdy interpretation.[81] However, this was by no means explicit in the lyrics, rather like the innuendo-dependent joke delivered by Dolly Scannell's Sweet Harry.

The historiography of the music halls is diverse, and to engage with all its strands is beyond the scope of this analysis. The most relevant debate, that propelled by Stedman Jones, Bailey and many others, might be summed up simply as, who was music hall by, and who was it for? Did commodification dominate, rendering the working-class characters who populated the stage mere empty representations ('replicants', as Derek Scott describes the stage costermongers), or was there, as Bailey contends, space for something that demonstrated the competencies of the audience, their 'insider's knowledge' of the city?[82] The answer, inevitably, is complex, but Bailey's 'knowingness' is one effective starting point, and is certainly useful in understanding some of the biggest hit songs of the costermonger comic singers. The knowing, playful and complicit relationship between performer and audience made humour out of the encounters of urban life, and on the streets, as in the halls, costermongers were not the least cunning, resilient, independent and 'competent' characters. The remainder of this chapter will look in detail at the genre of costermonger performers, before reading closely several examples of individual performers and their songs, using Bailey's idea of the culture of competence as broadly consistent with Bakhtin's dialogism and grotesque folk humour, and Stallybrass and White's reading of the hybrid marketplace.

George Le Roy's 1952 memoir *Music Hall Stars of the Nineties* gives a good snapshot of the sort of performers who flourished at the end of the nineteenth century.[83] Le Roy describes acrobats, dancers, hypnotists, escapologists, magicians, musicians, comedians and singers, all highly paid and well known in their day. It was in the last category, as singers of both sentimental and comic songs (and of songs that combined the two modes in the popular 'serio-comic' style), that cockney, and more specifically costermonger, acts flourished, and Le Roy describes a number of such artists, including Alec Hurley, Charles Coborn, Bessie Bellwood, Joe Elvin, Kate Carney and Albert Chevalier.[84] Other cockney-costermonger singers included Gus Elen, J. W. Rowley and Fanny Wentworth, and from a somewhat earlier period there were Hyram Travers and Alfred Vance.[85] Many of the 1890s stars described by Le Roy continued their careers well into the interwar period, and Kate Carney was still performing just before her death in 1950. Thus for almost all of the period under discussion in this book, costermongers existed both on the street and on the stage.

Not all these performers stuck to a costermonger, or even a cockney, identity all the time. Alfred Vance ('The Great Vance') was one of the 'lion comiques' who flourished from the 1860s, performing 'swell' songs that celebrated and satirised upper-class high living and fashionable dress. His 'Chickaleary Cove' (1870) was a specifically costermonger-cockney variation on the theme, in the character of a street seller boasting (in market back-slang) of his sharp tailoring.[86]

Bessie Bellwood's biggest hit was 'Wot Cheer 'Ria', about a 'a girl what's a-doing wery well in the weagetable line', who, like Vance's Chickaleary Cove, dresses herself up in showy new clothes.[87] However, Bellwood, who was best appreciated for the fiercely combative humour of her interactions with the audience, didn't always sing in costermonger character. Even within the cockney idiom the costermonger was not the sole occupation represented – however, it was the most celebrated, largely due to the efforts of Albert Chevalier, Gus Elen, Alec Hurley and Kate Carney, who all dedicated the majority of their performances to this theme, and wore pearl-button costumes, following in the footsteps of earlier performances by Vance and Travers.[88] Chevalier identified the costermonger as an ideal-type of the London working classes; 'I take the Coster pure as the typical cockney ... and the cab-driver, the omnibus-conductor, the loafer: all these are variations only of the cockney type.'[89] W. Macqueen-Pope, in a nostalgic 1950 history, made a similar attribution in discussing Kate Carney, who he described as 'the type that sold flowers around Eros in Piccadilly Circus ... or attended Covent Garden Market in the early morning to buy their wares' and was 'the embodiment of the people of London'.[90]

Although performers such as Chevalier and Carney took the costermonger figure and made it central to their depictions in song of working-class London, none stuck to the persona entirely without variation. Chevalier started his career as an actor on the 'legitimate' stage, and although his biggest successes were all achieved with costermonger songs, throughout his career he always took on a variety of roles.[91] Gus Elen, who also scored his biggest hits with costermonger material, started as a blackface minstrel (a common genre of the period), whereas Kate Carney sang Irish songs, another established genre.[92] Both blackface 'coon' songs and the Irish ballad were genres based on ethnicity, and it is difficult to escape the conclusion that the costermonger too was performed as an ethnic as well as a class identity, with typically parodic elements. Elen combined blackface and cockney in the song 'New Cut Coon', in which he took the role of a coal heaver with a dirt-blackened face who is mistakenly thought to be ethnically black.[93] The stage performance of the costermonger recalls the social identity of street sellers dating back to Mayhew and beyond in which they were marked by difference and seen as other and alien, a 'distinct race'.

What was the social background of those artists who performed as costermongers? Did any of them come from the streets or street markets that they depicted on stage? Perhaps the closest was Bessie Bellwood, who may have started her working life as a rabbit skinner in the New Cut, working in one of the most unpleasant and exploitative sweated trades in the vicinity of the notoriously rough street market.[94] Hyram Travers was a shipyard ironworker from East London, and Kate Carney came from a music hall family, although she was sent to work as a milliner by her mother (who was desperate to keep her out of the halls) and thereby claimed to know the life of the 'working girl' that she depicted.[95] Gus Elen came from a working-class background and worked variously as an egg packer and a draper's assistant while he performed in singing saloons in the evening, trying to establish himself as a performer.[96] However, none of these singers seemed tempted to carry their actual occupation or origin with them on to the stage – they chose instead a costermonger persona, unequivocally working-class but which came ready-made with an element of flamboyant performativity and visible social identity, a voice and a look. W. Macqueen-Pope's nostalgic and eulogistic description of Carney situated her within this identity, claiming that she represented street people,

> who wore their own type of clothes ... who faced their difficulties with a laugh and a joke ... whose idea of revelry was to change hats and do a special kind of tribal dance sacred to the coster ... and who spoke their own tongue with their own accent and had their own native slang.[97]

Carney had clearly, for Macqueen-Pope, become the thing she performed for so long, the very type of the working-class Londoner represented best of all by the costermonger on the street. The stage costermonger started as an act, the adoption of a stock character. It became enormously successful, and the following analysis of the three best-known costermonger performers, with examples of their hit songs, attempts to ascertain why.

Albert Chevalier was the best-known of the music hall acts who performed costermonger characters, a huge star in his day and a figure widely discussed in the historiography of the music hall, largely, in more recent works, as the most prominent example of the appropriation of working-class characters by bourgeois performers. Chevalier was very far in social origin from the characters he portrayed: he was born in London into a middle-class family (his French father was a teacher of languages), and spent the early part of his career, with reasonable success, as a straight actor on the 'legitimate' stage. He wrote and performed cockney-costermonger songs for his own amusement and that of friends, and it was only in 1891 that he tried these out in public, in the music hall. There followed a string of hits, written by Chevalier, often in partnership with other writers, several of which are among the best-remembered artefacts of the music hall cockney-costermonger genre. The cover artwork for an 1890s collection of Chevalier's songs depicts him as an artist in a studio, an impeccably dressed middle-class gentleman (albeit with the exaggeratedly large head of the caricature mode) – suave, refined and upright (see plate 8). His costermonger creations are shown in paintings and drawings around him, to one of which he is about to apply a dab of paint. The implication is clear: Chevalier as artist created his costermonger characters in their pearly suits, but distinguished himself from them socially. The slouching pose and leering expression of the costermonger character on which the artist Chevalier works is reminiscent of the costermonger as a 'distinct race', marked by physical difference.

This complex image supports the view of Chevalier as originator of the costermonger-cockney as 'replicant', a middle-class, sentimentalised impersonation of the costermonger that downplayed the less palatable aspects of street-selling life, and introduced strong strains of both humour and pathos.

The pathos is most vehemently expressed in Chevalier's song 'My Old Dutch', in which an elderly costermonger looks back on his long years of marriage to his 'dutch' or wife:

> We've been together now for forty years,
> An' it don't seem a day too much;
> There ain't a lady livin' in the land
> As I'd 'swop' for my dear old Dutch.[98]

The song ends by pushing sentiment to its maximum as the costermonger hopes that 'when we've to part, as part we must ... Death may come and take me fust': he can't bear to live without his 'pal'. The sentimentality of 'My Old Dutch' is unashamed, and effective, recalling Noel Coward's later epigram on the potency of 'cheap music'.

Some commentators, even in his own day, saw Chevalier's act as phoney, having little resemblance to any real character: William Archer described his 'representations of coster-life' as 'either absolutely trivial or grotesquely sentimentalised; they never get anywhere near the essence of their subject'.[99] Others, however, claimed for him a realism based on observation. A biography of 1895 quotes a review that likens Chevalier's work to the 'human documents' of the French realist novelist Emile Zola, with Chevalier depicting 'a genuine type: the East-end costermonger in his habit as he lives'.[100] Chevalier himself claimed the source of his characters to be the people he saw and the conversations he overheard on the streets of London. His famous costume, a 'flash' suit trimmed with velvet and pearl buttons, was, he said, purchased from an East End tailor, and for an interview in the *Sketch* magazine he showed the reporter a handbill from this tailor.[101] This was written in terms reminiscent of the tailor's advertisement quoted by Henry Mayhew and discussed in Chapter 4, confirming that this mode of dress was an established style and was not invented by Chevalier (although he may well have exaggerated it). Chevalier acknowledged the sentiment in his work, but identified it as a component of the realism, rather than being in contradiction to it. Writing in 1893, he judged that:

> the Variety audience ... are ready to digest some sentiment, some traits of deeper human life with their fare now ... They recognise and want something that is true to human nature, up or down the scale, and, whether it be laughable or pathetic, it must in the main be true.[102]

The American journalist Richard Harding Davis's assessment of Chevalier's version of 'the life of the Whitechapel coster' compared it with Israel Zangwill's treatment of the same theme in his bleakly realist novel, *The Children of the Ghetto* (1892), concluding that 'both are true and both untrue as showing only one side'.[103]

The most effective strategy in assessing Chevalier lies not in measuring either the distance of his origins from the characters he portrayed, or the realism or otherwise of those characters, but in considering the response of his audiences. His characters may have been only partially related to any figure to be found in London's street markets, but whether wholly 'true' or not, the very success of Chevalier's songs suggests that they connected with those who heard them, expressing something that London audiences *wanted* to be true, or found interesting or amusing. Harding Davis noted that Chevalier and the working-class parts of his audience were of 'wholly different class', but that the songs nevertheless 'were hailed and adopted unanimously by the people of the class about which they were written', citing as a parallel the adoption by British soldiers in India of Kipling's 'Barrack Room Ballads'.[104] A song does not have to originate within a community in order to take deep root there, and popular songs may be simultaneously open to 'sentimental and commercial appropriation' *and* possessed of 'a particular resonance' with their audiences.[105]

Bailey's idea of a culture of competence helps us to explain how the working-class sections of Chevalier's audience recognised themselves in his songs, which included comic as well as sentimental creations. 'Knock'd 'em in the Old Kent Road' cheerfully satirises a working-class couple who inherit a 'donkey shay' (a costermonger's donkey and cart), and come in for mockery from their neighbours for this rise in their fortunes and their adventures with the stubborn donkey. The chorus demonstrates how an audience might be invited to laugh both *with* and *at* the competence of the performed character, who simultaneously satirises and celebrates his own good fortune:

> 'Wot cher!' All the neighbours cried,
> 'Who're yer goin' to meet, Bill?
> Have yer bought the street, Bill?'
> Laugh! I thought I should 'ave died,
> Knock'd 'em in the Old Kent Road.[106]

Apart from his appeal to the working classes, we can also credit Chevalier with moving the figure of the costermonger more widely into mainstream culture, making the type palatable to a cross-class audience from his base in the music halls. He even performed in fashionable West End drawing rooms, as illustrated in the *Graphic* in 1892 (see figure 36). Chevalier, as a middle-class actor portraying a costermonger, was a safe importation into this grand, upper-class setting. The move lacked the dangerous frisson of George Augustus Sala's trip to the New Cut, and aligns with Stallybrass and White's view that 'carnival was too disgusting for bourgeois life to endure except as sentimental spectacle'.[107] The fact that Chevalier's tamed version of the working-class figure of the costermonger was now an acceptable source of amusement and sentiment in this milieu shows how he smoothed the way for the costermonger-cockney to move confidently into place as the accepted mythic centre of London working-class character, a portrayal that was to be repeated again and again in the following decades. Chevalier's act was a very long way from Mayhew's delineation of this class as a threatening problem half a century or more before,

36 'Mr Albert Chevalier singing one of his coster songs in a West-End drawing-room', *The Graphic*, 29 October 1892

although it had precedents in James Greenwood's journalistic versions of the costermonger-cockney from the 1860s and 1870s.

In the historiography of the music hall, if Chevalier is often criticised as an 'inauthentic' version of the costermonger, then Gus Elen, who also performed a string of costermonger hits from the early 1890s onwards, is seen to 'pass the acid test of putative authenticity', with his preference for 'the sardonic over the sentimental'.[108] One of Elen's most popular songs was 'If It Wasn't for the 'Ouses in Between' (see plate 9), the tale of a costermonger living in cramped conditions in the East End of London who nevertheless aspires to create a rural idyll in his back yard.[109] The song sets up many layers of improbability in the coster's claim to have a 'wery pretty garden', describing how he plants out unsold vegetables, teaches his donkey to moo like a cow, and recreates a comic approximation of a beehive with 'beetles in a pail'. The view from this ersatz cottage garden is appropriately expansive, or at least potentially so: all it would take, it is claimed, is 'a ladder and some glasses' (field glasses or binoculars) to 'see to 'Ackney Marshes' (the nearest open space to the East End of London, but hardly rolling countryside). However, the final impediment to the comically exaggerated rural pretensions of the costermonger furnishes the punchline to every verse – 'if it wasn't for the 'ouses in between'. Even with the help of the ladder and glasses, the view is blocked by intervening urban sprawl. The song manages to be both touching in its modest aspirations to a country life, and humorous in the gap – or multiple gaps – between what is claimed and what is real.

The inventiveness, persistence and self-aware humour with which the costermonger pursues his *rus in urb* project echoes Bailey's culture of competence. It also draws on the connection, however attenuated, between country and city. George Dodd's *The Food of London* (1856) captures the moment at which railway transport and the growing size of London determined that those street sellers who had once sourced food directly in the rural periphery to trade into the city no longer did so: the wholesale markets took over entirely the role of importing supplies, and the street sellers distributed them from there.[110] Nevertheless, as Stallybrass and White note, the market is always the sign and the means of the connection between the city's centre and its periphery: it might be located deep within the city, but it is also marginal, as the meeting point between inside and outside.[111] The costermongers and street sellers continued to be perceived as the conduit by which fruit and vegetables were circulated from London's productive hinterland into its congested streets, the marginality of the role doubly emphasised by the street markets' informality. In Elen's song the costermonger is comically aware of his position betwixt and between city and country, and 'If It Wasn't for the 'Ouses in Between' is just the best-known of many songs that derived both humour and sentiment from the interstitial function of the market and the costermonger, between nature and culture. Other examples include Alec Hurley's 'My London Country Lane', which imagines the bucolic origins behind the goods for sale in Drury Lane, and Chevalier's 'My Country Cousin', which compares city and country, to the city's advantage.[112] There was a rich vein of humour and pathos in this subject. One of its roots lay in the mid-nineteenth-century free-and-easy predecessors of the music hall where, as Phil Eva has shown, nostalgic Irish songs of exile were resonant for urban English audiences alienated and distressed by the dislocations brought by rapid urbanisation.[113]

Kate Carney started her career as a stage costermonger at almost the same time as Chevalier and Elen, but she carried on longer than either, until the late 1940s. She was called variously the 'Queen of Cockneys', 'London's coster queen', 'the female Chevalier' or even 'the spindle side of the submerged tenth' (a reference to the 'residuum' or underclass that was identified among London's casually employed and semi-criminal poor in the late nineteenth century).[114] Carney often performed with a costermonger's barrow on stage (and sometimes even a donkey), in character as a seller of oysters and whelks, hot potatoes or flowers.[115] Her costume frequently featured plentiful pearl buttons and feathers in her hat (see figure 37).[116]

37 Kate Carney in costume as a costermonger, 1890s

Carney's first big success was scored in the mid-1890s with a song called 'When the Summer Comes Again', or 'Three Pots a Shilling' (plate 10). This starts in the mode of a conventionally polite drawing room ballad, sung by Carney in the voice of a male costermonger describing how he and his sweetheart (also a costermonger) will leave the city and roam the countryside, selling flowers. As Peter Bailey has pointed out, 'the content of a song or act ... was important, but its resonance with an audience was inseparable from the manner of its performance'. Lyrics from song-sheets alone cannot tell the whole story and we have to imagine the stage business and inflection, the 'knowingness' that accompanied and emphasised the published lyrics. These lyrics suggest that Carney commenced her performance in the sweetly romantic drawing-room mode (although here she is ventriloquising the male costermonger) – 'When the summer comes again, and the pretty flowr's are growing;/ The sunshine after rain, the summer breezes blowing;/ Then to roam around the country with a girl who's ever willing' – before, half way through the final line, upping the volume and transitioning to a full-bodied market cry, in the voice of the female costermonger: 'I can buy and she can cry, "Three pots a shilling"'. The joke lay in the transition from one social situation or voice to another in the 'serio-comic' mode that was exploited by female performers in particular,[117] and which veered wildly between the sentimental and conventional, and the ribald and subversive. In Carney's song this contrast is expressed in the jump from the modest and modulated drawing-room ballad to the market voice of the cry, uninhibited, immoderate and commercial in intent. The diarist Fred Bason, who saw Carney perform many times, described her as 'a big fat plain looking woman with a big chest and a large heart ... She had a loud voice and loud ways.'[118] 'Three Pots a Shilling' engages in the ancient and moralising strain of humour that finds amusement in a woman (and particularly a large woman) being unrestrainedly noisy – a version of Bakhtin's female grotesque. The noisy woman is frequently located in the marketplace; George Augustus Sala described with heavy sarcasm the 'pleasant cataract of "chaff" [that] comes plashing down' between a fishwife and a costermonger in Billingsgate market, with similar humorous intent.[119] George Bernard Shaw, in *Pygmalion*, takes a street flower seller and constructs humour and drama from the attempt to teach her to leave behind her market voice.

Carney's approach was a knowing one, so that many members of the audience would recognise how, as well as the 'low' spectacle of the noisy woman, the market cry signalled the realities of life and exposed the thin sentimentality of a drawing-room gentility that was only available to a minority of women with social and economic privilege.[120] The fact that the joke worked, on all its levels, is emphasised not just by the popularity of the song, which was a staple of Carney's act throughout her long career, but also by the fact that she repeated the strategy in another song, this time in character as an oyster seller. This has a four-line chorus with exactly the same structure; the first three lines are in conventional drawing-room mode ('stars are peeping' and 'cloud is creeping') before it ends with a rousing cry of 'sixpence the half-a-dozen'.[121] On this song's published sheet music (see plate 11), the illustrated cover shows Carney making an inviting gesture to her stall, but the loud cry is transferred to the figure of a young boy, who has his hand cupped around his gaping mouth. This was perhaps an attempt on the part of the artist to visually mute the impact of Carney's market cries – demonstrating the contested nature of noise in the marketplace, particularly, in this instance, in relation to gender.

The costermonger and the street seller were a rich source for the construction of music hall characters because of the distinctive nature of the informal street cultures, populated by types with a well-established reputation for independence and self-determination, for their noisy, performative and visually spectacular command of certain streets, their reputation for resilience and humour. Performers such as Chevalier, Elen and Carney dramatised, exaggerated, sentimentalised and mythologised the street seller, in representations that were both visual and linguistic, shaped in costume, in animating gesture and the words of their songs. One final example is a song by Vesta Victoria, who adopted, like Kate Carney, the female market voice. The character Victoria performs is a costermonger girl from the East End of London who attempts to describe a visit to the country.[122] She can only speak of what she sees with reference to what she knows, and her starting point for naming each place, plant and animal is the city site it resembles or the market commodity that is its analogue (complete with price). Thus lambs are described as 'sheeps' heads with their bodies on … skipping all the day', and cows are an agglomeration of 'cowheels' and 'rumps' at 'fourteen pence a pound'. The ground is inexplicably stuffed with 'three-pound-tuppence 'taturs', and the whole is summed up in the punchline repeated at the end of each verse: 'Well it's absolutely 'Ackney with the 'ouses took away'. The direction of her understanding reverses the flow of the commodity, pushing it back from market to farm, so that the world is turned upside down, culture becomes prior to nature – and the costermonger is not merely a liminal figure who carries the country and its produce into the city, but also infects the rural world with the market voice. It was this market voice that became the most powerful characteristic in the representation of working-class London into the interwar period and beyond.

* * *

The music hall acts that performed the costermongers on the stage hybridised with other developing forms of mass culture and entertainment, as variety performance was taken up in film and radio (and eventually television), before in the end being eclipsed by them all. As early as 1915 Albert Chevalier starred in a film melodrama based on his hit song 'My Old Dutch', with a reviewer for *Variety* magazine claiming that at a press screening 'there was not a dry eye in the whole assemblage'.[123] This film was remade twice, in 1926 and 1934, as the costermonger-cockney type was seized upon in performance over and over again, in the music hall and beyond.[124] One of its most notable versions came in 1937 when a new West End musical opened which featured comic actor Lupino Lane as Bill Snibson, a Lambeth costermonger who unexpectedly finds that he is heir to an aristocratic title and a country estate.[125] *Me and My Girl*'s big number was 'The Lambeth Walk', a song named after a market street.[126] The street market in Lambeth Walk, close to the south bank of the Thames, probably dated from the 1860s and had 91 stalls when London County Council surveyed it in 1893.[127] When Lambeth borough council issued licences there in 1928, 151 marked pitches were occupied by sellers of goods from fruit to furniture: this was the supposed setting for the market scenes in *Me and My Girl*.[128] The Lambeth Walk also referred, supposedly, to a distinctive physical characteristic of the people of the streets and street markets of London, a mode of moving and occupying space. 'While he sings, Lupino Lane walks up and down the stage with a swagger and roll of the shoulders which represents the cockney walk' (see plate 12), reported an essay by Mass Observation, which researched the subject as part of its large-scale ethnography of British everyday life.[129] Mass Observation captured in detail how the Lambeth Walk grew into a dance craze that swept Britain and then the world in 1938, after choreographer Adele England invented steps to go with the song and taught them to dancers in the Locarno chain of ballrooms. In 1939 photographer Bill Brandt pictured a girl on an East End street performing the dance for the amusement of her friends (figure 38).

Mass Observation attributed the success of the Lambeth Walk to multiple origins – Lupino Lane and Adele England, the song's composers, the 'cockneys of Lambeth and elsewhere whose walk Lane imitated', and the BBC and the newspapers that drove the craze by reporting on it. Their ethnographic observers documented the trajectory of the song and dance as it spread, recording where people thought it had come from; some knew about *Me and My Girl*, whereas others assumed origins going directly back to 'authentic' cockney traditions: 'I understand the Lambeth Walk is a coster dance, and I imagine it originated with the costers and girls promenading.'[130] Many of the people Mass Observation questioned liked the Lambeth Walk, but a significant proportion did not, and were suspicious of its role in articulating class relations:

> I resent … the presentation of the personal life of the lower classes as being amusing. It leads to the viewing of slum-life with all its poverty, dirt and misery through the rosy spectacles of the wise-cracking Cockney and the glamorous Pearly King. It is a common dodge to make us laugh at our miseries and put them out of mind that way.[131]

Yet if the Lambeth Walk trivialised the working classes (and it is interesting to note how the pearly king was a figure of suspicion in this respect), it also satirised the aristocracy. In the play, Bill Snibson's snooty new associates are eventually drawn into 'doing the Lambeth Walk' themselves, and surrendering their upper-class manners and inhibitions. As Raphael Samuel and Alison Light have noted, *Me and My Girl* 're-enacted, albeit in the setting of the theatre rather

38 Bill Brandt, 'East End Girl Dancing the "Lambeth Walk"', 1939

than that of the market place … the enthronement of the Lord of Misrule'.¹³² Mass Observation reported that many of those who liked the Lambeth Walk did so because of the dance's informality – its impromptu nature and the scope for free interpretations of the dance steps: 'I have danced the Lambeth Walk several times, and rather like it. Its main appeal is in its informality. I cannot do better than quote the words of the lyric, "Everything's free and easy".'¹³³ The informality alluded to here is a rather more general social characteristic than the legal, economic and subsequently cultural informality through which I have examined the street markets, but nonetheless it shares certain features with it, in self-determination and a relaxed attitude to set rules.

The other feature that lay behind the popularity of the Lambeth Walk was that, as well as a dance, it was also a performance. Dancers imitated the character of the costermonger-cockney, and even vocalised it with repeated exclamations of 'Oi!' at various punctuation points in the song and the dance. 'A big proportion of observers mentioned as an outstanding feature of the dance that it includes gesture, speech and action, and is therefore more like acting or impersonation than other dances.'[134] Mass Observation reported how, in the summer of 1938, dancers of all classes, including guests at a 'big private do' in Carlton House Terrace, Mayfair, enjoyed not just watching the performance of the street market, as they had with Albert Chevalier's drawing room performance of 1892, but joining in with it too.

In 1939 *Me and My Girl* was made into a film, retitled *The Lambeth Walk*, and the popularity of the Lambeth Walk as a dance continued into the war years.[135] As Samuel and Light note, '*Me and My Girl* rehearses what was to be a major theme of wartime propaganda – cross-class fraternization – "all in it together", and the pleasing illusion that "ordinary people" had come into their own'.[136] This was the continued trajectory of the costermonger-cockney into the postwar period, in a succession of representations and performances that continue down to the street market in the BBC soap opera *Eastenders*, and which have all kept a certain sort of London identity pinned to characteristics plucked from or inspired by the street market and the costermonger – or perhaps just imagined using these raw materials as a starting point.

Notes

1 M. de Certeau, L. Giard and P. Mayol, *The Practice of Everyday Life*, Vol. 2, trans. T. J. Tomasik (Minneapolis, MN: University of Minnesota Press, 1998), p. 107.
2 M. Benedetta, *The Street Markets of London* (London: John Miles, 1936), p. 178.
3 J.-C. Agnew, *Worlds Apart: The Market and the Theatre in Anglo-American Thought, 1550–1750* (Cambridge: Cambridge University Press, 1986), p. 34; M. Casson and J. S. Lee, 'The origin and development of markets: a business history perspective', *Business History Review*, 85 (2011), 9–37, p. 16.
4 For an early and clear definition of the coexistence and overlap of market and fair in the developing medieval city, see H. Pirenne, 'Medieval cities' (1925), in R. T. LeGates and F. Stout (eds), *The City Reader* (London: Routledge, 2016), p. 48.
5 G. Sims, *How the Poor Live* (London: Chatto and Windus, 1883), p. 49.
6 G. A. Sala, *Twice Round the Clock: or the Hours of the Day and Night in London* (London: J. and R. Maxwell, 1859), p. 274.
7 Agnew, *Worlds Apart*, p. 40.
8 M. Bakhtin, *Rabelais and his World*, trans. H. Iswolsky (Bloomington, IN: Indiana

University Press, 1984 [1965]). See, for instance, p. 146, where all three terms are deployed in a single paragraph.

9 English translations of Bakhtin denote this language with a word derived from one of London's oldest authorised markets, the fish market at Billingsgate. The original Russian text uses a more general term describing obscene language as the speech genre of the market square or marketplace. The fact that English translators had the term 'billingsgate' to draw upon to name a certain sort of speech indicates an association in English of markets with rough language that coincides both with Bakhtin's analysis and Rabelais's joyful immersion in the colourful language of the marketplace. (I am very grateful to Professor Craig Brandist at the University of Sheffield's Bakhtin Centre for guidance on this point.)
10 Bakhtin, *Rabelais*, pp. 153–4, 160.
11 P. Stallybrass and A. White, *The Politics and Poetics of Transgression* (London: Routledge, 1986).
12 P. Joyce, *The Rule of Freedom: Liberalism and the Modern City* (London: Verso, 2003), pp. 77–80. See also I. MacLachlan, 'A bloody offal nuisance: the persistence of private slaughter-houses in nineteenth-century London', *Urban History*, 34 (2007); and C. Otter, 'Cleansing and clarifying: technology and perception in nineteenth-century London', *Journal of British Studies*, 43 (2004).
13 Joyce, *Rule of Freedom*, pp. 76–82.
14 T. Eagleton, in Stallybrass and White, *Politics and Poetics*, p. 13.
15 Stallybrass and White, *Politics and Poetics*, pp. 3, 19.
16 Stallybrass and White, *Politics and Poetics*, pp. 176–9; C. Dickens, *Sketches by Boz* (London: Chapman and Hall, 1854 [1839]), pp. 67–71; J. Greenwood, *Low-Life Deeps: An Account of the Strange Fish to be Found There* (London: Chatto and Windus, 1876), p. 308.
17 Stallybrass and White, *Politics and Poetics*, p. 178.
18 Bakhtin, *Rabelais*, pp. 6, 10.
19 Stallybrass and White, *Politics and Poetics*, pp. 35–8.
20 Bakhtin, *Rabelais*, p. 10.
21 Sala, *Twice Round the Clock*, p. 274.
22 Sala, *Twice Round the Clock*, pp. 268–75.
23 Stallybrass and White, *Politics and Poetics*, p. 5.
24 G. B. Shaw, *Pygmalion: A Romance in Five Acts* (London: Longmans, Green, 1957 [1913]), p. 26.
25 R. Harding Davis, *Our English Cousins* (New York: Harper and Brothers, 1894), p. 215.
26 'Saturday Night in the East End', *Good Words*, November 1868, p. 695.
27 'Saturday Night in the East End', p. 696.
28 Stallybrass and White, *Politics and Poetics*, p. 191.
29 Stallybrass and White, *Politics and Poetics*, p. 30.
30 Stallybrass and White, *Politics and Poetics*, p. 27.
31 D. Scannell, *Mother Knew Best: An East-End Childhood* (London: Pan, 1975), p. 34.
32 Scannell, *Mother Knew Best*, p. 36.
33 B. Magee, *Clouds of Glory: A Hoxton Childhood* (London: Pimlico, 2004), p. 56.
34 C. Booth, *Life and Labour of the People in London*, Series I, Vol. I (London: Macmillan, 1902–03), p. 68.

35 Magee, *Clouds of Glory*, pp. 61–2.
36 M. M. Smith, *Sensing the Past: Seeing, Hearing, Smelling, Tasting, and Touching in History* (Berkeley, CA: University of California Press, 2007), p. 9.
37 Magee, *Clouds of Glory*, pp. 55–60.
38 A. Corbin, *Village Bells: Sound and Meaning in the Nineteenth-century French Countryside*, trans. M. Thom (New York: Columbia University Press, 1998), pp. 95–6.
39 G. Gissing, *Workers in the Dawn*, Vol. I (London: Remington, 1880), p. 1. For similar accounts, see, for instance, Sims, *How the Poor Live*, p. 49; Booth, *Life and Labour*, Series I, Vol. I, p. 182.
40 A. Corbin, 'Charting the cultural history of the senses', in D. Howes (ed.), *Empire of the Senses: The Sensual Culture Reader* (Oxford: Berg, 2005), pp. 128–39.
41 M. Paterson, 'Haptic geographies: ethnography, haptic knowledges and sensuous dispositions', *Progress in Human Geography*, 33.6 (2009), 766–88, p. 771.
42 J. Winter, *London's Teeming Streets 1830–1914* (London: Routledge, 1993), p. 69.
43 A London Physician, *The Nuisance of Street Music; Or a Plea for the Sick, the Sensitive and the Studious* (London: Henry Renshaw, 1869), p. 4.
44 P. Bailey, *Popular Culture and Performance in the Victorian City* (Cambridge: Cambridge University Press, 1998), p. 201.
45 Bakhtin, *Rabelais*, p. 182.
46 *Londres, manuel du voyageur* (Coblenz: K. Bædeker, 1866), pp. xxiii–xxiv, translated by the author.
47 *Londres, manuel du voyageur*, pp. xxiii–xxiv.
48 T. Richards, *The Commodity Culture of Victorian England: Advertising and Spectacle 1851–1914* (London: Verso, 1991), pp. 249–51.
49 I. Armstrong, *Victorian Glassworlds: Glass, Culture and the Imagination 1830–1860* (Oxford: Oxford University Press, 2008), p. 139.
50 Scannell, *Mother Knew Best*, pp. 37, 38, 40.
51 Magee, *Clouds of Glory*, pp. 58–9.
52 I. F. Marcosson, *Wherever Men Trade: The Romance of the Cash Register* (New York: Dodd, Mead, 1945), p. 6.
53 'Wings of business' (advertising brochure for Lamson pneumatic cash handling system), Harrods Archive.
54 Corbin, 'Cultural history of the senses', p. 137.
55 'The Bye-laws of Columbia Square Market', printed poster, Tower Hamlets Local History Library and Archives, Press Cuttings Box 652.3–652.34, 1869.
56 Bakhtin, *Rabelais*, p. 187.
57 Columbia Market Bye-laws.
58 Harding Davis, *Our English Cousins*, p. 218.
59 Bakhtin, *Rabelais*, p. 319.
60 Corbin, 'Cultural history of the senses', p. 137.
61 Harding Davis, *Our English Cousins*, p. 216.
62 Scannell, *Mother Knew Best*, pp. 39–40.
63 R. Finn, *No Tears in Aldgate* (London: Robert Hale, 1963), pp. 41–2.
64 P. Bailey (ed.), *Music Hall: The Business of Pleasure* (Milton Keynes: Open University Press, 1986), p. xviii.
65 Scannell, *Mother Knew Best*, p. 36.
66 T. Burke, *Nights in London* (New York: Henry Holt, 1918), p. 148.

67 Bailey, *Popular Culture*, pp. 131–2.
68 J. Ewing Ritchie, *The Night Side of London* (London: William Tweedie, 1857), pp. 195–6.
69 Bailey (ed.), *Music Hall*, p. x.
70 A. Chevalier, 'On costers and music halls', *The English Illustrated Magazine*, April 1893, pp. 480, 488; 'A chat with Hyram Travers', *Era*, 19 October 1895, p. 17.
71 Chevalier, 'On costers', p. 479.
72 W. Archer, 'The music hall: past and future', *Living Age*, autumn 1916, p. 99.
73 W. Archer, 'The county council and the music halls', *Contemporary Review*, March 1895, pp. 317–21; H. G. Hibbert, *Fifty Years of a Londoner's Life* (London: Grant Richards, 1916), p. 33.
74 Archer, 'Music hall', p. 99; Archer 'County council', pp. 318–19; see also C. Radcliffe, 'Theatrical hierarchy, cultural capital and the legitimate/illegitimate divide', in P. Yeandle, K. Newey and J. Richards (eds), *Politics, Performance and Popular Culture* (Manchester: Manchester University Press, 2016), pp. 75–95.
75 Chevalier, 'On costers', p. 481.
76 Bailey, *Popular Culture*, p. 133.
77 H. Mayhew, *London Labour and the London Poor*, Vol. I (London: Griffin, Bohn and Co., 1861 [1851]), p. 40.
78 G. Stedman Jones, 'Working-class culture and working-class politics in London: notes on the remaking of a working class', *Journal of Social History*, 7.4 (1974), 460–508; Bailey (ed.), *Music Hall*, p. xviii.
79 Bailey, *Popular Culture*, p. 128.
80 Bailey, *Popular Culture*, p. 149.
81 A. Bennett, *Journals*, 2 January 1910, extracted in T. Elborough and N. Rennison (eds), *A London Year: 365 Days of City Life in Diaries, Journals and Letters* (London: Frances Lincoln, 2013), p. 16.
82 D. B. Scott, 'The music-hall cockney: flesh and blood, or replicant?', *Music & Letters*, 83.2 (2002), 237–58; Bailey, *Popular Culture*, p. 137.
83 G. Le Roy, *Music Hall Stars of the Nineties* (London: British Technical and General Press, 1952).
84 Le Roy, *Music Hall Stars of the Nineties*.
85 'A chat with Hyram Travers', p. 17; R. A. Baker, *British Music Hall: An Illustrated History* (Barnsley: Pen and Sword History: 2014), pp. 18–19; R. H. Lindo, 'The Coster's Confession', sung by Fanny Wentworth (London: Francis, Day and Hunter, 1895); F. Egerton, 'A Costermonger's Wife', sung by J.W. Rowley (London: Francis, Day and Hunter, 1894).
86 Baker, *British Music Hall*, pp. 18–19.
87 W. Herbert, 'What Cheer 'Ria', sung by Bessie Bellwood (London: Hopwood and Crew, 1887).
88 'A chat with Hyram Travers', p. 17.
89 Chevalier, 'On costers', p. 482.
90 W. Macqueen-Pope, *The Melodies Linger On: The Story of Music Hall* (London: W. H. Allen, 1950), pp. 342–3.
91 Various press cuttings, Albert Chevalier biographical file, Victoria and Albert Museum Theatre and Performance Archive.
92 T. Barker, 'Gus Elen', typescript biography, Gus Elen biographical file, Victoria and

Albert Museum Theatre and Performance Archive, p. 86; Baker, *British Music Hall*, pp. 175–6.
93 C. Collins and E. Bateman, 'The New Cut Coon', sung by Gus Elen (London: Francis, Day and Hunter, 1899).
94 Hibbert, *Fifty Years*, p. 55.
95 'A chat with Hyram Travers', p. 17; Baker, *British Music Hall*, p. 175.
96 T. Barker, 'Gus Elen', typescript biography, Gus Elen biographical file, Victoria and Albert Museum Theatre and Performance Archive.
97 Macqueen-Pope, *The Melodies Linger On*, pp. 342–3.
98 A. Chevalier and C. Ingle, 'My Old Dutch', sung by Albert Chevalier (London: Reynolds, 1893).
99 Archer, 'County council', p. 326.
100 A. Chevalier (with Brian Daly), *Albert Chevalier, A Record by Himself* (London: John MacQueen, 1895), p. 116–7.
101 'Mr Albert Chevalier', *Sketch*, 24 May 1893, p. 179.
102 Chevalier, 'On costers', p. 487.
103 Harding Davis, *Our English Cousins*, p. 227.
104 Harding Davis, *Our English Cousins*, p. 28; Kipling was an admirer of the music hall and the cockney-costermonger performers (P. J. Keating, *The Working Classes in Victorian Fiction* (London: Routledge and Kegan Paul, 1971), pp. 159–61).
105 P. Eva, 'Home sweet home? The "culture of exile" in mid-Victorian popular song', *Popular Music*, 16.2 (1997), 131–50, p. 14.
106 C. Chevalier and C. Ingle, 'Wot cher! Or, Knock'd 'em in the Old Kent Road', sung by Albert Chevalier (London: Reynolds, 1892).
107 Stallybrass and White, *Politics and Poetics*, p. 183.
108 Bailey, *Popular Culture*, p. 129.
109 G. Le Brunn and E. Bateman, 'If it Wasn't for the 'Ouses in Between', sung by Gus Elen (London: Francis, Day and Hunter, 1894).
110 G. Dodd, *The Food of London* (London: Longman, Brown, Green, and Longmans, 1856), pp. 521–2, 379–80.
111 Stallybrass and White, *Politics and Poetics*, p. 27; see also Agnew, *Worlds Apart*, pp. 22–3.
112 E. Bateman and A. Perry, 'My London Country Lane', sung by Alec Hurley (London: Francis, Day and Hunter, 1900); A. Chevalier and A. H. West, 'My Country Cousin', sung by Albert Chevalier (London: Reynolds, 1894).
113 Eva, 'Home sweet home?'
114 'Miss Kate Carney at Bristol', *Bristol Mercury*, quoted in the *Era*, 1 October 1898, p. 18; 'Kate Carney and crooners', *Telegraph*, 7 October 1935 (unpaginated press cutting in Kate Carney biographical file, V&A Theatre and Performance Archive); 'Kate Carney at the Met', *Era*, 5 December 1934, p. 17; 'The Standard', *Era*, 27 July 1895, p. 14.
115 'The Standard', p. 14; 'The music halls', *Lloyd's Weekly Newspaper*, 1 January 1899, p. 7; 'Miss Kate Carney at Bristol', p. 18.
116 '50 years of Kate', *The Illustrated*, 3 April 1948, p. 16.
117 Hibbert, *Fifty Years*, pp. 35–6.
118 F. Bason, *Diary*, 3 January 1950, extracted in Elborough and Rennison (eds), *A London Year*, p. 18.

119 Sala, *Twice Round the Clock*, p. 14.
120 For examples of drawing-room ballad lyrics, see D. B. Scott, *The Singing Bourgeois: Songs of the Victorian Drawing Room and Parlour* (Abingdon: Routledge, 2017 [1989]), ch. 3.
121 C. Collins, 'Sixpence the Half-a-dozen', sung by Kate Carney (London: Francis, Day and Hunter, 1898).
122 G. Le Brunn and E. Bateman, 'Ackney with the 'Ouses Took Away', sung by Vesta Victoria (London: Francis, Day and Hunter, 1900).
123 'Jolo', 'My Old Dutch', *Variety*, 2 July 1915, p. 19.
124 British Film Institute Online Collections (http://collections-search.bfi.org.uk/web).
125 C. Madge and T. Harrisson, 'Doing the Lambeth Walk', in *Britain by Mass Observation* (London: Faber and Faber, 2009 [1939]), pp. 140–1.
126 The music hall performer Alec Hurley had performed a different song also entitled 'The Lambeth Walk' in 1899 (Spellman Collection of Victorian Music Covers, University of Reading, accessed via VADS, www.vads.ac.uk).
127 London County Council Public Control Department, *London Markets, Special Report of the Public Control Committee Relative to Existing Markets and Market Rights and as to the Expediency of Establishing New Markets in or Near the Administrative County of London* (London: London County Council, 1893), Appendix B.
128 Appendix to Report on the Regulation of Street Trading, Lambeth Borough Council Town Clerk's Department Street Trading files, Lambeth Archives, MBL/TC/R/268, 1928.
129 Madge and Harrisson, 'Doing the Lambeth Walk', p. 141.
130 Madge and Harrisson, 'Doing the Lambeth Walk', p. 166.
131 Madge and Harrisson, 'Doing the Lambeth Walk', p. 169.
132 R. Samuel and A. Light, 'Doing the Lambeth Walk', in R. Samuel, *Theatres of Memory: Past and Present in Contemporary Culture* (London: Verso, 1994), p. 392.
133 Madge and Harrisson, 'Doing the Lambeth Walk', p. 171.
134 Madge and Harrisson, 'Doing the Lambeth Walk', p. 173.
135 *The Lambeth Walk*, directed by Albert de Courville, UK, 1939.
136 Samuel and Light, 'Doing the Lambeth Walk', p. 397.

Conclusion

In November 1868 *Good Words* magazine published a picture of an East End street market at night (see figure 1). I used this image at the outset, to accompany Henry Mayhew's description of a Saturday night street market, and it seems fitting to return to it to conclude, because it contains many of the themes that run through the history of the London street markets from the mid-nineteenth century onwards. The requisite cast of characters is here: the street sellers are represented by a costermonger selling fish, loudly crying his wares from a barrow, and a butcher – prosperous, sturdy and more than slightly menacing with his two sharp knives – who stands beside his counter. Customers are predominantly female, and suggest the market as the chief site of working-class consumption, a place where family budgets were deployed, perhaps recklessly, more often with care, and where some pleasure was to be found in the social interactions that took place around the act of shopping. It is a male figure who suggests sociability and pleasure most strongly, a working man who is cheerful in his enjoyment of the sensory stimulation and entertainment provided by the Saturday-night market. His stance (hands in pockets and pipe jutting) shows him to be at ease in experiencing the market as a space not just of exchange but also of leisure. A family of beggars occupies the foreground of the picture; we can't hide from the fact that the street market was a place where plenty and poverty collided, a mingling point of excess and abjection. This theme is reinforced by the aloof figure of an upper-class observer (perhaps a journalist like George Augustus Sala or James Greenwood), who has resorted to the street market for a thrilling, voyeuristic glimpse of working-class life that is both picturesque and degraded. As in so many depictions of the street markets, a police constable observes from the periphery, indicating that this is a place on the margins of legality, requiring surveillance.

The material culture of the scene is as suggestive as the people. The street is blocked by the market's bustle, which has substituted the circulation of traffic with that of goods, in a tangle of encounters. The scene is lit dramatically;

street lamps represent official light and order, but are less vivid than the costermonger's naphtha flare, with its spouting jet of naked flame. The products on display are heaped up and plentiful, although the picture gives away nothing as to their quality or price. Just meat and fish are shown here, but we have seen how London's street markets provided 'nearly everything required for personal consumption or home use'.[1] The costermonger's kerbside barrow is representative of his flexible and independent mode of business and his low overheads, while the butcher's counter opposite is the extension of a fixed shop out into the street. These two stalls together dramatise a potential conflict, the sometimes antagonistic relationship between street sellers and neighbouring rate-paying shopkeepers. For the customers, however, the two together provided a single retail environment, a rich mix of stalls and shops in which traditional modes of selling coexisted with newer ones, and where novel goods were increasingly to be found. From the mid-nineteenth to the mid-twentieth centuries the street markets were integrated into consumer modernity, not superseded by it – and recognising this fact allows us to see the geographies of London differently.

London's street markets, as I have argued throughout, can best be understood by recognising their informality, their position on the fringes of the normative structures of the law and the economy. Lacking legal frameworks and operating on the casual edges of the labour market, they were located in subaltern opposition to more dominant and recognised formal institutions – ancient and legally chartered authorised markets, permanent shop-based retailing, waged employment and prevailing conceptions of the street as a route of circulation. Yet I have tried to show how the street markets were not just peripheral but also central, deeply embedded in the life and economy of the city. They were informal, and informality may have been in opposition to the normative structures of formal institutions – but it was also utterly normal and ordinary for many people (as it continues to be in many contemporary societies). Throughout London, the everyday fabric of life was shaped as much by informal practices as by formal ones, and the street markets are the richest case study of this fact, opening up new views of the nineteenth- and early twentieth-century city.

The street markets were both humdrum and spectacular, and constituted the central node, meeting point and place of exchange in many urban localities. As such, they were culturally productive. Their informality produced a persistent impermanence, patterned by arrival and departure, with the temporary illumination of naphtha flares leading an array of sensory affects. They were peopled by costermongers who practised a performative mode of selling that used the voice as its chief means of promotion. Representations of the street markets and the street sellers generated performances in the music halls and set in motion a conveyor belt of characters, moving from the markets into wider culture and seeming to sum up the essential nature of the working-class Londoner as quick-witted, humorous, noisy, truculent, independent and resilient. The costermonger and street seller are members of a cast of traditional London 'types', alongside the city gent and the black cab driver, the London policeman and the East End gangster, and the market and its people continued to recur in creative depictions well beyond the chronological reach of this study.

Gareth Stedman Jones (whose work has been an important point of reference at many points in this research) wrote in the 1980s of his wariness of the cockney, the broader type wherein the costermonger is located as a central, defining figure. He was fearful of the stereotype – a nostalgic, conservative and sentimental version of the Londoner. This is an anxiety that has haunted me too in the writing of this book. The preconceptions that surround the subject have always made me nervous, and the one thing that I did not want to do was to produce a history that uncritically reproduced the London myth of the cockney market trader as a 'cheeky chappy', a 'wide boy' or a comic type, romantically and affectionately depicted in popular culture. Recognising (and critically dissecting) this cultural end-point of the street markets' story must be part of my analysis, but it is only part, and there is a great deal more to be said that is more complex and less comfortably familiar (or less uncomfortably clichéd).

As history, I hope that what I have said has avoided cliché: does it have any relevance as commentary on the present world (which all historical writing always contains, whether consciously or not)? Stedman Jones was writing in the 1980s, and the place of the cockney was unsure in the class and ethnic politics of that decade, seeming to signal a monolithic identity that was in the process of being rendered obsolete by multiculturalism and the reconfiguration of class. Three decades later a stuttering economy, the erosion of labour rights and the emergence of the urban 'precariat' have all served to make small-scale entrepreneurialism, on the streets or elsewhere, a topical issue, and not an inevitably nostalgic one. Stedman Jones raised the (for him) unresolved question of whether immigrants (he names the Irish and Jewish specifically) were incorporated into or excluded from the idea of the 'cockney'. I have argued that the historical street markets always retained the potential to hybridise culture across ethnicity, but in the present too mass movements of global migration again point to the persistence of the informal economy, and the relevance of recognising it as a means by which migrants support themselves and cultures mingle. I am loath to reach too confidently for simplistic parallels between the informality that burgeoned in the street markets of the 1850–1939 period and its contemporary repercussions; my chief aim has been to document and to a modest extent elucidate the historical subject of the London street market. In doing so, I have drawn attention to informal economic activities, to lives lived in robust disregard of legitimate and legally established categories and institutions. My claim is simply that such lives deserve to be noticed, and their potential for cultural fertility recognised – in the past and in the present.

Note

1 London County Council, *London Markets: Special Report of the Public Control Committee Relative to Existing Markets and Market Rights and as to the Expediency of Establishing New Markets in or Near the Administrative County of London* (London: London County Council, 1893), p. 56.

Select bibliography

Published primary sources

Anon., *The City of London: The Times Book* (London: Times Publishing, 1927)
Archer, W., 'The county council and the music halls', *Contemporary Review*, March 1895
Archer, W., 'The music hall: past and future', *Living Age*, autumn 1916
Baillie, E., *The Shabby Paradise: The Autobiography of a Decade* (London: Hutchinson, 1958)
Benedetta, M., *The Street Markets of London* (London: John Miles, 1936)
Booth, C., *Labour and Life of the People* (London: Williams and Norgate, 1889)
Booth, C., *Life and Labour of the People in London* (London: Macmillan, 1903)
Booth, W., *In Darkest England and the Way Out* (London: Salvation Army, 1890)
Bosanquet, H., *Rich and Poor* (London: Macmillan, 1896)
Burke, T., *The London Spy: A Book of Town Travels* (London: Thornton Butterworth, 1922)
Burke, T., *Nights in London* (New York: Henry Holt, 1918)
Chevalier, A. (with B. Daly), *Albert Chevalier, A Record by Himself* (London: John MacQueen, 1895)
Chevalier, A., *Before I Forget* (London: T. Fisher Unwin, 1901)
Chevalier, A., 'On costers and music halls', *The English Illustrated Magazine*, April 1893
Dickens, C., *Sketches by Boz* (London: Chapman and Hall, 1854 [1839])
Dickens, C., Jr, *Dickens's Dictionary of London* (London: Macmillan, 1879)
Dodd, G., *The Food of London* (London: Longman, Brown, Green, and Longmans, 1856)
Doré, G., and B. Jerrold, *London: A Pilgrimage* (London: Grant and Co., 1872)
Ewing Ritchie, J., *The Night Side of London* (London: William Tweedie, 1857)
Finn, R., *No Tears in Aldgate* (London: Robert Hale, 1963)
Flint, E., *Hot Bread and Chips* (London: Museum Press, 1963)
Foakes, G., *Between High Walls: A London Childhood* (London: Shepheard-Walwyn, 1972)
Fraser, J. F., 'Birmingham and its jewellery', *The Windsor Magazine*, 6 (1897), 463–73
Gissing, G., *Workers in the Dawn* (London: Remington, 1880)
Greenwood, J., 'Evidence to Food Committee', *Journal of the Society of Arts*, 27 December 1867
Greenwood, J., *Low-Life Deeps: An Account of the Strange Fish to be Found There* (London: Chatto and Windus, 1876)

Select bibliography

Greenwood, J., *Unsentimental Journeys: Or, Byways of the Modern Babylon* (London: Ward, Lock and Tyler, 1867)
Harding Davis, R., *Our English Cousins* (New York: Harper and Brothers, 1894)
Hartog, A., *Born to Sing: Memoirs of an East End Mantle Presser* (London: Brick Lane Books, 1979)
Hebert, L., *The Engineer's and Mechanic's Encyclopaedia* (London: Thomas Kelly, 1836)
Hibbert, H. G., *Fifty Years of a Londoner's Life* (London: Grant Richards, 1916)
Hotten, J. C., *The Slang Dictionary* (London: John Camden Hotten, 1869)
Jenkins, V., *Where I was Young* (London: Granada, 1976)
Knight, C., *Knight's Cyclopædia of London* (London: George Woodfall, 1851)
Le Roy, G., *Music Hall Stars of the Nineties* (London: British Technical and General Press, 1952)
London County Council Public Control Department, *London Markets, Special Report of the Public Control Committee Relative to Existing Markets and Market Rights and as to the Expediency of Establishing New Markets in or Near the Administrative County of London* (London: London County Council, 1893)
London County Council Public Control Department, *Street markets: report of the chief officer of the public control department as to the street markets in the county of London* (London: London County Council, 1901)
A London Physician, *The Nuisance of Street Music; Or a Plea for the Sick, the Sensitive and the Studious* (London: Henry Renshaw, 1869)
London School of Economics, *New Survey of London Life and Labour* (London: P. S. King, 1932)
Luckiesh, M., *Artificial Light: Its Influence Upon Civilization* (New York: Century, 1920)
Macqueen-Pope, W., *The Melodies Linger On: The Story of Music Hall* (London: W. H. Allen, 1950)
Madge, C., and T. Harrisson, 'Doing the Lambeth Walk', in *Britain by Mass Observation* (London: Faber and Faber, 2009 [1939])
Magee, B., *Clouds of Glory: A Hoxton Childhood* (London: Pimlico, 2004)
Malvery, O., *The Soul Market* (London: Hutchinson, 1907)
Mannin, E., *Confessions and Impressions* (London: Hutchinson, 1936 [1930])
Mayhew, H., *London Labour and the London Poor* (London: Griffin, Bohn and Co., 1861 [1851])
Meldola, R., *Coal and What We Get from It* (London: SPCK, 1891)
Miller, A., *The Earl of Petticoat Lane* (London: Random House, 2006)
Morton, H. V., *The Spell of London* (London: Methuen, 1935 [1926])
Page, W. (ed.), *The Victoria History of the County of Kent*, Vol. III (London: St Catherine's Press, 1932)
Parrish, H., *Pease and Chitty's Law of Markets and Fairs*, 2nd edn (London: Charles Knight and Co., 1958)
Passingham, W. J., *London's Markets: Their Origin and History* (London: Sampson Low, Marston, 1935)
Pease, J. G., and H. Chitty, *Law of Markets and Fairs* (London: Knight and Co., 1899)
Rag, Jack, *Streetology of London* (London: James S. Hodson, 1837)
Royal Commission on Alien Immigration (London: HMSO, 1903)
Royal Commission on Market Rights and Tolls (London: HMSO, 1891)
Sala, G. A., *Gaslight and Daylight* (London: Chapman and Hall, 1859)

Sala, G. A., *Twice Round the Clock: Or the Hours of the Day and Night in London* (London: J. and R. Maxwell, 1859)
Scannell, D., *Mother Knew Best: An East-End Childhood* (London: Pan, 1975)
Shaw, G. B., *Pygmalion: A Romance in Five Acts* (London: Longmans, Green, 1957 [1913])
Sims, G., *How the Poor Live* (London: Chatto and Windus, 1883)
Sims, G. (ed.), *Living London: Its Work and Its Play, Its Humour and Its Pathos, Its Sights and Its Scenes* (London: Cassell, 1901)
Smith, J. T., *The Cries of London: Itinerant Traders of Antient and Modern Times* (London: John Bowyer Nichols, 1839)
Southgate, W., *That's the Way it Was: A Working-class Autobiography, 1890–1950* (London: New Clarion Press/History Workshop, 1982)
Sullivan, J. W., *Markets for the People: The Consumer's Part* (New York: Macmillan, 1913)
Thomson, J., and A. Smith, *Street Life in London* (London: Sampson Low, Marston, Searle and Rivington, 1877)
Thornbury, W., and E. Walford, *Old and New London*, Vol. III (London: Cassell, Petter and Galpin, 1878)
Webb, S., *The Scandal of London's Markets*, Fabian Tract no. 36 (London: Fabian Society, 1891)
Woolf, V., 'The Oxford Street tide', in *The London Scene* (London: Snowbooks, 2004 [1932])

Archives

British Film Institute National Archive
British Library newspaper collections
British Library sheet music collections
Hansard: The Official Report of all Parliamentary Debates (https://hansard.parliament.uk/)
Lambeth Archives
Legislation.gov.uk: The Official Home of UK Legislation
Lewisham Local History and Archives Centre
London Metropolitan Archives
London School of Economics, Charles Booth Online Archive (http://booth.lse.ac.uk)
Tower Hamlets Local History Library and Archives (including records from the former London metropolitan boroughs of Bethnal Green, Stepney and Whitechapel)
Victoria and Albert Museum Theatre and Performance Archive
City of Westminster Archives Centre (including records from the former London metropolitan boroughs of Paddington, St Marylebone, and the City of Westminster)

Secondary sources

Agnew, J.-C., *Worlds Apart: The Market and the Theatre in Anglo-American Thought, 1550–1750* (Cambridge: Cambridge University Press, 1986)
Archer, I., C. Barron and V. Harding (eds), *Hugh Alley's Caveat: The Markets of London in 1598* (London: London Topographical Society, 1988)
Armstrong, I., *Victorian Glassworlds: Glass, Culture and the Imagination 1830–1860* (Oxford: Oxford University Press, 2008)

Select bibliography

Atkins, P. J., *Liquid Materialities: A History of Milk, Science and the Law* (Routledge: London, 2010)
Atkins, P. J., '"A tale of two cities": a comparison of food supply in London and Paris in the 1850s', in P. J. Atkins, P. Lummel and D. J. Oddy (eds), *Food and the City in Europe since 1800* (Abingdon: Routledge, 2016 [2007]), pp. 25–38
Bailey, P., *Popular Culture and Performance in the Victorian City* (Cambridge: Cambridge University Press, 1998)
Bailey, P. (ed.), *Music Hall: The Business of Pleasure* (Milton Keynes: Open University Press, 1986)
Baker, R. A., *British Music Hall: An Illustrated History* (Barnsley: Pen and Sword History, 2014)
Bakhtin, M., *Rabelais and his World*, trans. H. Iswolsky (Bloomington, IN: Indiana University Press, 1984 [1965])
Ball, M., and D. Sunderland, *An Economic History of London 1800–1914* (London: Routledge, 2001)
Basu, A., 'Immigrant entrepreneurs in the food sector: breaking the mould', in A. Kershen (ed.), *Food in the Migrant Experience* (Aldershot: Ashgate, 2002), pp. 149–71
Benson, J., *The Penny Capitalists: A Study of Nineteenth-century Working-class Entrepreneurs* (Dublin: Gill and Macmillan, 1983)
Benson, J., and G. Shaw (eds), *The Evolution of Retail Systems* (Leicester: Leicester University Press, 1992)
Benson, J., and G. Shaw (eds), *The Retailing Industry, Volume II: The Coming of the Mass Market 1800–1945* (London: I. B. Tauris, 1999)
Bille, M., and T. Flohr Sørensen, 'An anthropology of luminosity: the agency of light', *Journal of Material Culture*, 12.3 (2007), 263–84
Binder, P., *The Pearlies: A Social Record* (London: Jupiter Books, 1975)
Blackman, J., 'The food supply of an industrial town: a study of Sheffield's public markets 1780–1900', *Business History*, 5 (1963), 83–97
Boast, M., *The Story of Walworth* (London: London Borough of Southwark, 1993)
Breward, C., *Fashioning London: Clothing and the Modern Metropolis* (London: Berg, 2004)
Brodie, M., '"Jaunty individualists" or Labour activists? Costermongers, trade unions and the politics of the poor', *Labour History Review*, 66.2 (2001), 147–64
Brooks, P. F., *Pearly Kings and Queens in Britain* (Chichester: Barry Rose, 1974)
Buchner, T., and P. R. Hoffmann-Rehnitz (eds), *Shadow Economies and Irregular Work in Urban Europe, Sixteenth to Early Twentieth Centuries* (Vienna and Münster: Lit Verlag, 2011)
Burchell, G., C. Gordon and P. Miller (eds), *The Foucault Effect: Studies in Governmentality* (Chicago: University of Chicago Press, 1991)
Burnett, J., *Plenty and Want: A Social History of Food in England from 1815 to the Present Day* (London: Routledge, 1989 [1966])
Calaresu, M., and D. van den Heuvel (eds), *Food Hawkers: Selling in the Streets from Antiquity to the Present* (London: Routledge, 2016)
Carnevali, F., 'Luxury for the masses: jewellery and jewellers in London and Birmingham in the nineteenth century', *Entreprises et Histoire*, 46.1 (2007), 56–70
Casson, M., and J. S. Lee, 'The origin and development of markets: a business history perspective', *Business History Review*, 85 (2011), 9–37

de Certeau, M., L. Giard and P. Mayol, *The Practice of Everyday Life*, Vol. 2, trans. T. J. Tomasik (Minneapolis, MN: University of Minnesota Press, 1998)

Cleaver, T., 'Sic semper monopoliis: modernising the law of markets and fairs', Bar Council Law Reform Essay Competition winner 2009, http://www.barcouncil.org.uk/2374.aspx

Conroy, J. D., 'Intimations of Keith Hart's "informal economy" in the work of Henry Mayhew, P. T. Bauer and Richard Salisbury', 12 March 2012, SSRN: http://dx.doi.org/10.2139/ssrn.2031291

Corbin, A., 'Charting the cultural history of the senses', in D. Howes (ed.), *Empire of the Senses: The Sensual Culture Reader* (Oxford: Berg, 2005), pp. 128–39

Corbin, A., *Village Bells: Sound and Meaning in the Nineteenth-century French Countryside*, trans M. Thom (New York: Columbia University Press, 1998)

Daunton, M., 'Industry in London: revisions and reflections', *London Journal*, 21.1 (1996), 1–8

Dean, M., *Governmentality: Power and Rule in Modern Society* (London: Sage, 2010)

Dennis, R., *Cities in Modernity: Representations and Productions of Metropolitan Space, 1840–1930* (Cambridge: Cambridge University Press, 2008)

Deriu, D., '"Don't look down!": a short history of rooftopping photography', *Journal of Architecture*, 21.7 (2016), 1033–61

Deriu, D., 'The photogenic city: aerial photography and urban visions in Europe, 1914–1945', unpublished PhD thesis, Bartlett School of Architecture, University of London, 2004

Edensor, T., 'Light design and atmosphere', *Visual Communication*, 14.3 (2015), 331–50

Elborough, T., and N. Rennison (eds), *A London Year: 365 Days of City Life in Diaries, Journals and Letters* (London: Frances Lincoln, 2013)

Englander, D, 'Booth's Jews: the presentation of Jews and Judaism in *Life and Labour of the People in London*', *Victorian Studies*, 32 (1989), 551–71

Englander, D., and R. O'Day (eds), *Retrieved Riches: Social Investigation in Britain 1840–1914* (Aldershot: Ashgate, 1998)

Epstein Nord, D., *Walking the Victorian Streets: Women, Representation and the City* (Ithaca, NY: Cornell University Press, 1995)

Eva, P., 'Home sweet home? The "culture of exile" in mid-Victorian popular song', *Popular Music*, 16.2 (1997), 131–50

Fishman, W. J., *The Streets of East London* (London: Five Leaves, 2006 [1979])

Fiske, J., *Understanding Popular Culture* (London: Routledge, 2011 [1989])

Floud, P., and P. Johnson (eds), *The Cambridge Economic History of Modern Britain*, Vol. II (Cambridge: Cambridge University Press, 2004)

Gerritsen, A., and G. Riello (eds), *Writing Material Culture History* (London: Bloomsbury, 2014)

Girouard, M., *The English Town: A History of Urban Life* (New Haven, CT: Yale University Press, 1990)

Godley, A., 'Immigrant entrepreneurs and the emergence of London's East End as an industrial district', *London Journal*, 21.1 (1996), 38–45

Godley, A., *Jewish Immigrant Entrepreneurship in London and New York, 1880–1914* (Basingstoke: Palgrave, 2001)

Green, D. R., 'The nineteenth-century metropolitan economy: a revisionist interpretation', *London Journal*, 21.1 (1996), 9–26

Green, D. R., 'Street trading in London: a case study of casual labour 1830–60', in J. H. Johnson and C. G. Pooley (eds), *The Structure of Nineteenth-Century Cities* (London: Croom Helm, 1982), pp. 129–51

Green, N. L., 'Immigrant Jews in Paris, London and New York: a comparative approach', *Judaism*, 49.3 (2000), 280–91

Hart, K., 'Informal income opportunities and urban employment in Ghana', *Journal of Modern African Studies*, 11.1 (1973), 61–89

Herbert, C., *Culture and Anomie: Ethnographic Imagination in the Nineteenth Century* (Chicago: University of Chicago Press, 1991)

Hetherington, K., *Capitalism's Eye: Cultural Spaces of the Commodity* (London: Routledge, 2007)

Highmore, B., 'Street life in London: towards a rhythmanalysis of London in the late nineteenth century', *New Formations*, 47 (2002), 171–93

Hobsbawm, E., and T. Ranger (eds), *The Invention of Tradition* (Cambridge: Cambridge University Press, 1992 [1983])

Hodson, D., 'The municipal store: adaptation and development in the retail markets of nineteenth-century urban Lancashire', *Business History*, 40 (1998), 94–114

Horrocks, S. M., 'Quality control and research: the role of scientists in the British food industry, 1870–1939', in J. Burnett and D. J. Oddy (eds), *The Origins and Development of Food Policies in Europe* (Leicester: Leicester University Press, 1994), pp. 130–45

Howes, D. (ed.), *Empire of the Senses: The Sensual Culture Reader* (Oxford: Berg, 2005)

Hudson, P., *The Industrial Revolution* (London: Arnold, 2005 [1992])

Isenstadt, S., 'The spaces of shopping: a historical overview', in D. C. Andrews (ed.) *Shopping: Material Culture Perspectives* (Newark, DE: University of Delaware Press, 2015), pp. 1–32

Jefferys, J. B., *Retail Trading in Britain 1850–1950* (Cambridge: Cambridge University Press, 1954)

Johnson, P., 'Conspicuous consumption and working-class culture in late-Victorian and Edwardian Britain', *Transactions of the Royal Historical Society*, 38 (1988), 27–42

Johnson, P., 'Economic development and industrial dynamism in Victorian London', *London Journal*, 21.1 (1996), 27–37

Jones, P., 'Redressing reform narratives: Victorian London's street markets and the informal supply lines of urban modernity', *London Journal*, 41.1 (2016), 60–81

Joseph, A., *King of the Pearly Kings: The Story of Henry Croft* (London: Cockney Museum, n.d.)

Joyce, P., *The Rule of Freedom: Liberalism and the Modern City* (London: Verso, 2003)

Keating, P. J., *The Working Classes in Victorian Fiction* (London: Routledge and Kegan Paul, 1971)

Kelley, V., 'Home and work: housework and paid work in British homes', in J. Hamlett (ed.), *A Cultural History of the Home* (London: Bloomsbury, 2019)

Kelley, V., *Soap and Water: Cleanliness, Dirt and the Working Classes in Victorian and Edwardian Britain* (London: I. B. Tauris, 2010)

Kershen, A. J., 'Jewish and Muslim married women don't work: immigrant wives and home-work in the late nineteenth and late twentieth centuries', *Home Cultures*, 8.2 (2011), 119–32

Kershen, A. J., 'Morris Cohen and the origins of the women's wholesale clothing industry in the East End', *Textile History*, 28 (1997), 39–46

Kift, D., *Victorian Music Hall: Culture, Class and Conflict* (Cambridge: Cambridge University Press, 1996)

Kronenburg, R., *Transportable Environments: Theory, Context, Design, and Technology* (London: Spon Press, 1999)

Kushner, T., 'Jew and non-Jew in the East End of London: towards an anthropology of "everyday" relations', in G. Alderman and C. Holmes (eds), *Outsiders and Outcasts: Essays in Honour of William J. Fishman* (London: Duckworth, 1993), pp. 32–52

Lancaster, B., *The Department Store: A Social History* (Leicester: Leicester University Press, 1995)

Lefebvre, H., *Key Writings*, ed. S. Elden, E. Lebas and E. Kofman (London: Continuum, 2003)

Lefebvre, H., *Rhythmanalysis: Space, Time and Everyday Life*, trans. S. Elden (London: Bloomsbury, 2013)

Leonard, M., 'Coping strategies in developed and developing societies: the workings of the informal economy', *Journal of International Development*, 12.8 (2000), 1069–85

Lewis, S. S., 'The artistic and architectural patronage of Angela Burdett Coutts', PhD thesis, Royal Holloway University of London, 2012

Lysack, K., 'Goblin markets: Victorian women shoppers at Liberty's oriental bazaar', *Nineteenth-Century Contexts*, 27.2 (2005), 139–65

MacRaild, D., *The Irish Diaspora in Britain, 1750–1939* (Basingstoke: Palgrave Macmillan, 2011 [1999])

Marsh, A. I., and J. Smethurst, *Historical Directory of Trade Unions* (Aldershot: Ashgate, 2006)

McKibbin, R., *The Ideologies of Class: Social Relations in Britain 1880–1950* (Oxford: Clarendon Press, 1990)

Mendelsohn, A. D., *The Rag Race: How Jews Sewed Their Way to Success in America and the British Empire* (New York: New York University Press, 2015)

Mitchell, I., 'Retail markets in Northern and Midland England, 1870–1914: civic icon, municipal white elephant, or consumer paradise?', *Economic History Review*, 71.4 (2018), 1270–90, doi.org/10.1111/ehr.12653

Mitchell, I., *Tradition and Innovation in English Retailing 1700–1850* (Farnham: Ashgate, 2014)

Morrison, K. A., *English Shops and Shopping* (New Haven, CT: Yale University Press, 2003)

Mui, H.-C., and L. Mui, *Shops and Shopkeeping in Eighteenth-century England* (London: Routledge, 1989)

Nead, L., *Victorian Babylon: People, Streets and Images in Nineteenth-century London* (New Haven, CT: Yale University Press, 2000)

Nora, P., 'Between memory and history: les lieux de mémoire', *Representations*, 26 (1989), 7–24

Orr, E., 'Designing display in the department store', PhD thesis, Royal College of Art, 2017

Orton, D., *Made of Gold: A Biography of Angela Burdett Coutts* (London: Hamish Hamilton, 1980)

Otter, C., *The Victorian Eye: A Political History of Light and Vision in Britain, 1800–1910* (Chicago: University of Chicago Press, 2008)

Pallasmaa, J., 'Hapticity and time: notes on fragile architecture', *Architectural Review*, 207 (May 2000), 78–84

Panayi, P., *Spicing up Britain: The Multicultural History of British Food* (London: Reaktion, 2008)

Paterson, M., 'Haptic geographies: ethnography, haptic knowledges and sensuous dispositions', *Progress in Human Geography*, 33.6 (2009), 766–88

Phillips, M., 'The evolution of markets and shops in Britain', in J. Benson and G. Shaw (eds), *The Evolution of Retail Systems* (Leicester: Leicester University Press, 1992), pp. 53–75

Pirenne, H., 'Medieval cities' (1925), in R. T. LeGates and F. Stout (eds), *The City Reader* (London: Routledge, 2016), pp. 45–52

Radcliffe, C., 'Theatrical hierarchy, cultural capital and the legitimate/illegitimate divide', in P. Yeandle, K. Newey and J. Richards (eds), *Politics, Performance and Popular Culture* (Manchester: Manchester University Press, 2016), pp. 75–95

Rappaport, E. D., *Shopping for Pleasure: Women in the Making of London's West End* (Princeton, NJ: Princeton University Press, 2000)

Richards, T., *The Commodity Culture of Victorian England: Advertising and Spectacle 1851–1914* (London: Verso, 1991)

Riello, G., 'Boundless competition: subcontracting and the London economy in the late nineteenth century', *Enterprise and Society*, 13.3 (2012), 504–37

Roddy, S., J.-M. Strange and B. Taithe, 'Henry Mayhew at 200: the "other Victorian bicentenary"', *Journal of Victorian Culture*, 19.4 (2014), 482–96

Ross, E., *Slum Travelers: Ladies and London Poverty 1860–1920* (Berkeley, CA: University of California Press, 2007)

Samuel, R., *Theatres of Memory: Past and Present in Contemporary Culture* (London: Verso, 1994)

Sassen, S., 'The informal economy: between new developments and old regulations', *Yale Law Journal*, 103.8 (1994), 2289–304

Saunders, R., *Democracy and the Vote in British Politics, 1848–1867* (Aldershot: Ashgate, 2013)

Schivelbusch, W., *Disenchanted Night: The Industrialisation of Light in the Nineteenth Century* (Oxford: Berg, 1988 [1983])

Schlör, J., *Nights in the Big City: Paris, Berlin, London 1840–1930*, trans. P. G. Imhof and D. R. Roberts (London: Reaktion, 1998 [1991])

Schmiechen, J., and K. Carls, *The British Market Hall: A Social and Architectural History* (New Haven, CT: Yale University Press, 1999)

Scola, R., *Feeding the Victorian City: The Food Supply of Manchester, 1770–1870* (Manchester: Manchester University Press, 1992)

Scott, D. B., 'The music-hall cockney: flesh and blood, or replicant?', *Music & Letters*, 83.2 (2002), 237–58

Scott, D. B., *The Singing Bourgeois: Songs of the Victorian Drawing Room and Parlour* (Abingdon: Routledge, 2017 [1989])

Scott, J., *Seeing Like a State* (New Haven, CT: Yale University Press, 1998)

Seed, J., 'Did the subaltern speak? Mayhew and the coster-girl', *Journal of Victorian Culture*, 19.4 (2014), 536–49

Shaw, G., and M. T. Wild, 'Retail patterns in the Victorian city', in J. Benson and G. Shaw (eds), *The Retailing Industry, Volume II: The Coming of the Mass Market 1800–1945* (London: I. B. Tauris, 1999), pp. 99–114

Shesgreen, S., *Images of the Outcast: The Urban Poor in the Cries of London* (Manchester: Manchester University Press, 2002)

Smith, K., 'Sensing design and workmanship: the haptic skills of shoppers in eighteenth-century London', *Journal of Design History*, 25.1 (2012), 1–10

Smith, L. D., 'Greeners and sweaters: Jewish immigration and the cabinet-making trade in East London, 1880–1914', *Jewish Historical Studies*, 39 (2004), 103–20

Smith, M. M., *Sensing the Past: Seeing, Hearing, Smelling, Tasting, and Touching in History* (Berkeley, CA: University of California Press, 2007)

Stallybrass, P., and A. White, *The Politics and Poetics of Transgression* (London: Routledge, 1986)

Stedman Jones, G., 'The "cockney" and the nation, 1780–1988', in D. Feldman and G. Stedman Jones (eds), *Metropolis London: Histories and Representations since 1800* (London: Routledge, 1989), pp. 272–322

Stedman Jones, G., *Outcast London: A Study in the Relationship Between Classes in Victorian Society* (London: Penguin, 1984 [1971])

Stedman Jones, G., 'Working-class culture and working-class politics in London: notes on the remaking of a working class', *Journal of Social History*, 7.4 (1974), 460–509

Stedman Jones, G., and R. Samuel, 'Pearly kings and queens', in R. Samuel (ed.), *Patriotism: The Making and Unmaking of British National Identity*, Vol. 3 (London: Routledge, 1989) [AQ]

Steedman, C., 'Mayhew: on reading, about writing', *Journal of Victorian Culture*, 19.4 (2014), 550–61

Stern, W. M, 'The baroness's market: the history of a noble failure', *Guildhall Miscellany*, 3.8 (1966), 353–66

Stobart, J., and I. Van Damme, 'Introduction: markets in modernization: transformations in urban market space and practice, c.1800–c.1970', *Urban History*, 43.3 (2016), 358–71

Strother, Z. S., 'Architecture against the state: the virtues of impermanence in the kibulu of Easter Pende chiefs in Central Africa', *Journal of the Society of Architectural Historians*, 63.3 (2004), 272–95

Swift, R., *Irish Migrants in Britain 1815–1914: A Documentary History* (Cork: Cork University Press, 2002)

Tames, R., *Feeding London: A Taste of History* (London: Historical Publications, 2003)

Tarr, C., 'Covent goblin market', *Victorian Poetry*, 50.3 (2012), 297–316

Thompson, E. P., and E. Yeo (eds), *Unknown Mayhew: Selections from the Morning Chronicle, 1849–50* (London: Merlin, 1971)

Tucker, H. F., 'Rossetti's goblin marketing: sweet to tongue and sound to eye', *Representations*, 82 (2003), 117–33

Turton, J., 'Mayhew's Irish: the Irish poor in mid nineteenth-century London', in R. Swift and S. Gilley (eds), *The Irish in Victorian Britain: The Local Dimension* (Dublin: Four Courts Press, 1999), pp. 122–55

Valverde, M., 'Police science, British style: pub licensing and knowledge of urban disorder', *Economy and Society*, 32.2 (2011), 234–52

Valverde, M., 'Seeing like a city: the dialectic of modern and pre-modern ways of seeing in urban governance', *Law & Society Review*, 45.2 (2011), 277–312

van den Heuvel, D., 'Selling in the shadows: peddlers and hawkers in early modern Europe', in M. M. van der Linden and L. Lucassen (eds), *Studies in Global Social History, Volume 9: Working on Labour: Essays in Honour of Jan Lucassen* (Leiden: Brill, 2012), pp. 125–51

Select bibliography

Walkowitz, J., *City of Dreadful Delight: Narratives of Sexual Danger in Late-Victorian London* (Chicago: University of Chicago Press, 1992)
Walkowitz, J., *Nights Out: Life in Cosmopolitan London* (New Haven, CT: Yale University Press, 2012)
White, J., *London in the Nineteenth Century: 'A Human Awful Wonder of God'* (London: Vintage, 2008 [2007])
White, J., *London in the Twentieth Century: A City and its People* (London: Vintage, 2008 [2001])
Williams, K., *From Pauperism to Poverty* (London: Routledge and Kegan Paul, 1981)
Williams, S. C., *Religious Belief and Popular Culture in Southwark, c.1880–1939* (Oxford: Clarendon Press, 1999)
Winter, J., *London's Teeming Streets 1830–1914* (London: Routledge, 1993)
Wright, P., *On Living in an Old Country: The National Past in Contemporary Britain* (London: Verso, 1985)

Index

Note: page numbers in italics refer to illustrations

''Ackney with the 'ouses took away' 178
Agnew, Jean-Christophe 153
architecture and street markets 76, 95–103
    fragile architecture 76, 95, 98, 99, 103
    impermanent architecture 76, 98
    interiority 92–5, *94*, 100, 103
authorised and unauthorised markets 8, 9, 17–18, 20–5, 32, 41–2, 51–2, 155–6, 188
    see also markets (London), authorised; markets (London), unauthorised

Bailey, Peter 161, 165–9, 173, 175, 177
Bakhtin, Mikhail 11, 76, 98, 153–6, 158–9, 161, 163–5, 167, 168, 169, 177
Barnet Fair 133–4
barrows, and stalls 23, 24, 25, 26, 31, 95–7, *96*, *97*, 175, 187–8
    design 95
    dimensions 27–8, 33–4, 40, 95–6, 99–100
    hire 65, 95–6, 116, 125
Bartholomew Fair 3, 152, 154, 155
beggars 83, 115, 121, 187
Bellwood, Bessie 169, 170
Benedetta, Mary 5, 13n.3, 52, 57, *58*, *59*, 60, 64–6, *78*, 83, 91, 99, 100, *101*, 143–5, *144*
Benson, John 9–10, 115
'billingsgate' (low speech) 154, 164, 182n.9

for Billingsgate Market *see* markets (London), authorised
Binder, Pearl 135, 136, 139, 141–2
blackface 170
Booth, Charles 13n.3, 24, 39, 50, 54, 61, 63, 65, 74, 85–6, 124–5, 141, 142, 147n.50, 159
Booth, William 85
Bosanquet, Helen 52, 55–6, 61, 62, 64–6, 76, 86, 102–3, 126
branded goods 56, 66, 67, 162
Brandt, Bill *179*, *180*
Buchner, Thomas and Hoffmann-Rehnitz, Philip 10, 18–19, 24, 26
Burdett-Coutts, Angela 28, 30, 32, 125, 163
    see also Columbia Market
Burke, Thomas 91, 94–5, 98, 99, 102, 103, 141, 166
butchers 3, 53, 55, 83, 103, 133, 161, 187–8

Carney, Kate 169, 170–1, 175–8, *176*, *plates 10 & 11*
carnival and the carnivalesque 11, 76, 98, 133–4, 138, 153–9, 168, 173
cash handling 163
    cash railways and pneumatic tubes 163
    cash registers 163
    in markets 163
Cheapside and East Cheap 4

Chevalier, Albert 136, *137*, 139–40,
    167–75, *174*, 178, 181, *plate 8*
circulation
  of goods 23–4, 50–3, 67–8, 80–1, 187
  of traffic 25, 34, 76–80, 84, 187
clothing
  manufacture 62–7
  retailing 1–3, 48, 57–60, *59*, 64–5, 66,
    72n.91, 87, *88*, 117, *118*, 129–30,
    131, 132, 142, 164, 166
  see also costermongers, dress
Coborn, Charles 169
cockneys 4, 134–42, 155, 165–81, 189
Cohen, Jack 57, 129
  see also shops, Tesco
commodities *see* goods sold in London
  street markets
Corbin, Alain 160, 163–4
Corporation of London 21–4, 30, 34–5,
  40, 123, 155
costermongers 1, 4, 13n.1, 18, 20, 23,
  24–8, 33–4
  business practices 50–5, 64–7, 79–82,
    95, *97*, 113–17, 125
  class identity 127
  dress 113, 126, 134, 140–1, 172
  ethnographic and journalistic accounts
    60, 109, 110–28, *114*, *118*, 133–5,
    140
  in film 178, 181
  hereditary nature 113–14, 123, 125–6,
    141
  in music hall 135–8, *137*, 153, 165–78,
    174, *176*, *plates 6, 8, 9, 10, 11 & 12*
  mutual support 127–8
  politics 127–8
  and race 109–10, 117–21, 119, 120, 121,
    125–6, 130, 131, 132, 170, 171
  unions 20, 127
Cries, London 117, 121–2, 123, 161, *plate 5*
  see also market cries
Cries, Paris 161, 163
Croft, Henry 136–42

department stores 5, 7, 53, 64, 84–5,
  99–102, 158, 162, 163
  Harrods 99–100
  Liberty 85
  Selfridge 85
Dickens, Charles 134, 155
districts of London
  Bethnal Green 28, 70n.38

Borough 79
Chiswick 99
Elephant and Castle 79
Greenwich 155
Hammersmith 76, *77*
Hampstead 134, 138
Lambeth 29, 47n.105, 75, 81, 143, 167,
  179
Lewisham 53, 54, 75, 143, 145
Marylebone 47n.106, 113
Peckham 75
Poplar 32, 40–1, 75, 91, 102, 159, 164
Soho 3, 6, 61, 74
Somers Town 111, 136, 138, 139, 141
Southwark 75, 111
Stepney 53, 75, 128, 143–5
Walworth 67, *68*, 79, 94, 162, *162*
Westminster *37*, *38*, 47n.106, 74–5,
Woolwich 46n.75
see also East End; West End
Dodd, George 22, 48, 50–2, 55, 175
donkeys 81, *114*, 120, 121, 125, 133, 138,
  173, *174*, 175, *plates 6, 9 & 10*
Doré, Gustave and Jerrold, Blanchard,
  31, 33
Dutch auctions 159, 163

East End 3, *3*, 4, 18, 28, 32, 42, 52, 55–6,
  57, 61–2, 64–7, 75, 85–6, 91, 94,
  103, 128–33, 141, 145, 157–8, 172,
  174–5, 178, 179, *180*, 187–9, *plate 3*
Elen, Gus 169–70, 174–5, 178, *plates 6 & 9*
Elvin, Joe, 169
England, Adele 179

fairs 4, 34, 8, 91, 98, 151, 153–8
  see also Barnet Fair; Bartholomew Fair;
    Greenwich Fair
Feldman, Henry 66–7, 129
'free and easies' 167–8, 175

Gissing, George 92–4, 160
goods sold in London street markets
  consumer goods 1–3, 41, 57–67, 162
  fish 1, 23, 41, 48, 51–3, 55, 56, 81, 87,
    113–16, 159
  fruit 1, 23, 41, 48, 50–3, 70n.26, 81, 175
  jewellery 60–2, *60*, 83
  old clothes 3, 48, 57, 64, 117, *118*
  price of 51–6, 64–5, 83, 97, 115–16,
    159–61, 178
  quality of 51–3, 55–6, 61, 67, 83, 87, 133

ready-made clothes 62–8
stolen and/or counterfeit goods 66
vegetables 1, 23, 41, 48, 50–1, 53, 56, 70n.26, 175
governmentality 11, 35–6
Greenwich Fair 155
Greenwood, James 52, 82–4, 125, 133–4, 155, 174, 187

Harding Davis, Richard 4, 48–9, 76, *121*, 126, 140, 157, 164, *172*–3
Hart, Keith 8–9, 18, 36, 117
high and low culture 11, 155–9
humour *see* market cries
Hurley, Alec 169–70, 175, 186n.126
hybridity 11, 117–18, 130–3, 157, 158, 169, 189
hygiene 22, 56, 102

'If it wasn't for the 'ouses in between' 174–5, *plate 9*
industry in London
  flexible specialisation 63–4, 66, 129
  'immiserisation' 63
  sweated labour 111, 63, 128–9, 170
  workshops and subcontracting 62–7

Jones, Horace 22–3
Joyce, Patrick 11, 154

Kipling, Rudyard 173, 185n.104
'Knock'd 'em in the Old Kent Road' 173

'The Lambeth Walk' 4, 178–181, *180*, *plate 12*
Lane, Lupino 193
LCC General Powers Act (1927) 39–40, 41, 47n.109, 51–2, 65, 79, 143–5
Lefebvre, Henri 10, 75, 80, 82
legibility/illegibility 35–40
liberalism 11, 35–8, 79–80, 90
licensing of markets *see* LCC General Powers Act (1927)
lighting 82, 84–95, 160
  electric light 85, 87, 90, 91
  gas light 82, 83, 85, 87, 90
  and mapping the city 84–6
  street lights 91, 187
  see also naphtha flares
Lloyd, Marie 168
London County Council (LCC) 7, 21, 34–40, 79, 99

  see also London County Council, *London Markets* report, 1893; London County Council, *London Markets* report, 1901
London County Council, *London Markets* report (1893) 1, 13n.3, 2, 17, 25, 31, 32, 33, 35, 36–40, *37*, *38*, 64, 70n.34, 72n.91, 76, 80
London County Council, *London Markets* report (1901) 13n.3, 33, 37

Magee, Bryan 55, 56, 66, 159–60, 162–3
Malvery, Olive 97, *97*, 127, 128, 130
Mannin, Ethel 86, 87, 91, 103
markets (London), authorised
  Billingsgate Market 17, 18, 22, 30, 42n.2, 51, 52, 55, 81, 177, 182n.9
    see also 'billingsgate' (low speech)
  Borough Market 17
  Columbia Market 28–33, *29*, *30*, 35, 99, 125, 126, 156, 163–4
    see also Burdett-Coutts, Angela
  Covent Garden Market 8, 17, 18, 21, 22, 42n.2, 51, 81, 122, 125, 170, *plate 1*
  Hungerford Market 22
  Leadenhall Market 17
  London Central Markets 22
    see also Smithfield
  Metropolitan Cattle Market 22
  Newgate Market 22
  Newport Market 22
  Oxford Market 22
  Randall's Market 32
  Smithfield 17, 22, 23, 42n.2, 154, 168–9
  Spitalfields Market 17, 18, 22, 27, 42n.2, 44n.27
    see also London Central Markets
  Whitechapel Hay Market 18, 79
  see also authorised and unauthorised markets
markets (London), street or unauthorised
  Berwick Street 5, 6, *59*, 61, 62, 74
  The Brill 111
  Caledonian Market 49
  Chalton Street 139
  Chapel Street 27–8, 34, 53, 99
  Chiswick 99
  Chrisp Street 1, 32, 40–1, 75, 91, 116, 159, 164, 166
  Clare Market 32, 36–7
  Commercial Road 58

markets (London), street or unauthorised (*cont.*)
   East Street 68, 79, 162, *162*
   Hammersmith 76, *77*
   Hoxton Street 66, 159
   Lambeth Walk 47n.105, 143, 179–80
     see also 'The Lambeth Walk'
   Lavender Hill 86, 103
   Leather Lane 36–7, 84
   Lewisham 53, *54*, 75, 143, 145
   Lower Marsh 54–5, 143
   Malden Road 53
   Middlesex Street 18, 75, 130, 145
     see also Petticoat Lane
   New Cut 29, 33, 60, 75, 81, *88*, 103, 111, 115, 142, 143, 152, 157, 170, 173
   Petticoat Lane 18, 57, 64–7, 75, 76–7, *78*, 94, *101*, 129–30, *131*, *132*, *134*, *135*, 143–5, *144*, 164, 165, 166
   see also Middlesex Street; Wentworth Street
   Queen's Crescent 53
   Salmon Lane 103, 166
   'Squalors' Market' 82, 83, 133–4
     see also Whitecross Street
   Strutton Ground 36, *37*, *38*, 74–5
   Walworth Road 79
   Watney Street 53, 75, 86
   Wentworth Street 75
     see also Petticoat Lane
   Whitechapel Road 79, 91, 93
   Whitecross Street 6, 52, 66, 82, 83, 133–4, 160
     see also 'Squalors' Market'
   see also authorised and unauthorised markets
market cries 53, 83, 86, 91, 103, 159–65, 167, 168, 177–8
   and Bakhtinian grotesque 154, 155–6, 158, 164, 169, 177
   and dialogic speech 156, 159, 163–4, 169
   and humour 130, 153–9, 163–5, 177, 178
market halls 20–1, 33, 36–8, *37*, *38*, 41, 63, 99
Mass Observation 179–81
Mayhew, Henry 1, 2, 13n.3, 18, 23, 25, 48, 52, 61, 64, 70n.26, 88, 109, 110–23, 114, *118*, 124, 140, 142, 168
'Me and My Girl' 4, 179–81, plate 12

Metropolis Management Act (1855) 24
Metropolitan Board of Works 7
Metropolitan Boroughs 13n.3, 35, 39–40, 47n.105, 51, 143
   see also districts of London
Metropolitan Paving Act (Michael Angelo Taylor's Act) (1817) 24
Metropolitan Police 24, 25, 26–8, 33–4, 38, 41, 79, 116, 127, 130, 156, 157, 187
   see also surveillance
Metropolitan Police Act (1839) 24
Metropolitan Streets Act (1867) 25–8, 32, 33, 35, 42, 79, 95, 99, 116, 118–19, 141, 156
migration and migrants 9, 56–7, 63–7, 75, 109–10, 116–23, 128–33, 141, 145, 189
   Irish 20, 109–10, 116–19, *119*, *120*, 126, 128, 130, 145, 170, 175, 189
   Jewish 41, 56–7, 57–60, 63–7, 75, 109–10, 117–18, *118*, 122, 128–33, *131*, *132*, 141, 142, 143–5, 164, 166, 189
Moholy-Nagy, Laszlo 5, 57, 58, 59, 76–7, *78*, 100, *101*, 144
music hall 135–40, 153, 157, 165–78
'My Old Dutch' 172, 178

naphtha flares 3, 4, 41, 75–6, 82, 84–95, *88*, *89*, *92*, *93*, 98, 103, 160, 187–8
Nead, Lynda 85, 123
New Survey of London Life and Labour 1, 3, 4, 13n.3, 40, 52–3, 57–60, 64, 143
noise *see* sound; market cries; Cries, London; Cries, Paris
Nora, Pierre 139
nostalgia 12, 94, 135–6, 138–9, 153, 154–5, 160, 170–1, 175, 189
nuisance 36–9

Oxford Street 74, 84, 85

Pallasmaa, Juhani 98–9, 103
pearly kings and queens 110, 134–42, *135*, 153, 165–6, 170, 171, 172, *174*, 175, *176*, 179, plate 7
Piccadilly 85, 170
population growth in London 1, 6, 51

Rabelais, François 154, 156, 161, 164, 189n.9

Rappaport, Erica Diane 84, 102
Regent Street 74, 84
rhythm, urban 75, 76–84
   see also rhythmanalysis; space-time
rhythmanalysis 10, 75, 80, 82, 98
Rossetti, Christina 122–3
Rowley, J. W. 169
Royal Commission on Alien Immigration 127
Royal Commission on Market Rights and Tolls 9, 13n.3, 17–18, 27–8, 35–6

Sala, George Augustus 81, 87, 91, 98, 152, 157, 177, 187
Samuel, Raphael 135, 138, 139, 179–80
Saturday night markets 1, 3, 4, 23, 41, 48, 54–5, 76, 82–4, 86, 102–3, 93, 116, 157–8, 164, 187–8
Scannell, Dolly 41, 102–3, 130, 159, 164, 166
senses, and street markets 10, 103
   smell 86, 87, 103, 160
   taste 103, 160
   touch 103, 160
   see also sound
sensory history 10, 75–6, 84, 103, 153, 159–61, 163–4, 187, 188
shops 4–6, 42, 52–3, 65, 76, 84–5, 129, 130, 162–3, 188
   Home and Colonial 53
   Lipton's 53
   Marks and Spencer 53
   Maypole Dairies 53
   Sainsbury's 53, 57
   Tesco 57
   Woolworths 53
   see also department stores
shop windows 85, 102, 162
Sims, George 83–4, 85, *89*, 91, *92*, *93*, 96, 128–9, 152
sound 91, 103, 147n.40, 153, 159–65, 177
   see also market cries

space-time 10, 39–40, 75, 81–3, 154, 155–6
   see also rhythm, urban; rhythmanalysis
Stallybrass, Peter and White, Allon 11, 98, 154–6, 157, 158, 165, 173, 175
Stedman Jones 9–10, 18, 135–41, 168–9, 189
subcontracting see industry in London
suburbs 3, 6, 75, 81, 85
Sullivan, J. W. 13n.3, 35, 51, 56, 80–1
Sunday markets and Sunday trading 24, 28, 29, 31, 41, 76, 115, 129, 130, 131, 135, 145, 157
surveillance (police) 3, 4, 28, 37–8, *88*, *93*, 130, *131*, 132, 187
sweated labour see industry in London

Thomson, John and Smith, Adolphe 51, 60–2, *60*, 65, 80
tradition, the invention of 136, 138, 139, 141, 152, 165
Travers, Hyram 136, 139, 169, 170

Valverde, Mariana 27, 36–40
Vance, Alfred 136, 139, 169–70
visibility/invisibility 23, 35–40, 156

Walkowitz, Judith 6, 62, 85
Wentworth, Fanny 169
West End 7, 42, 55–6, 74–6, 84–5, 87, 100, 102, 158, 167, 173, *174*
'When the Stars are Peeping' 177, *plate 11*
'When the Summer Comes Again' 177, *plate 10*
Winter, James 6, 25, 34, 77, 79–80, 160–1
women in London street markets 9, 55, 65–6, 87, 102–3, 113, 126
Woolf, Virginia 85
Wright, Patrick 139

Zangwill, Israel 172

EU authorised representative for GPSR:
Easy Access System Europe, Mustamäe tee 50,
10621 Tallinn, Estonia
gpsr.requests@easproject.com

www.ingramcontent.com/pod-product-compliance
Lightning Source LLC
Chambersburg PA
CBHW040931240426
43672CB00022B/2998